The Psyc
Confessions Of A
Primal Screamer

(The Tambourine Years 1984 – 87)

By
Martin St. John

Copyright © 2016 Martin St. John

All rights reserved, including the right to reproduce this book, or portions thereof in any form. No part of this text may be reproduced, transmitted, downloaded, decompiled, reverse engineered, or stored, in any form or introduced into any information storage and retrieval system, in any form or by any means, whether electronic or mechanical without the express written permission of the author.

ISBN: 978-1-326-76775-4

Thank you friends

First of all many tanx to Ruth Blakley, Maybole's finest typist in showing great patience in word processing the whole script(not an easy task)Frank Brown for his witty synopsis come back cover blurb. Tommy Cherry for his psychedelically designed front cover and scanning of book photographs. Also a big shout out to everyone who gave me their time especially Joyce X (all truth/no bullshit) Tam Mc Gurk (tales of on the road) Chris Davidson (Greenock Go-Getter) Billy Thompson (Splash One/Neighbour reminisces) Derek Lee (Cumbernauld garage tales) Paul Mac Neil (Action House shenanigans) Sheer Taft (Greenock promoter hi-jinks) Leigh Morrison (Psychic Tv gig chat) Joe Foster (Fitzrovian tales) Jeff Barrett (Plymouthian promoter yarns) And last but not least special tanx to Michelle Carr and Peter Callaghan for their collection of rare 1980s independent fanzines that were a gas to read and proved real useful in providing insightful information of the early 1980s indie scene in Glasgow. A special correction goes to ex neighbour Grant Mc Dougall who was thee actual main man and point of contact in promoting Sonic Youth,s first ever appearance in Glasgow,s Splash One club early 1986 and not Bob G and Mc Gee who i initially thought were the promoters. I can't leave the section without giving special mention to my all time musical heroes who made my life that little bit more interesting but who are now all sadly gone on this here earth but will be whooping it up in rock n roll heaven forever-i give you:Alex Chilton! Lux Interior! Jeffrey Lee Pierce! Joe Strummer! Syd Barrett! Arthur Lee! Rowland S Howard! And now as I'm writing this piece up Alan Vega has also sadly departed- a true solid gone ghost rider of the sky....Amen

ODE TO PRIMAL SCREAM
(ORIGINAL GANG 1984 – 87)

Six buttoned-up, zonked-out Glaswegian garage nuts hell-bent on acid, leather strides and hard kicks with jumpin'-in-the-night Rickenbacker harmonies to die for.

A walkin' Z movie of power-poppin' sonic youths in a perpetual dawn of fish-eye contempt.

Cascading pulsating rhythms on a Gentle Tuesday producing velvet guitar crescendos of shimmering sounds.

Carpet crawling, system smashing, psyche heads or stroppy malcontents digging the trash aesthetic.

Interstellar social misfits with a mystic eye aiming a kick in the eye to the dullsville 9-5.

Intoxicated spontaneous delinquent rainbow-chasers wigging out in a euphoric rave-up in Crystal Crescent.

Blow yer toes and shake some goddamn action.

Primals on patrol in bubblegum land.

Primal Scream/Jesus And Mary Chain gig poster from October 1984 – co-headliners.

THE BIRTH OF A TAMBOURINE MAN

The date: October 11th 1984. The place: Glasgow, The Venue. The bands: Primal Scream! The Jesus And Mary Chain! Biff Bang Pow! Ochre 5! Meat Whiplash!

At the time, I was working in a dead-end piss factory in Bridgeton, the gutter east end, on the nightshift as a bottler. It was a total soul destroying nightmare of a job with no stimulating of the senses whatsoever. Watching bottles going round and round endlessly on a never-ending loop, till one of the fuckers fell over on the merry-go-round and then pressing stop! If you've ever watched the 1920s futuristic flick "Metropolis" of the workers toiling away 'down below', you'll get the picture of abject misery I had to endure on a nightly basis. One recurring vision still pops up in my head of that particular period. This enormous fuck off clock that was situated bang right in the centre of the miserable workplace. Talk about ramming the intimidating tedium down your throat? These warlords of the workplace were supreme masochists of the first order. Thank the heavens above for psychedelic garage punk from the 1960s appearing in my life at this point in time as salvation. I was already known in the workplace as "The Psychedelic Kid" due to my penchant for wearing a blue paisley-patterned shirt along with my ever growing shaggy moptop sprouting up all over the place.

The A4 poster advertising the gig contained a striking, captivating image lifted from the life changing 1968 film IF….. with the classic blurb emblazoned "Whose Side Are You On?" with an angelic image of Malcolm McDowell with his schoolbooks on one side and on the other a snotty enraged image of Mick Travis brandishing a machine gun defiantly in the face of adversity. The other mesmerising slogan that we never used was "One Hand Grenade Of A Film" which could've perfectly captured the spirit of the assembled bill for this particular night's musical entertainment. Alongside us, the other four bands performing were The Jesus And Mary Jane (current press darlings), Biff Bang Pow! (Alan McGee's powerpop combo), Ochre 5 (Supercomic Grant Morrison's band) and Meat Whiplash (East Kilbride teenage upstarts).

After a non-eventful soundcheck, we all retired to The Griffin pub across the road to sink a few foaming ales to conjure up some Dutch courage to cool the nerves, as for most people it was to be the first time that we'd all set a Chelsea boot on a real live stage. In the pub we bumped into a few of the Cumbernauld music lovers who told us that they were hitting Nite Moves to see Flesh For Lulu. We tried to persuade them to come along to our night in The Venue but they'd already bought their tickets – no luck guys! Bob G at this point had been over the road taking care of business when all of a sudden he burst into The Griffin to tell us that he'd been getting a bit of grief off some assholes outside The Venue. The ever-willing posse of Tam, Dungo and Beattie were rounded up and sent over with myself and Bob G remaining in the pub supping our drinks. Within minutes, the posse were back, problem solved.

After a few beers, we all headed back over to The Venue, whereby I hit the toilet first and proceeded to bump into Meat Whiplash who were busy tuning/de-tuning their guitars. No sound check for these guys – they were real raw! They were the first band on and played a real short, feral set of manic numbers to get us all in the mood. Next up were Ochre 5 and I can't remember a darn thing of their set, the same for Biff Bang Pow. I must've been tanning the meagre supply of beers in our 'rider' to calm the impending nerves, as we were the headline band all of a sudden as The Jesus And Mary Chain didn't want the headline slot. As they hit the stage, the crowd had now swelled to around 100 sweaty, heaving bodies creating a feverish buzz of energy and excitement. This was their second gig in Glasgow and by this time they'd already whipped up some precious press reviews concerning the fact they'd just signed to Creation Records with their first release 'Upside Down', ready to be unleashed on 7-inch single real soon. Again their feedback drenched set was short and shambolic complete with lots of drunken stop/start moments that had a bemused crowd hollering and cheering them on to the end. It didn't help that Dino (the sound man) was at the helm, producing his usual muddled gig sound. The Jesus And Mary Chain sure were different in attitude and sound but were still to convince me that they were the real, rocking 100% deal.

After a couple of rehearsals in Beattie's spare room and one in The Hellfire Studios to produce a workable set of tunes – our moment had come! We proceeded to work our way through our scanty, short set list of songs, culminating in the Subway Sect cover of 'Nobody's Scare' for an encore. I dropped the tambourine and produced Lux's mouth organ for this number as we blasted our way through a real neat, hot-wired version that brought the gig to its final conclusion. Being on stage was frightening and thrilling at the same time, especially when you looked out in to the crowd and spotted all your friends half pished, grinning away like Cheshire cats, cheering you on. The set list is quite vague after the years rolling by but probably featured early versions of 'It Happens', 'I Love You', 'Aftermath', 'Leaves' and 'Subterranean'. If Gary Barrett (The Bootleg King) was alive today, somewhere deep in his musical vaults gathering dust, there would be a dusty tape recording of this gig as Gary had recorded nearly every important gig in Glasgow from the punky 1977 years onwards.

I remember playing our version of 'Nobody's Scared' which was a complete blast as we could relax then and bust loose as it was the final song of the night. It was a real buzz afterwards with other band members and friends coming over to backslap and congratulate you on an excellent night – it was to be another important year in music for me again – year zero 11 October 1984. One of our mates that night, Grant, took some live photographs of The Primals on stage and there's one of myself in mid-tambourine-bashing-flow grinning away and that for me sums up the night perfectly.

Taking to Jim Beattie later on as we were packing our kit away, he collared me and asked Right! Do you wanna join us? He didn't have to ask me twice, and since The Cramps didn't have a job vacancy for tambourinist/maraca shaker I thought why the hell not! He didn't really have to ask me as on that stage, I already felt part of the group dynamics and couldn't wait for the next gig to happen – let's execute the fantasy now! The cacophony of noise being on a stage had gripped my psyche and there was to be no turning back now.

The line up for The Venue gig in October 1984 is: Bobby Gillespie (vocals), Jim Beattie (chiming guitar), Robert Young (bass man), Tam McGurk (whiplash drummer) and myself Martin St John (tambourine/mouth organ).

COME TOGETHER

The previous year of 1983 was the first time that Primal Scream had actually performed, in the Alan McGee promoted club night The Living Room, set in a London boozer called 'The Adam Arms'. This was the original fresh-faced, pre-flyte two-piece act that had been conceived by Jim Beattie who then invited his old school buddy Bobby Gillespie to join him, resplendent in their short, shaven-headed New Order style haircuts. The music itself from this period matched the hairdos and from the recently discovered bootleg recording of the actual gig it sounds totally different to what Primal Scream would sound like one year later when I first started rehearsing with them. That jingle jangle morning was still a distant echo away back then. Primal Scream on this night supported Alan McGee's 'Laughing Apple', who themselves one year later also, would also be musically transformed, this time under the rowdy pop art attack of Biff Bang Pow!

I'm glad the embryonic Primal Scream sobered up quick style and ditched that 1983 look and sound and got in to that 12-string jingle jangle Byrdsian groove, as there was no way I could've envisioned myself in that earlier incarnation rattling off my tambourine!

As the group was forming and changing, Primal Scream produced a song called 'The Orchard' which was sung by Judith Boyle, Beattie's chick at the time. This record was to be an early record release on Creation Records but for reasons now lost in the psychedelic mists of time, Beattie decided to burn the original master tape as he thought the song didn't come up to the standard that he required off in quality control. I remember hearing the tape at the time and didn't think it was as bad as he made it out to be. (It's now on YouTube pop kids). Maybe Beattie thought the vocals were too nice and twee cos the next you know Bob G is the singer and the song and full-time songwriter alongside Beattie – let the games begin!

When you think of the band name of Primal Scream your mind instantly conjures up visions of a pitiful gothic Batcave style band and not a group of five delightful, Glaswegian delinquents on a modern day 1980s style Byrds kick. It all came back to Arthur Lee naming his band Love but who were the opposite – hate! Five thuggish, acid-drenched punks from the 1966 Sunset Strip scene of Los Angeles USA. The name Primal Scream itself was actually blagged off an Arthur Janov novel of the same name which consisted of theoretical writings and musings of various people engaged in primal therapy sessions unleashing their inner thoughts of fear, truth and childhood memories. Definitely an apt name for the 5 of us thrown together!

The name of a band can instantly define your outlook and attitude and over the years some of my all time favourite groups have possessed eye-catching, thought-provoking band names to die for: The Velvet Underground! The 13th Floor Elevators! The Sex Pistols! – with names that distinctive, how could you disappoint?

I was also a major fan of the more obscure end of punk group names too, especially ones that possessed a black-humoured, devilish viewpoint such as The Dead Kennedys, Alternative Tv!, The Desperate Bicycles and the all-time warped, sicko classic The Butthole Surfers! Coming across these particular bands in the music weeklies or on album sleeves, instantly grabbed your attention and contained a certain outlook and attitude in a blinding flash of inspiration. To back up the name, all you need then is the songs to back up the image – along with a healthy dose of delusion, cockiness, arrogance and swagger!

Jim Beattie, Bobby Gillespie and Robert 'Dungo' Young all knew each other previously from growing up together, frequenting the local King's Park Secondary School in Glasgow's Southside district. Interesting fact fans – all original 5 members of Primal Scream were born within a 5-miles radius of Glasgow city centre when they first came together! This gang of three had already bonded together by the time I came to meet them through going to the footy, catching gigs and messing about in various bands. This all-singing, guitar, bass combo now needed a snappy drummer – introducing one Tam McGurk from the street tough ghetto of Penilee. Initially I thought that Tam had joined the Primals through Dungo as they seemed to have formed a close buddy relationship but it transpires he joined Primal Scream through meeting a certain Paul Harte via a college friend Gary Mooney when both were studying at Springburn College. Paul Harte was a mate of Bob G who sent out the feelers for a drummer – voila – instant karma! The Primals were now the gang of 4 and all they lacked now was an all dancing, tambourine-rattling, maraca-shaking garage head to complete the picture.....

Around the hazy summer days of 1983 my mate The Doug would always bump into this other musique idiote on his way to work, who hated the dreaded 9 – 5 treadmill as much as himself. His name was Bobby Gillespie and at that time he worked in a local printers in Shawlands. When The Doug described him, I recalled seeing him on a few fleeting occasions but not really speaking to him. The first time was outside The Glasgow Apollo trying to get tickets for the Siouxsie And The Banshees gig only to find out that they'd split up the night before in Aberdeen! The next time I remember seeing Bob G was onstage in The Plaza in a band called The Wake who were supporting New Order that night. I didn't pay much attention to them but The Doug was a fan. Most people were there to check out New Order, who had still to find their live groove and were pretty rank into the bargain that night if truth be told!

Around the autumn days of 1983 Bob G had left The Wake by then and had just hooked up with Jim Beattie in the embryonic Primal Scream. Bob G and The Doug were massive Factory Records freaks but Bob G also mentioned that he'd started to listen to a lot of new 1960s records such as The Byrds, Love and Pebbles Garage Compilations – brand new second hand sounds, just ripe for a new pissed off generation! When I next met up with The Doug and he mentioned this guy and these sounds I told him I'd like to meet him for proper this time, to find out if we were on the same deranged, newly discovered musical wavelength. The Doug's quote at the time was 'He's beginning to listen all that psychedelic pish that you're banging on about now as well'. As you can tell The Doug was not a fan of this particular breed of psychedelic garage punk sounds from another era. After initially meeting up with Bob G for a rap and getting along great, little did I know that this was to be the beginning of a 3-year roller coaster ride of male bonding, psyching in to each other's freewheeling minds on a psychedelic garage trip to the underworld and back – strap yourself in – you're in for a bumpy ride!

By the start of 1984 I had been slung back on the signing on slagheap once more as my temporary nightshift job had ended in December my sweet lord! Bob G joined me also as he'd had enough of his soul destroying printers job and now was a free man who could dedicate all his spare time to the Primal Scream cause 100% plus his drummer boy role in The Jesus And Mary Chain for live gigs, was taking up a large chunk of his free time also. From then on, me and Bob G started to hang out with each other on a regular weekly basis. He was still living in King's Park at the time with Robert Gillespie senior (well quoted Union Rep. of the Labour Party) whose left wing principles had rubbed off on the young Bob G's mind and left a permanent impression. Also living with them was Gringo, his lookalike younger brother. I thought at the time that Bob G senior possessed a healthy black humoured outlook on life, straight outta the mean streets of the Gorbals where he had been brought up. He still vividly had love and hate tattooed on his knuckles from his old gangland years and at that particular time also he was going out with a young, frisky dolly bird half his age much to the disgust of a sneering Bob G junior!

One moment still sticks out in my memory box of that time. As we were blasting out Subway Sects – 'Nobody's Scared' (for the 100th time) on Bob G's battered dansette stereo, out of nowhere Bob G senior appeared and started to strip off his strides, meanwhile talking ten to the dozen about his work, spinning real funny stories a la Billy Connolly style, sending me into raptures. Bob G junior seemed nonplussed about the whole thing as he just didn't find his stories that funny. At times he was real intense and uptight, what he needed was some lsd to unwind his mind, loosen up a bit and to unlock the hidden demons inside his critical mindshaft. Once the springtime sunshine appeared we would hit 'The Queenie' (local park) with Bob G's ever faithful blazing red cassette player to blast out a constant stream of new found ear shredding psychedelic garage sounds – No summer of love 1984 crap going down here daddio, just demented mindrocking 60s garage sounds – Syd Barrett! Love! The Seeds! 13th Floor Elevators and The Chocolate Watchband! At that time I don't think anyone else up 'The Queenie' possessed such a more beautiful, fucked up collection of totally wired sounds booming out of their boombox in the blazing, supercool hot sunshine. At one point goofing off, playing at pitch and putt golf we noticed another shaggy haired moptop dude, who was playing grass bowls at the time. This was Jim Lambie (soon to be pop art supremo) who at the time was in a band called The Boy Hairdresser along with one Norman Blake (soon to be Teenage Fanny). Jim was living in a sprawling mansion of a flat in Langside Road and as we got chatting, he invited us to a house party at their gaff on the following Saturday. Also there that night was everyone's favourite indie darling Jean McClure who was romantically attached to Stewart (aka The Wolfman) then – so it was strictly hands off she's mine guys!

I didn't live too far from Jim's gaff and 'The Queenie' and one sunny day I invited Bob G over to mine for a cuppa and a record session. I don't think Bob G really knew what he was letting himself in for, as I told him about my mum and 'The Joker' – a ventriloquist double act that blew his mind to explosive pieces! In the summer of 1983 I went to the South of France on holiday and brought back this joker doll figure for my wee sister Sarah. My mum instantly fell in love with The Joker's ever smiling fizzog and from that day on, claimed it as her own, very rarely leaving her side in the year to come. From that instant my mum then claimed to be of French origin like 'The Joker' and totally disowned her Irish roots and upbringing! Bob G sat dumbfounded on the couch as my mum went into her full 'Dead Of Night' routine act along with the rest of the family joining in, humouring her, as it kept our mum upbeat and happy. If Govanhill's most famous frontier psychiatrist Ronnie Lang had just dropped into our family home at that very point in time, he would've thrown himself right over the first floor landing! Speaking to Bob G outside after 'The Joker' experience, I don't think he could quite comprehend what had actually happened back in my house and that was without the drugs! He never ever set foot in my family home again! From now on we tended to mostly hang out in Beattie's house of fun, fun, fun!

Around this time in spring 1984, Beattie's sunshine playroom became the main hangout drag for record sessions and songwriting. Since his parents and brother worked all day and Beattie could skive off from his day job (as a budding apprentice architect), it gave him more free time to indulge in some 12-string Frippertronics with the rest of us blasting out some kicking garage sounds. By the time I'd met Jim Beattie I was already hooked on the psychedelic soundscape of Pink Floyd's 'Piper At The Gates of Dawn'. I then soon found out that Beattie went deeper into the Floyd underground and was already a total Syd Barrett nut who then awakened me to the dark side of Pink Floyd and in particular the songwriting genius of Syd Barrett. I was already fried on 'Lucifer Sam', 'Bike' and 'Astronomy Domine' without realising that they'd been penned by the tortured beauty of Syd. Beattie then turned me on to his 2 damaged solo albums along with a track called 'Jughand Blues' of Floyd's second album 'A Saucerful of Secrets'. He also possessed the super rare 'Terrapin' fanzine which enlightened me even more about the lifestyle of this unsung, forgotten music visionary. Then he produced this dodgily named 'Masters Of Rock' compilation that you could snaffle up for a pretty pound or two in the bargain bins. This album had a barrowful of even more psychedelic delights to rediscover and all mostly written by Syd. 'Arnold Layne' was a progressive slab of proto punk psyche dealing with the unusual subject matter of a transvestite stealing woman's clothes off a moonshine washing line. No wonder this superb tune didn't dent the Top 20 at the time of its release! The b-side was just as deranged, the deliciously named 'Candy And A Currant Bun' – a stuff your eyes with wonder instant classic. Syd's second penned attempt at gatecrashing the Top 20 was the delightful 'See Emily Play' which just bursts into a kaleidoscopic joy of colour and explodes with beautiful summer of '67 vibes. Beattie was definitely turning me on to a different side of the dark side of the goon that's for sure! For Syd's Floyd swansong he conjured up a track called 'Jugband Blues' which actually has a Salvation Army Band marching halfway through the record, to create a total derangement of the senses. By this time in Pink Floyd, Syd's acid soaked mind was already on a one way ticket to doomsville and this particular track perfectly captured Syd's impending dislocation from the rest of the Floyd due to his ongoing mental health state of mind and the copious amount of heavy duty lsd which Syd was gobbling up on a daily basis. Beattie also played me this Syd Barrett bootleg album he possessed which contained two stand out unreleased tracks in 'Scream Thy Last Scream' and 'Vegetable Man'. This latter song was a sinister, stomping punker with Syd's lyrics taking the listener through another dimension in time of his sheer vitriol and put down of the psychedelic happening scene at the time. Syd was ten years ahead of his time at least; he should've ripped up his paisley patterned shirt and put it back together again with safety pins – punks! After obliterating my mind with Syd's time in Pink Floyd, Beattie then gave me a loan of Syd's two solo lp's – 'The Madcap Laughs' and 'Barrett'. After the recording of these albums, Syd then disappeared to the safety of his old Cambridge home hideout, never to record again before being re-discovered by The Television Personalities who penned a homage to Syd called 'I Know Where Syd Barrett Lives'. During the recordings of his two solo albums, Syd at times was totally zapped on acid and incapable of finishing some of the recordings. At one point his fellow bandmates tried to arrange a meeting with R D Laing (that man again!) to assess Syd's mental state of mind. Apparently he had read a recent interview of Syd in a music magazine and declared him incurable! 'The Madcap Laughs' contains my favourite Syd solo track in 'Golden Hair' (adapted from a James Joyce poem) which he initially wrote when he was 16 years old. It's hauntingly sung in a double-tracked Syd whisper which still sends a shiver down the tingler to this very day. Two other songs that grab your attention are 'Octopus' and 'Terrapin' which possesses a real slow, barbiturate stoner groove that sends your mind into an instant blissful state of nirvana. The second solo lp from Syd called 'Barrett' is slightly more unhinged and downright creepsville at times especially the real horror show rantings of 'Rats'. Alongside this track are two bounce pop classics in 'Baby Lemonade' and 'Gigolo Aunt' which took me that little bit further into the psychedelic void. Syd's childlike songs resonated big-style in my own personal headspace at that time in my life. He spoke to that lost, innocent kid in all of us and took me on an unforgettable 'Alice in Wonderland' adventure of tripped out pleasures. Listening to the whole collection of Syd Barrett written songs blew away the whole laborious prog-rocking self indulgence of previous Pink Floyd tracks that I had been subjected to over the 1970s period. God bless you Syd – shine on you crazy nugget! LOVE SYD – HATE FLOYD! (I think there could be a tee shirt idea in there?!?)

Meeting the other group members Tam and Dungo wasn't quite as dramatic as meeting up with Bob G and Beattie. I think the first time I'd met them was at Hellfire Recording Studios come rehearsal space in the summer of 1984. My initial thoughts of Tam and Dungo were that they were the quiet ones of the group, slightly reserved but as the story turns out – it was the opposite!

MY FLASH ON YOU

It's kinda strange to ponder on that when I first met Bob G and Beattie and I was rapping on about the musical influences that turned me on, that they'd never really heard much of The Cramps and other real cool trash bands such as Panther Burns! The Gun Club! The Birthday Party and Suicide. These bands were my kind of rock n roll animals: sleazy, provocative, dangerous and dynamic especially in a live gig setting. They'd been synched in to the same music weeklies such as NME! Sounds! and Melody Maker but these fave rave bands of mine went right over their heads. The internet and YouTube were still distant memories of the future so the only way you could turn someone on to these musical forbidden fruits (without giving your precious albums away) was to concoct some mindsnapping C90 cassette mix-tapes.

By the time Bob G had worked his way to The Cramps' 'Psychedelic Jungle' album he was hooked all the way gator! The lp possessed a certain lysergic, voodoo quality which was perfect for 1984 and how could you go wrong with 'Green Fuzz', 'Beautiful Gardens' and 'Under The Wires' for truly warped grooves to behold? Through that album release, from 1981, I had started to see the names The Seeds and The 13th Floor Elevators pop up more frequently whenever Lux Interior was interviewed and asked about his current influences. This certainly pricked up my ears in wanting to discover even more unknown and arcane groups that were lost in time but were once more ripe for discovery. When I caught The Cramps live in May '84 they had already included a kicking version of 'Hungry' by Paul Revere And The Raiders which would've fitted in nicely on 'The Psychedelic Jungle' album or the mini 'Smell Of Female' lp. And who can forget their mighty, insane version of 'Strychnine' from The Sonics which popped up on the second side of their first album – 'Songs The Lord Taught Us'. It's that epic it even surpasses the original – it's that fucking great! One other album that resonated in Bob G's psyche was The Gun Club's 'Fire Of Love' lp.

This album was never off his dansette stereo and whenever I hear the track 'Sex Beat' I am instantly transported to Plymouth Ziggy's nightclub in 1985. As we were packing our gear away after the gig, someone slapped a cassette on in the tour van and 'Sex Beat' came pounding out at full volume and the next you know the band and the fans start bopping away like lunatics as we're humphing the dancing guitars, drums and amps in to the back of the transit – may the power of music compel you brothers and sisters! The other stone cold classic track that warped Bob G's twisted mind was 'Jack On Fire' with its deep south, sex-fuelled lyrics of necromancy that sent him spiralling into a deep fried funk! If those two bands hadn't destroyed his brain cells, I then made him up a mix-tape of Suicide's two glorious albums plus various Alan Vega solo lp's to tantalize his tastebuds. I think by this point in time New Order and The Fire Engines were but fading memories.....Listening to the killer electronic boogie of 'Ghost Rider' and 'I Remember' he couldn't believe that he hadn't heard this futuristic groove of minimalist sounds. Bob G did admit that he saw Suicide supporting The Clash but hadn't really taken any notice of them?!?! How he came to that conclusion astounds me as I was also there and Suicide ripped my mind to pieces. The narrow-minded Clash City Rockers despised the electronic rockabilly sounds even though Alan Vega kept shouting back at them (dodging bottles and cans) "Me and you – we're on the same side". Suicide were definitely well ahead of the curve – I wonder how many blockheads at that particular gig ended up buying Suicide records many years later?

My Suicide/Vega albums still take pride of place in my ever-growing vinyl archive and even if Paul McCartney offered me The Beatles 'Butchers Covers' lp in return, I would gladly reject his handsome deal. I also introduced Bob G and Beattie to Alan Vega's spaced out moderne rockabilly albums especially Collision Drive which possessed a throbbing, dynamic reconstruction of Suicide's 'Ghost Rider' from the first album – total genius!

At rehearsals sometimes the Primals would take on 'I Remember' with myself on drums keeping up a never say die propulsive beat with Bob G rappin' the vocals over the top of the groove and notta bad version it was too if I recall? Another major influence that took root in the Primal Scream sound was the young bold boy genius of Alex Chilton – straight out of Memphis! He'd produced the first Cramps album but at the time I hadn't realised that this guy had already created some of the most heart-wrenching beautiful fucked up sounds to ever hit a turntable. He also popped up on Panther Burns 'Behind The Magnolia Curtain' album on guitar and effects. But the eureka moment came with the discovery of Alex Chilton's Big Star – 'Sister Lovers' album which I snaffled at a record store pronto, after reading a recent interview about its re-release date. 'Sister Lovers' for me is one record that deserves the title of unsurpassable greatness. I instantly made up a cassette tape to Bob G and Beattie and the rest to check out this tortured beauty of an lp. It was first released in 1975 and no one bought it at the time, just like the first Velvet Underground album in 1966. The record is a total masterpiece of unknown pop magic of the toppermost. Kangaroo! Holocaust! and Jesus Christ were the crucial tracks that remained permanently on my stereo for at least one year solid. Everyone who came within our sphere gotta severe earbashing of this mysterious album of tortured genius at work. Through the 'Sister Lovers' album I then discovered the first 2 Big Star lp's – 'No. 1 Record' and 'Radio City' that contained a supreme collection of Byrdsian chiming, rhyming tunes that were very different in sound to 'Sister Lovers'. I actually acquired the 2 albums of Stephen Pastel who wanted my Users 7-inch single 'Kicks In Style' in return – result! We were hoovering up so much amazing undiscovered gems of albums that our well-worn hi-fi's and turntables could barely keep up with the maximum rock 'n' roll damage that we were inflicting on them...

There was one band in particular that we were all universally in love with and that was The Byrds and one person for us stood out in the band and that was Gene Clark with his beautiful aching, soulful songs. He was the top Byrd for us, eager-to-learn jangle groovers, who touched our melancholic souls deeply. I especially identified with Gene Clark personally myself as he was my 'tambourine god' who just happened to be a shit hot songwriter also. I never tired of practicing my tambourine playing along to the first two Byrds albums – 'Mr Tambourine Man' and 'Turn Turn Turn' in my bedroom.

Gene Clark, the man, came from solid Irish/American stock along with a sensation of the Native American in his make up and it's this historical attachment and fiery Celtic soul that makes his songs and voice totally unique in my mind. In his personal life, he was a notorious, rebellious hellraiser who throughout his short life constantly battled the boozed up demons which flew about him. Gazing at pictures of him in The Byrds with his youthful, rugged Prince Valiant looks and then comparing them with his older self at 47, he has the looks of a haunted, ravaged lifestyle that had taken its toll on his body way too early in life.

The one regret we all had around his later years was missing out on seeing him live in a small, intimate club setting. He was playing in London somewhere but it clashed with one of our own gigs. It was a real opportunity missed as shortly after, he died. On his grave is the fitting epitaph 'No Other' – you can't argue with that! It was around that time that Bob G made me up a cassette copy of his 'White Light' album and one track we all flipped on was 'Because Of You'. When I'm dead and gone and everyone's having a rock 'n' roll riot dancing on my grave, this is the song I want to be played to bring it down and make people reflect on the lyrics and Gene's superfluous vocal. After that bittersweet touch of reflection, get the dj then to bang on 'You're Gonna Miss Me' by The 13th Floor Elevators – if you're gonna go, you might as well go out on a high!

Back to some of his recordings again, his mogadon version of 'She Don't Care About Time' on his solo 'Roadmaster' album brings it on home what a superb angelic voice he possessed. On the 'Mr Tambourine Man' lp the unsung gem for me is the 'I'd Knew I'd Want You' track that contains one mighty relaxed Gene Clark harmonic vocal to die for with evocative lyrics about finding that perfect, elusive partner of your dreams – majestic pop at its most glorious. On the second Byrds album 'Turn Turn Turn' Gene Clark turns in another classy performance with 'If You're Gone' which has the most divine, harmonic heavenly choir backing vocals floating over his vocal, sending the listener in to raptures of unknown pleasures. Before he flew the Byrds nest, Gene had a hand in writing the psychedelic raga epic 'Eight Miles High'. The imagery and lyrics are pretty cryptic and drug-fuelled with double meanings a go-go throughout the song. We'll never know for sure how much of a hand he had in the writing of these lyrics as they're certainly a departure in songwriting for Gene Clark. His fear of flying was supposedly one of the reasons for fleeing The Byrds and David Corsby even penned a song about his phobia called 'Psychodrama City'. Gene Clark certainly lived up to the tag as 'The Byrd Who Flew' – in more ways than one. GOD SAVE THE GENE CLARK APPRECIATION SOCIETY!

TALES FROM THE MUSICAL DRUG ATTIC

In December 1983's NME, Julian Cope was featured in an article called 'Tales From The Drug Attic' with a piece on esoteric, undiscovered lost vinyl treasures from mostly the 1965 – 67 time period. Little did I realise at the time that myself, Bob G, Beattie and thousands of other garage heads worldwide were all reading this very same article and were inspired to then go out and discover this brand new kind of music (well, to our young ears anyway) for ourselves. The way Julian Cope waxed lyrical about The Seeds! Electric Prunes! 13th Floor Elevators! Chocolate Watchband and Pebbles Compilations was truly inspiring and awakened in us all a new psychedelic-garage punk dawn to discover. Lucky for us around that time, quite a few re-issue labels had mushroomed also and they then began a major tsunami of record releases to satisfy a new generation of psyched-out punks wanting and demanding a new kind of kick. The labels Rhino! Edsel! and Bam Caruso unearthed momentous slices of freakbeat sounds along with tantalising, informative liner notes and beautifully conceived works of art records sleeves especially from the Bam Caruso label who were out on their own in this genre. It certainly saved us skinteroonie garage cats a pretty penny or two as snaffling up the original releases were well outta our price range. Try some of these compilations on for size: 'Back From The Grave' – 'What A Way To Die' – 'Mindrocker' – 'Scum Of The Earth' – 'The Psychedelic Snarl' – 'The Acid Gallery' and my personal twisted fave 'Chocolate Soup For Diabetics' – blast yer skull with those for starters! I do believe it was the Bam Caruso label that first appeared with the 'freakbeat' moniker – that perfecto moment in time – 1966 to be precise where 1960s beat grooves met psychedelia head on in one glorious tilt a whirl moment in time. The Namdam's description of this particular period in time as pre hippy hits it bang on the button! Certain stories stick out in my mind of the Julian Cope article. It was the first time I'd read about Tommy

Hall's electric jug playing in The 13th Floor Elevators which proceeded to blast it's crazed, epileptic sound all the way through their first album – 'The Psychedelic Sounds Of...' This to me sounded like utter derangement of the first order! And just who the hell was 'Suzy Creamchese'? Frank Zappa wrote it but Teddy And The Patcher covered it in their own psychotic flower punk distinctive style.

1965 – 1966 were the important years for these magical psyched out tunes, before the mainstream media jumped on the summer of love 1967 bandwagon and music turned into one long oh so boring masturbatory jam – man!!! This article turned into a massive influence on our new found tastes in psychedelic garage punk sounds. It opened up a new avenue of discovery called 'The Psychedelic Twilight Zone' – enter if you dare....This elegant, chaotic new world music was at our fingertips and right then we couldn't wait to hit the next Record Fair in town to pick up some more of these vinyl gems.

Around 1984 Record Fairs were about the only gig in town if you wanted to dig deep down into the psychedelic catacombs, to start purchasing these obscure nuggets of vinyl treasures. Most of the High Street record shops such as Virgin and Tower Records at the time only dealt in Greatest Hits and mainstream compilations. If you were lucky De Courcy's in Argyle Street Market might have a rare odd item now and again such as Scott Walker's – 'God Like Genius In The Sky' album compiled by one Julian Cope – freakoids!

Sometimes at the Record Fairs it would turn into a competition to see who could produce the rarest out of print Tim Buckley – Lee Hazelwood – Gene Clark lp in amongst all the other psychedelic punk compilations. At one point I bought the third Seeds album 'Future', Bob G bought 'A Web Of Sound' and Beattie gotta hold of the first Seeds lp, to vary it out and stretch the vinyl budget a little bit more. There was always one dude (step forward Lowdy) who could afford to buy the lot in one go but us poor tykes could only afford to snaffle up a few at a time so we then had to wait till the next Record

Fair rolled into town once more, usually six months later if I remember? One record that everyone bought and had to own was Nancy Sinatra/Lee Hazelwood's 'Some Velvet Morning' which for myself personally is one of the most majestic original songs ever recorded. It just didn't belong in any category whatsoever and contained a most unusual psychedelic warped, waltzing rhythm with Nancy's voice tripping us all out in a dreamlike state until Lee Hazelwood's menacing drawl drifted in Johnny Cash style in a slightly sinister manner. Years later Primal Scream attempted a pathetic version with that Croydon strumpet Kate Moss wailing away like a detuned cat from hell! If you wanna create a decent version, listen to Lydia Lunch/Rowland S Howard's attempt for inspiration, an updated wonky waltz that Tom Waits would've been proud of. One garage compilation that instantly turned our heads was 'The Best Of The Chocolate Watchband'. We were already massive Stones freaks and to discover a band that actually out-stoned The Rolling Stones was a total mindsnapper! Their snarling lead singer Dave Aguilar was that convincing in his swaggering vocals and rubber-lipped looks that he was convinced Mick Jagger came along and stole his look! It was as if ol' rubber lips had passed the garage baton to The Watchband in 1966 and they ran with it to the glorious end producing a pulsating high energy beat to a shakin' maraca groove. Dig some of these tracks for starters: 'Sweet Young Thing', 'Let's Talk About Girls', 'Milkcow Blues', 'Gone And Passes By' and everyone's fave rave up Kinks loner anthem 'I'm Not Like Everybody Else' which they make their own. These songs were that good The Stones should have covered them instead of the other way round – every one a driving-maraca hip-shaking classic to the end!

In amongst the superb finds at the Record Fairs there would appear the odd howler of a compilation – 'Houston Hallucinations' anyone? Precisely!

Within a year, between the three of us (me, Beattie and Bob G) we'd purchased every Byrds – Seeds – Love – Elevators – Watchband album going we were that insatiable and god only knows where we found the ready cash to buy 'em, living at home with no job in sight... After we'd binged out on these vinyl delights we'd then descend on Beattie's sunshine playroom for one almighty blast of garage psyche heaven. Nothing else semed to matter at that point in time, family and old friends were falling by the wayside in rapid succession, as we were subsumed by these new sounds.

IT'S A PSYCHEDELIC WORLD

Also around this time it had seemed that all the old punk bands of the 1977 period had all popped a tab of acid by 1984 (marching backwards into the future!) and turned all psychedelic on us.

Emanating from year zero and vapourising from the overground Siouxsie And The Banshees continued their Beatles fixation by once more delving into 'The White Album' (remember 'Helter Skelter' little piggies?) and producing a neat chiming, uptempo version of 'Dear Prudence' that shot like a neon bolt straight into the straight-laced Top 10 charts. The Banshees shot at 'This Wheel's on Fire' a couple of years later never quite achieved the joys of 'Dear Prudence's' chart placing and in time their psychedelic notion faded away into the ether of obscurity.

The Damned also donned their crushed velvet capes and stormed the Top 20 charts with a gothic high tempo version of Love's superlative latino tinged 'Alone Again Or' track. The hipsters and flipsters on the music scene already knew that the chief psychedelic warlord in The Damned was one Captain Sensible (The Electric Rebel) who by the looks of that furry get-up that he sports onstage had definitely chewed on a few electric sugarcubes out in his interstellar Croydon hideaway.

It was in 1984 that The Damned took a trip to the subterranean recesses of their mind and emerged in full psyched out guise mode as Naz Nomad And The Nightmares producing their one and only album 'Give Daddy The Knife Cindy' in homage to Pink Floyd's 'Careful With That Axe Eugene'. Their psyche garage attempts at 'Action Woman', 'The Trip' and 'Get Me To The World On Time' don't come anywhere near the tripped out, deranged originals. For me personally they should've stuck to their own psyche flavoured tunes such as 'I Just Can't Be Happy Today' which is a perfect example. One band who did produce a stomping razor sharp version of The Electric Prunes 'Get Me To the World On Time' was London's Clapham South Escalators who cut a real mean punkabilly one-off classic!

    Swindon's finest purveyors of psyche punk pop thrills XTC also joined the psychedelic dance party concocting two excellent mini albums under the supercool moniker of The Dukes Of Stratosphear in '25 O Clock' and 'Psonic Psunspots'. These enigmatic freakoids captured the psychedelic bubble down beat to a tee in their new guise producing instant stone cold classics in 'You're My Drug, Brainiacs' 'Daughter' and the enchanting 'Vanishing Girl' – a track so pop, Prince should've covered it! These dudes had certainly swallowed the right microdot, conjuring up sparkling, pastiche homages to The Hollies, Beach Boys, Syd Barrett, The Kinks and The Zombies. By 1988 The Dukes had dropped out of the time machine and metmorphosized straight back into XTC mode once more. Life certainly begins at the hop!

    Who would've thought that The Ramones would also jump onboard the psychedelic garage punk bandwagon in the late 1980s producing a heady brew of covers called 'Acid Eaters' (neat name). Again this album failed to convince me that their versions of 'My Back Pages', 'Out Of Time' and '7 And 7 Is' were better conceived than the outstanding originals. Only their version of The Stones 'Out Of Time' comes close. Surprisingly Alice Cooper also churned out a version of Love's '7 And 7 Is', that was brutal to listen to also. Just how could you even attempt to capture the essence of the original insane version with a spitting Arthur Lee vocal, that frenetic 100mph Snoopy drumbeat and those truly surreal lyrics. I just hoped Arthur's dog survived the trip!

    The 1980s period was definitely a bit hit and miss concerning turning on to the psychedelic groove and that includes Marc Almond's torturous attempt at 'The Days of Pearly Spencer' which came a bit later – dearie me, pass the mushrooms please!

IN THAT JINGLE JANGLE MORNING

What's my name? John Martin actually but not that boring old folkie with the same name! His second name was spelt with a y instead of an i – thank god! My own name didn't really particularly resonate within myself; it wasn't exotic or rock 'n' roll enough so I decided to change it to Martin St John instead. I simply reversed my full name and stuck a saint in the middle, to give it a hint of distinction. It was funny when John Peel once read out the members of Primal Scream for a radio session and he called me 'Martin Sinjin John' – ha! The name was also a bit of a nod and homage to the 13th Floor Elevators' mysterious songwriter John St Powell who by the second album 'Easter Everywhere' had reverted to Powell St John! There were no pictures of this dude on any of the Elevators' record sleeves but he'd written a couple of truly inspiring sinister tracks that had wormed by brain called 'Kingdom Of Heaven' and 'Monkey Island'. On 'Easter Everywhere' as Powell St John now, he penned the twisted psyche gem 'Slide Machine'. Maybe someday I'll get to meet the dude and ask him "Just why did you change your name for the second album?" Answers on a postcard please. Martin St John ain't quite up there with Joe Strummer! Richard Hell! Polystyrene or even Aeriel Bender (all time classic) for supreme inspirational rock 'n' roll namepieces but it's only rock 'n' roll and I like it......

Believe it or not but I actually practiced my tambourine playing for live gigs, radio sessions and recordings! No kid on Bez maraca behaviour from me. My fave rave albums to bash my tambourine along to were the first albums of The Byrds! Love and The Seeds. The tambourine was high in the mix and their jangling beats were great to get yer tamby groove thing on. Every 60s garage band worth their salt had a guy or girl grooving away on the beat and looking killer!

Flicking through the back pages of my mind I can recall a John Peel radio session once in Maida Vale at the BBC studios and at the production helm was that hoary ol Mott rocker Dale Griffin. This guy actually banished me to the outside of the main recording studio as I was supposedly playing out of time with Tam the drummer and was putting everyone else of their rhythm according to his finely tuned lugholes. When I played the tambourine I actually followed the abstract beat in my own head whereby I didn't follow the drummer's groove but Beattic's actual guitar rhythms! I was off the beat but on the beat at the same time and it only made perfect sense to myself and no one else in the band. It definitely produced a good bout of head scratching among the other members of the band at the time.

Anyway back to some of the greatest tambourine flavoured songs from the 1960s jingle jangle heyday. On Love's version of the Manfred Mann penned 'My Little Red Book', Arthur Lee's red right hand introduces the song, accentuating the rhythm with a slamming never say die groove not letting up until the final conclusion – an easy one to practice along to ha!

On the ultimate freakbeat 45 'Makin Time' by Creation, the tambourine takes a while to appear as the song builds up in to a tension packed uber mean beat until a couple of verses pass and then the tamby appears out of nowheresville as it drives the crazed, schizoid rhythm to its shimmering orgasmic climax. Hearing The Velvet Underground's 'Pale Blue Eyes' in all its minimalist glory of just guitar and the voice of Lou Reed you can't help but notice how the tambourine is the only rhythmic instrument in town as it keeps a solid intoxicating groove along to the actual song. And who could forget that iconic photograph of Andy Warhol defiantly holding up his prized shimmering tambourine to advertise the first Velvets 'banana' album?

A special mention must also go to Motown Records who place the tambourine to the forefront on every one of their hip clickin, supersnazzy pop soul numbers. Two records in particular stick out in my memory box. The first is the Supremes – 'Reflections' with its spooked out sound effects and atmospheric strung out stoned vocals of Diana Ross cooing lasciviously in to your stereo speakers as a glorious greatness and perfection tambourine beat cruises the rhythm underneath. The other Motown tambourine classic is the more obscure 'Let's Go Somewhere' by R Dean Taylor, a 7-inch single that kicks in with some serious jingle jangling rhythmic beats before it explodes in to breakneck speed as it send dancers out on the floor, spinning around in ecstasy – it's one killer beat with one killer tambourine!

I can't finish this piece without mentioning the two hit singles from the 1960s which had tambourine in the title – Bob Dylan's 'Mr Tambourine Man' and The Lemon Pipers' swirlin pop gem 'Green Tambourine' (how apt). I've always preferred The Byrds' version of 'Tambourine Man' if truth be told. They bring the track alive with their electric Rickenbacker guitar style compared to Dylan's stripped down acoustic version. There's also another ace version out there by Dylan's Gospel who put a really nice gospel soul spin on it. The fact that The Byrds had a real life 'Mr Tambourine' aka Gene Clark on stage bashing his tamby makes the song even more special and poignant to me. The Lemon Pipers' 'Green Tambourine' is another joyful blast of sunshine pop with more drug infused lyrics to chew on. This song was relased in the acid drenched late 60s whereby lyricists were opening up their minds to more imaginative lyrical word pieces when it came to songwriting. Billy McKenzie (ex Associates) also produced a neat cover of 'Green Tambourine' which is tucked away somewhere, on an obscure b-side solo single if my memory serves me right.

Before I depart and give my digits a much earned rest, I've got to mention the Panther Burns tracks 'Tina The Go-Go Queen' who apparently shakes her fanny like a tambourine – wowsa! Gustav Falco is American but over here that means something else differently! His version in the bad ol USA means shaking your ass/tush like a tambourine – which I kinda prefer! One last piece of useless information in to the amazing world of tambourines. Did ya know that the metal jingles on them are called zils? Gimme some skin before I start to untangle the jingle from the jangle tamby cats!

THE GRIFFIN BAR

One summery night in late May, The Primals gang (and the two Pauls) found ourselves in our local hang out pub – The Griffin. After acquiring several 'pink pyramid tabs' (lsd) we decided to hit the exotic night life off Sauchiehall Street aka The Art School Friday night disco which we managed to gatecrash our way through. By the time we arrived there, we were completely 'fleeing' outta our skulls and in a wild, raucous devil may care mode. The dj was playing real blando sounds so we bugged him and requested 'any 60s garage punk' and lo and behold he spinned a few discs to the utter joy of ourselves but to utter bemusement of the assembled arty crafty students who fled the dancefloor quickstyle as we took over the whole floor, bouncing about like deranged chipmunks on heat. Someone grassed us to the monkey men bouncers who then proceeded to bounce us right on to the garage gutter outside. As we assembled outside (still well up on the trips), Tam pounced up on a car bonnet and then others joined in as they proceeded to hop, skip and jump on a procession of parked buggys to our amusement in our acid riddled mindstate ha!

As we wandered about heading into the City Centre someone piped up "Where will we go now?" There was only one suggestion and that was to head back to Beattie's spare living room for a secret undercover of the night record session. All 7 of us hailed a couple black cabs to continue the trip in merry Mount Florida. As Syd Barrett was blasting our stupefied minds, someone decided to roll up Big Paul in a carpet rug that was lying around forra silly laugh just as Dungo planted a clock on his forehead and just at that point, out of nowhere Beattie's mum appeared (rubbing her eyes) and told us all to turn down the music and the carry on, as we had awakened the whole Beattie household with our tripped out hi-jinks.

As Beattie's mum departed without realising the ridiculous stunts that were going on in her precious spare living room (Sunday guests only) we all burst into convulsions of laughter at the unfolding scene that Beattie's mum had missed out on. I think her serious tone of voice maybe had something to do with it too and the fact that the adult world hadn't a clue that we were goddamn tripping out of our gourds and loving every minute of it! Sorry Mrs B for being cheeky rapscallions of the night.....

Now back to the Griffin Bar and to tall ya the story of how we all tended to gravitate towards it on many a wasted weekend night. When me and The Doug discovered it for ourselves in Summer '79, it automatically felt like our second home and would be our main headquarters for the next ten years solid, a non-stop procession of propping up the bar every weekend without fail, Friday, Saturday and sometimes on a Sunday if we still had any cash left! The only menu in town in The Griffin at the time was their special deal of a pie and a pint all for £1 only. None of your gourmet, gastro nonsense and craft beer shit had taken hold in this particular bar yet. This was a pub for sociable drinking and drugging only!

The Griffin was peppered with a variety of kooky characters that took in your arty loafers, biker types, budding thesps, musique idiotes and yer locals – a myriad assortment on the outer fringes of society all locked in together. A special mention must also go to the doppelgangers that frequented the bar on a regular occurrence. Near the front entrance stood the local Anthony Perkins lookalike – straight outta The Bates Motel and released for the weekend to sup amongst us fearless denizens of the night. I'm sure when he had a few rums too many, me and The Doug could detect a mad twinkle in his eye which conjured up real gothic horror visions of stuffed birds, creepy mansions and powdered wigs – one to avoid strictly late at night he was....The other stand out clone in The Griffin that no one else seemed to notice (apart from me and The Doug) was the John Craven dude. He wasn't quite as intimidating as ol 'psycho' himself and kept himself to himself, keeping up a steady succession of foaming ales to banish away those newsround blues before once again donning that uptight BBC shirt and tie to hit us with some more ultra depressing news to bore the pants of us all. Another regular face there every weekend (but not a clone) near the comfy seats up the back, stood propping up the bar was 'The Sergeant Major', who was bar polishing up his half and a half in silent contemplation as all manic hell was being unleashed behind his back (false teeth in pints of lager on acid anyone?) one other major character of The Griffin was 'Irish John' the main chargehand behind the bar who just spontaneously barked out orders at people such as "Is that a swastika on your back there?" to some perplexed punkoid who was mightily offended. It was around these times that I heard a particularly nasty story involving 'Irish John'. Apparently he went to a party one night off duty and some sicko there decided to spike his drink with acid for a daft laugh!!! News got around that he flipped out on the trip and was reported missing in action for several weeks behind the bar. In my eyes this unfunny stunt was of a particular nasty streak. 'Irish John' was fruity enough without acid – a bad funk all round.

The Griffin around this time had started to pick up a reputation as a place that you could score your weekly pharmaceuticals for a small exchange of hard cash. Speed and acid were the main drugs of choice for the eager space cadets assembled. Acid came in small microdots pills or pink pyramid blotters that were of the strongest, mind bending quality. No barbs, codeine, smack or mandies on sale here – that was for downers only! At one point as I hit the cludgy for a 'single fish' I came across a leaflet warning the patrons not to buy speed off the local drug dealer as it was a bad batch and had been cut up with some straight strychnine. The bar staff had apparently got wind of the toxic batch, warning us regulars of the imminent dangers when snorted and had decided to flyer the gents and ladies toilets. How's that for customer care!!!

Bob G at this point in time (Summer of '84) still had the appearance of a fresh faced bumfluff youth and depending on who was serving behind the bar at the time he would sometimes have to produce his ID and since he was like 23 and never really ventured into pubs at the time, he very rarely carried his birth certificate with him. As he was sucking on a candy and a currant bun ice cream outside, we'd be inside, getting ripped on Sammy The Tripmaker's latest dynamite supply of lsd! This dude was our resident 'Mr Pharmacist' dealer along with a fellow biker (inna wheelchair) providing the 'sweets' on a regular occasion to satisfy our druggy lust for life. If these two street wise druggists hadn't appeared by about ten o'clock at night, panic would set in and a few of us would get kinda twitchy and leave The Griffin to hunt them down, in their other well known drug fuelled haunts at the time, namely 'Oceans Eleven' bar across the road in Sauchiehall Street and 'His Nibs' further on down off the main drag. By the time you found Sammy The Tripmaker, he was already high on his own supply and after some small talk gibberish he would finally come across with the goods for the night's entertainment – all for £1 each a pop!

There was always a cracking, energetic buzz about in The Griffin at the weekend, as you'd just show up with no masterplan in hand, and the next you know you could be boppin' up Nite Moves, skanking up The Tech or getting funky at Maestros usually as high as the proverbial kite either watching a band on stage or dancing your skinny ass off.

One night in The Griffin, that gang of 7 again, descended on Maestros with a handful of 7-inch records – all punk and no funk! Since the resident dj knew a few of our faces, he blasted some of the singles and totally killed the dancefloor vibe as the regular funkateers fled the dancefloor inna pissed off disdainful mood. I think hearing Wire's 'I Am The Fly' was the record that broke the camel's back. We were instantly sent to compost corner and fled once more into the dark night. The crazy thing was, that Maestros always played a varied mixture of tunes with The Banshees – 'Spellbound' back to back with Grandmaster Flash – 'The Message' blaring out, at times, during the early 80s period.

In the early 1980s The Griffin was also a major hangout for all the Postcard Records related bands such as Orange Juice and Aztec Camera but no one really made a fuss about seeing them at the time – they were treated as just another local band who frequented the bar on a regular basis like, for example, 'The Dreamboys' who were a permanent fixture in The Griffin Bar and at the time spawned Peter Capaldi and Craig Ferguson (two future tv stars) and a really cookin live band they were too!

It was kinda funny to see The Jesus And Mary Chain beginning to hang out there also, as they looked as though they hadn't seen the insides of a boozer for years! These dudes were bedroom punks with pale complexions with some serious wiggy wighats going down.

On a weekly basis you'd come across the same faces there, mostly from deepest Busby, outer Cumbernauld, scary Airdrie and punky Paisley! It was a great mix of people, fellow voyagers on the same trip, who sat on the same seats guaranteed every week waiting patiently for that club, gig or party to appear so that everyone could kickstart their whole fucked-up debauched, decadent weekend.

The fishbowl area in the bar was a popular haunt to hang out in and that's where Sammy The Tripmaker would hide out, wheeling and dealing away from the prying eyes of 'Irish John' and his cohorts. Also attached to The Griffin were two lounges, The Griffiny and The Griffinette which were of a more sombre, sedate affair – unlike the bar next door!

Looking back now the schizoid mix of different peoples assembled in The Griffin then created some kind of magical alchemy whereby we were all drawn there like a magnet for what seemed like a ten-year eternity.

I swear to this day that I once clocked Divine propping up the bar one Saturday night when he was gigging in town or maybe it was the polyester pink pyramid tabs at work?!?!

FLASHBACK CHECKPOINT

I'd first started to experiment with drugs around 1981 mostly of a hallucinogenic bent, ie acid and magic mushrooms which propelled me into a cosmic adventure of never-ending pleasure seeking weekend thrills. It certainly made a pleasant change of slugging half pints of stagger juice down my throat for the rest of my pissing social life. I certainly was not gonna be no stereotype drinking my age in pints! The discovery of these drugs of forbidden fruit tasted even better when you knew the straight 9-5 world hadn't a clue what the hell they were all about. We weren't on some enlightened Timothy Leary transcendental kick, it was more of a free form anything goes Ken Kesey trip into the unknown for us spaced out cats! It was a total escape into the inner world. It also seemed around this point in time that the whole of The Griffin was turning on (except the barstaff) to these zapped out chemical reactions to the old synapses.

Along with the spacey 'microdots' and 'pink pyramid' tabs being gobbled up, the magic mushrooms also began to sprout up their wigged out heads and hey! – they were free gratis (but more disgusting). The 'mushy season' usually appeared around the misty months of late September/early October if my fried mind serves me right. Then all of a sudden, it turned into open season as the lysergic word of mouth got around that the 'magic ones' (long stem, little teat on top) were suddenly out and were ripe for some freakin' picking. Out of nowhere all the flipped out acid heads would appear out of their autumnal bedrooms and descend on their nearest golf course (with imaginary golf bag in tow) to catch the early morning dew and collect the prized, free psychedelics. You'd be lucky to get a few days action out of them as the local killjoy park keeper would get sussed to the situation and would then spray some toxic pesticides on them to put a real bummer on the mushroom season trip! I still don't know if that crazy law exists whereby you can't be caught by the fuzz picking them, it was only when you actually cooked them and they had turned lysergic that you got busted!!! I would've loved to have heard the conversation in The House Of Lords about that little bill when they'd passed it?!?!

One thing is for sure and that was when you took them raw (about 50 zappers) they stunk bigstyle and left a disgusting taste in your gub. They were best cooked in an Indian curry or even inna cuppa tea but if you wanted an instant hit it was a simple case of wrapping them in a sheet of tissue and swallowing them quickstyle before you wretched the whole lot back up again. One time in my house, I was cooking up some 'mushies' in a pie and my mum suddenly appeared all quizzical "What's that funny smell?" "Don't worry, it's just one of those foreign pie things that I like!" My mum skulked away half believing me and left me to 'em.

By the timewarp year of 1984 and with the psychedelic garage scene ready to rise up from the underground, acid had taken over as the No. 1 drug of choice for a brand new artificial energy kick and we were the new psyched out pipers at the gates of dawn, ripe, for some new tripped out adventures. These drugs possessed a mystical gateway to unchartered, unhinged experiences of forbidden delights especially in the world of sound and vision. The acid certainly didn't work on everyone. If you were a fucked up, neurotic deep-thinking individual, the drug would wipe you out and leave your mind wriggling on the bedroom floor in a vegetable-like state. You had to trip out with the right people in the right setting, with a healthy state of mind – strictly hang-up free!

God knows what the original lsd 25 tabs of acid were like in the 1960s straight from the Sandoz labs of Switzerland? Once you popped that first tab, there was no way back crawling up those stairs – you were either on the magic bus or off it. We'd all bought the ticket and took the ride – Do You Dream In Colour?

To the tune of The Skids 'tv Stars' here's a little ditty I put together to commemorate famous acidheads of the big screen and small screen!

Cary Grant! R.D. Laing! Goldie Hawn! Barbarella! James Coburn! Norman Wisdom! George Clinton! ALBERT HOFFMAN!

THE 24-HOUR TECHNICOLOUR EAST KILBRIDE FREAK-OUT!

There were only a couple of bands around the Glasgow area who were tuning into the same 1960s psychedelic punk wavelength as ourselves. One was The Pastels, who already had been kicking around for a good few years on the Glasgow music scene and annoying the shit out of everyone. The other group was The Jesus And Mary Chain (JAMC for short) from merry go round East Kilbride on the outer fringes of Glasgow's ripped backside. I first came across these guys when Bob G had been handed a promo demo tape from Douglas (bass player). We had a good listen to it and thought it contained an energetic bastard mix of influences such as Generation X and Dr Mix And The Remix which were different at the time. It certainly struck a note with us and sounded different from the norm that was cutting about in the indie scene at the time. They were originally called 'The Daisy Chain' (tweeness incarnate) and comprised of Jim Reid on vocals and Douglas Hart on bass in their embryonic days till William Reid (Jim's brother) hooked up and plugged in on feedback drenched guitar effects. They also had a drummer called Murray Dalgleish on the drum stool. How they got their first gig was truly a buzzed up, word of mouth chain of events. Promoter Nick Lowe (not the Stiff dude) passed the well worn demo tape to Bob G who then passed it on to Tam Coyle who was then the promoter of gigs at Nite Moves. The JAMC first gig was on a boring nothing-to-do Tuesday night in June and I vividly remember at the time Douglas and co frantically out pasting up posters, before their first ever gig, outside of their bedroom. Around 30 bodies had turned up outta curiosity, to see The Mary Chain turn up on stage totally pished, stumbling about and lasting all of 15 shambolic minutes (3 songs) before being hauled off stage, thrown downstairs and slung head first into the back alley like a bunch of gutter rats –

take that for your feedback and explosions, you goddamn destructive, disciples of melody and mayhem! My first initial reaction on viewing this spectacle was "Are these guys for real or extracting the urine?" On that very same stage a couple of years before I had just witnessed the most exciting, shambolic, chaotic gig when The Birthday Party had torn the place up with one Rowland S Howard on drunken stumblin' feedback mayhem guitar. I was still to be convinced that JAMC were the real deal daddio, did they possess a tune as earth shatteringly great as 'The Friendcatcher'? I preferred the noise and tracks on the demo but so far as a live spectacle the garage psyched out jury was still out on these dudes for me personally. One aspect did appeal and that was the like it or lump it arrogant attitude which was kinda refreshing on the oh so staid Glasgow music scene at the time. For the next couple of weeks most of The Primals and JAMC would begin to see a bit more of each other hanging out in The Griffin and conspiring together to venture on a real psychedelic trip into the outer suburbs of East Kilbride. It was also a good excuse to give the clockwork Orange Parade a big bodyswerve in Glasgow for their annual hate fest freakshow parade.

It was on this scorching hot summer day in July 1984 that I found myself meeting up with Bob G, Beattie and the two Pauls to catch a bus from Battlefield that would take us to East Kilbride and one unbelievable twenty four hour acid fried trip later....To this very day, I still get a reality flashback to the surreal happenings that occurred on that memorable day in time – burning giraffes a go-go!

As we departed our magic bus and met up with the three fuzzy headed Mary Chain gang (ready to storm heaven and venture into a veritable no man's land of the unknown), I produced the microdot tabs and proceeded to dish them out to everyone, like totally excited kids trying out the new sweetie in town only these were no lemon sherberts! Douglas had brought along his old battered cassette player to really bring us up on the trip and to transport us to the goddamn freaky outer world on time – faster than a speeding mind – whoosh!!!!

The Mary Chain had decided that we should head for an old disused garage on the edges of East Kilbride to trip out in as it was in a remote quiet part of town. By the time we arrived there, the sun was belting down like a blazing comet and our brains were getting melted quickstyle as the acid kicked in and we were heading straight for the 99th floor as voices green and purple started to rear its wonky head. Once we got to the decrepit garage William and Jim went into full on auto destructive mode as they proceeded to smash and destroy the shit out of everything around them and this then triggered off Bob G, who out of nowhere had found a rope hanging from the rafters which he then started swinging on about Tarzan style, then proceeded to jump off and grab Douglas's fuzzy wig-hat hairdo tugging away at it and not letting go. I didn't quite dig the charged atmosphere at this point in time and started to get a bad dose of the paranoias. This was certainly no perfumed garden trip out here; it was more like a garden of unearthly delights unfolding before my very eyes. Myself, Beattie and Paul (half a tab) McNeil then went outside, to get away from the bad vibes inside and found ourselves in a quiet spot on the bottom of a golf course sitting about like a bunch of Syd-like gnomes spinning funny tales of previous acid trips and zoomerating like hell, trying to get something out of this mind melting experience that we found ourselves in. It doesn't matter where you're tripping, a panda cop car always seems to appear and as it slowed down surveying the scene, (ie three unkempt dudes rapping away at the bottom of the golf course), we started to get the 'paras' once more as we could still hear the gang inside still, creating merry mayhem so we decided to head back into the garage. Back in the psychedelic shack, we were truly floating on air by this time and I was beginning to visualize giant football boots in the burning orange skies above. I then split from the garage goings on and went for a casual stroll outside to get away from the still suffocating vibes from inside. As I came to this river I could literally hear the grass grow around me as I was suddenly rooted to the spot and then suddenly out of nowhere I was surrounded by hundreds of little bad ass demons (like the dwarf out of The Singing Ringing Tree x 100) at my feet looking up at me shouting "Get him!" Hellzapoppin! I suddenly realised I had to get out of there pronto and ran back to the garage relieved to have snapped out of that potential hellish bad trip scenario. When I arrived back at the garage, everyone was hanging about outside, sitting about trying to get into the psychedelic groove of Arthur Lee's Love but the sounds to my ears were beginning to sound real weird like. Either our batteries had run low or the cassettes? Something didn't sound quite right so we turned the sounds off. It was then around this time that Bob G started to have a major freak out and turn spazz on us. He took a complete psychotic reaction, broke on through to the other side, started to take down his strides and then proceeded to perform some weird out white rabbit impersonations bounding about like a freeform bunny lunatic which had the rest of us absolutely rolling about the ground in stitches. This space cadet had now turned into the king of chaos right before our disbelieving eyes, a dribbling fram Winker Watson from hell – he was suddenly rocket man incarnate! He still had a thing about tugging at Douglas's wighat and seemed to be getting out of hand so everyone split apart from myself and Paul McNeil, lumbered with a totally gonesville Bob G who was now rolling about in the dirt and still with his trousers at his ankles. Luckily for Bob G, myself and Big Paul were experienced trippers (the good, the bad and the ugly) whereas the rest of the gang here were relatively new to the acid experience and never had to deal with this sorta warped behaviour before. They just couldn't handle his erratic freakout bursts of madness as Bob G was so wrapped up in his own personal mind garden by now – total la-la land! He was soaring eight miles high and heading for oblivion so we decided to help the guy get his trousers back up again (as the joke was wearing thin) and get the hell out of there! We finally got him to lay still and as we started to pull up his strides, wriggling about, we (me and Paul) just both looked at each other and proceeded to burst out laughing at the totally ridiculous situation that we both found ourselves in. From a passers-'by point of view, it had looked as though we had just gang-raped this dude, stole his cash and were now helping him up with his trousers after the act! It was an unreal situation and Bob G just lay there like a little boy lost with not a care in the world. This guy was heading for a slow death right before our very eyes and let's get this

Crystal Crescent sparkling clear here, if it wasn't for myself and Big Paul rescuing Bob G at this point in time (as everyone else had given up on him and fucked off) there would have been no 'Velocity Girl'!, no 'Screamadelica'! and no 'Country Girl' – ahem!

After that little episode of freakout city, we managed to catch up with the rest of the gang or who was left of it. Everyone had come down off their magic cloud by now as Bob G had put a real bummer on everyone's trip with his major grade one meltdown. Even the patron saint of lost souls couldn't have saved this dude from scrambling his brains at this point in time. He was heading for a 19th nervous breakdown so we all decided to head for this peaceful river further down the country lane. By this time the two Reid brothers had split and wandered off into the ether. We heard the next day that they had both laid down in the boiling sun, fell asleep and awoke hours later to find out that Jim had acquired a burnt red stripe right across his gut due to going in to an acid induced coma in the sun. William also had a nasty experience as he had started seeing spiders in his eyelids. Along with Bob G, if Neal Cassady had suddenly come off the road and appeared here, he would've definitely skipped out giving these guys a diploma as they had spectacularly failed The Acid Tests bigstyle! Meanwhile down the lane, Bob G was back in abusive mode and getting in to a jaffa cake-like state once more, as he started to hurl a volley of abuse at passing joggers as they sped on by. As we finally arrived at the river, Bob G was just about to fall in when myself and Paul just grabbed him in the nick of time. To get to the other side of the river to cool down, you had a short jump over. Me and Big Paul just took an arm each and wheeched him over, as we all fell in to a crumpled heap on the ground. Just as we were cooling down in the acid heat we suddenly heard gunfire coming from god knows where? Holy Gadzooks! This was turning into one helluva killer trip! Some assassin, high up in the trees was firing at some birds and we all thought it was us he was firing at! Right then we all thought we were gonna die for our psychedelic sins. Douglas went over to the dude in the tree and explained to him that we were still tripping out of our trees and could he please refrain from firing bullets over our heads as we were still pretty much fried from all the previous goings on. Lucky for us, Douglas knew the guy and everything was then calm for a short while with me, Beattie, Douglas and the 2 Pauls chatting away amongst ourselves with Bob G sitting on his own in his own peculiar world. We then all decided it was time to hit the big road back to Glasgow. As we left the country fields of East Kilbride for the last time, I took a look back and right at that moment in time it was like looking at a perfect picture postcard of luscious green fields, glorious sunshine and little fluffy clouds – perfecto! We were still merrily tripping at this time but not as heavily as before in the early afternoon. It was now around 5 o'clock and we were still around 2,000 light years from home. We were still that zonked, we actually got on the wrong magic bus that was headed in the opposite direction of Glasgow, until someone noticed and we bailed off and crossed the road to wait at the correct bus stop to sanityville. Then out of nowhere we heard the dreaded flutes and drums of all these clockwork dudes in dodgy pinstripe trousers and overlarge hats heading over the hill, zooming in on our horizon. It was payback time, time to repent sinners and for them – it was just another Saturday but for us…..

We were struck silent as they glowered past us, shooting mean looks of disgust, looking like we had crawled up outta some kind 1960s underworld. Secretly we were all dying to laugh at the stupidity of this buncha Mr Benn characters all marching to the same innocuous beat of bigotry. Thank fuck, a bus finally came along to rescue us from this insane horroshow freakshow – destination Further!

I was still pretty much ripped on the acid when I got on the bus and gave the driver a whole load of change and acid gobbledygook about where we were heading as a bemused Paul looked on in astonishment.

On the bus Paul had told us all that it was okay to invade his mum's house to get a wash as he said that we all looked like a bunch of navvies who'd just finished up a dayshift at the local building site!

After a quick wash and bite to eat, me and the 2 Pauls decided to hit The Griffin to recant our trip to all the disbelievers in the bar. As we told the story of our totally surreal day out in East Kilbride they couldn't quite comprehend what we had experienced especially the Bob G freakout part. The next day when I phoned Bob G to find out how he was, he told me that him and Beattie were last seen at Shawlands X giving it sieg heil's down Kilmarnock Road to a busload of bewildered looking German tourists on their tour bus before heading their separate ways. When we arrived at The Griffin our faces were blazing hot, what with the combined effects of the scorching heat and the acid in us. By the time we got there, the acid effect had come down a notch and it then turned into a kool, glassy eyed, speed buzz without the scary distorted sounds and visuals appearing.

For a couple of weeks after the trip, it took us a while to play Love and those psychedelic garage records again, in a drug free normal state of mind. The whole lsd experience nearly backfired on us and as my mate Dougie once quoted "There's always one!" (ie freakout person). Looking back and reflecting on that day once more it was the most dangerous, hyper scary, exhilarating other worldly experience I've ever lived through – to this very day!!! It was as though you were stuck in an acid time bubble, with no escape route, a bit like Patrick McGoohan in The Prisoner trying to escape from the village in every episode of that insane tv series.

When I finally woke up next day on the Sunday afternoon, I felt glad to be back in the real world once more after that psychedelic trip to the inner world of madness. We certainly got higher than the bomb that day for sure.....

THE GROSVENOR PICTURE HOUSE DOUBLE BILLS

Throughout the whole summer of '84 myself and Bob G had got totally hooked on visiting The Grosvenor Cinema in the hipster West End to catch some truly mind altering double bills of mostly obscure 1960s slightly kooky, trashy flicks, with a couple of leftfield choices from the 1970s and 80s also thrown in. The first film that grabbed our attention was 'Beyond The Valley Of The Dolls' (which was the main feature) along with 'Valley Of The Dolls' which was not quite as out there. The main feature concerned the musical adventures of a super, slinky buxotic group of chicklets called 'The Carrie Nations' who take you on a rollercoaster ride of emotions and thrills in what it entails to be as a famous all girl garage pop band in the late 1960s. It was directed by Russ Meyer with a large, colourful all expenses Hollyweird budget and it certainly produced an eye-catching perspective from a female point of view concerning the pitfalls, with all sorts of strange scenes unfolding before your disbelieving eyes. 'The Carrie Nations' beat babes were managed by a parasitic, kinkoid dude called Ronnie 'Z Man' Bartell (after Phil Spector supposedly) and who actually – get this! possesses a goddamn pair of female tits – very bizarre! The film is definitely worth a gander for its campy, trashy take on pop stardom in the late 1960s. The next memorable double bill to suck up (along with Douglas Hart as well this time) was Midnight Cowboy and Barbarella. We definitely popped the tab for this mind shredding double bill of psychedelic weirdnesss that's for sure! One of our favourite scenes in Midnight Cowboy was the freaky psyched out party scene which was full of the New York underground glitterati having a freeform, tripped out helluva time. I remember reading once that The Velvet Underground were asked if they wanted to be the party band in the party scene but it fell through and went to Elephant's Memory instead – a major pity! Some of the Warholian entourage did make it into the film through as walk-on extras. In a café scene with Rizzo and Joe Buck, a striking New York freak appears, to hand them an invite to the party resplendent in a wild bouffant hairdo, leather trench coat jacket, black boots and black skirt – wowsa! That dude was at least ten years ahead of his time with that stylish kit that wouldn't looked outta place ten years later in the burgeoning punk rock scene. Next up was Barbarella and this film was conceived in the late 1960s for acid heads only – no debate! It starred a vampish Jane Fonda, as a space age sex kitten floating about in outer space dressed in the most revealing, kinkiest, furriest outfits to ever hit the cinema screen. At one point in the film she's actually being pummelled by a pumping organ like sex machine called 'The Orgasmatron' controlled by an evil badass, eyebrowed villain called Duran Duran (no sniggering now). Also starring in Barbarella was the ultimate supergroupie herself, Anita Pallenberg, who starred as the ultra saucy 'Black Queen' who was also kitted out in a variety of explicit kinky costumes that instantly sent all our libidos into outer space!. The scene where The Black Queen beckons Barbarella in to her 'Chamber of Dreams' is total bliss oh my brothers and sisters as she enters a mind warping super colour den, of psychedelic luminescent nirvana which Barbarella can't escape from. Currently on the cinema grapevine the word is out that they're gonna do a re-make of Barbarella – one piece of advice – don't! It would be totally impossible to replicate this wondrous one-off piece of psychedelia celluloid.

After that amazing double bill of late 1960s madness and still buzzing into the night, we hailed a taxi and hit Bob G's gaff to unwind with some kool sounds to soothe our mashed up heads. There was only so much technicolour visions your brain could handle in one night!

It was now turntable time and one particular track sticks out in my memory that Bob G spinned and that was The Electric Prunes 'Get Me To The World On Time'. At the point when the record goes into the mid section Diddleyesque maraca beat, I sprang up from the couch and started to cut loose, stripping off my top and shirt as I lost myself in the twistfrugwatusijerk beat – Holy ecstasy! I was suddenly possessed by the pounding beat as Bob G and Douglas looked on with startled expressions as if to say "Where the fuck did that come from?" Ha!

One film we went to and didn't dig was the Jimi Hendrix 'Live At The Isle Of Wight Festival'. I actually walked out in self disgust along with my psychedelic hombres in tow. That film was just one big self indulgent guitar solo of hippy nonsense that just bored the Z man tits off us all. It was just too heavy and not psychedelic enough for us young garage heads. Too much of a spliffo groove daddio going on, for our liking. We would've all preferred to have seen The Doors or The Seeds up there on the big screen instead of a well-past-his-peak Jimi Hendrix and his band of guitar gypsies wanking off in festival-land. Pass the biscuits please!

Another interesting double bill of note was 'Catch 22' and Slaughterhouse 5'. Both of these films were based on the respective bestselling books and were totally made for mind zapping pleasure heads only. I've watched both these films since then, drug free and I still don't know what the fuck is going on.....

The last of the Grosvenor double bills that we caught that hazy summer was 'Performance' and 'Dog Day Afternoon' – a strange pairing to behold. The latter film for me is Al Pacino's greatest acting performance of his career and that includes The Godfather – Serpico and Cruising. Al Pacino owns 'Dog Day Afternoon' and turns in a truly compelling performance as a gay male down on his street luck who requires some instant cash so that he can provide the money for his boyfriend's impending sex change. (Imagine trying to pitch that idea for a film in Hollywood nowadays?!?!) Along with his droopy-eyed accomplice (a doeful John Cazale) their attempts at a bank heist for a quick cash fix is doomed from the start. For me it possesses one of the most intense, nail-biting climaxes in a film that I've ever had the good fortune to watch over the years. The pizza delivery scene out on the streets with the baying crowd of onlookers all shouting Attica! Attica! Attica! Is one of the most joyful inspiring pieces of film to behold for the viewer.

Next up was 'Performance' – one truly bonkers of a film that is split in two halfs. The first half of the film is an explosive, ultra violent piece of Kray Twins inspired gangland shenanigans laced with touches of extreme black humour due to the inspired casting, of employing real life Cockney gangsters for these particular roles. The second half transforms into a magic mushroom freaky trip that takes place in a faded rock star's elegantly wasted pad in Notting Hill. The main cast comprised of Anthony Valentine, James Fox, Anita Pallenberg and Mick Jagger and possessed a menacing, druggy feel due to the judicious use of fast edit cuts adding to an extremely disorientated effect for the film viewer. It was filmed in 1968 and automatically got barred by the censors on its initial release. It finally got a cinema release in 1970. Apparently it completely fucked up one of the main actors, James Fox's life for years after the film. He disappeared for a number of years, found religion and eventually made a comeback later on in his years. That final scene in 'Performance' where James Fox takes a gun and plants a bullet right through the inner cortex of the brain of Mick Jagger's character 'Turner' still resonates to this day as an explosive image to view. Let It Bleed..... I sometimes wondered who was the person responsible for curating those truly wondrous double bills? Whoever it was – I salute your choices as it enlightened myself to an underground of superb thought-provoking delights that I would never have had the chance to watch due to their obscurity.

Two films that never made it on to The Grosvenor Double Bills, but should've were 'What's Good For The Goose' and 'Here We Go Round The Mulberry Bush'. This latter film by 1984, I had already viewed many times over the years by then. It stars Barry Evans parading about Stevenage new town, resplendent in a variety of paisley patterned shirts, dreaming of copping off with swinging girl about town Judy Geeson. Once more the psychedelic party scene steals the honours in the film with The Spencer Davis Group spinning round on a revolving stage playing some neat psyche beat numbers to the upbeat party people. Judy Geeson was every guy's wet dream in that film – oh to have been transported back in time to that particular Mulberry Bush.....

'What's Good For The Goose' is memorable for the fact that The Pretty Things were the psychedelic houseband for the club happening shindig, under the alias of 'The Electric Banana' – shot in swinging Southport!!! I'm still trying to banish the memory of seeing Normad Wisdom, out on the floor, jerking about, trying to 'get down' with the kids! This film starred Sally Geeson (Judy's sister) as the switched on dolly bird, who had been picked up hitchhiking by Norman Wisdom, who is in town for a tedious boring works conference. Since he's going through a mid life crisis himself, he's intrigued by Sally's 1960s freewheeling lifestyle and decides to check out the scene for himself, resulting in our Norman throwing some bizarre shapes out on the dancefloor to 'The Electric Banana'. It was definitely a bizarre flick for a major star to get wrapped up in and at times it did hit the peak and heights of utter ridiculousness – I almost prayed!

THE NON-EXISTENT, UNEXCITING GLASGOW MUSIC SCENE

In Glasgow around early 1984 there was an abundance of super, sterile plastic pop bands who just did not float my boat and were beginning to clog up High Street shop fronts and billboards everywhere you went in the City Centre. For a new kind of inspiring kick, I was all hopped up and ready to go, to enter my timewarp tardis, heading out on a journey, stamped Sunset Strip, Los Angeles 1966. All the local bands cutting about at the time were just too fucking smooth and sterile for my new found musical palette. I wanted unknown thrills, a spot of danger and some dirt in the eye to arouse some psychedelic fire in the belly. Hipsway, Hue And Cry, Wet, Wet, Wet and Love And Money were to my eyes a sorry excuse for the modern day pop star. I loved The Cramps with a passion and detested Duran Duran with a vengeance – there was to be no middle ground in my house!

The only local bands Primal Scream shared any influences with were The Jesus And Mary Chain and The Pastels, who were reviled as the most hated band in Glasgow at one point. By the time we were gripped by the garage/punk/psyche disease, the earlier Postcard groups had either achieved chart action by then or lost their original spunk. Orange Juice and Aztec Camera were now bona fide Top Of The Pops stars forlornly gazing out of Smash Hits and Record Mirror and were never to write another decent tune between them ever again. Altered Images were another local Glasgow pop group who detonated from nowhere to storm the charts in the early 1980s with 'Happy Birthday' (their worst number). They'd started out in the late 1970s hopping on board The Siouxsie And The Banshees bandwagon and conjured up a couple of nifty dark numbers in 'Dead Pop Starts' and 'Insects' before finding instant pop glory with ace, gum snapping pop magic such as 'See Those Eyes', 'I Could Be Happy' and 'Don't Talk To Me About Love'. Everyone's indie lovebomb darling Clare Grogan at the time was the saucy, bouncy minx who hypnotized thousands of teenage record buyers and also found acting fame in Gregory's Girl into the bargain, as a parallel career in acting took hold. The two acts that to me were the most exciting around that early 80s period came from enemy territory, 45 miles away in Edinburgh – The Fire Engines and Josef K. The Fire Engines never cut a record on Postcard Records (too untamed) but they did produce two poptastic singles in 'Candyskin' and 'Big Gold Dream' which should've stormed the gates of the Top 20 pop charts. They also created a mostly instrumental mini masterpiece album called 'Lubricate Your Living Room' (great title lads) which came in a groovy 1960s style polythene bag – excellent packaging! Somewhere deep in my tape vaults lies my C60 cassette of that album that Bob G made up at the time as him and Beattie were total fanatics of their discordant, schizoid racket. As a live act The Fire Engines cooked up one mighty, dynamite mix of thrashing guitars and cowbell bashing that proved to be an electric experience. Me and The Doug ended up on many a Fire Engines bootleg, screaming the place down and creating merry hell. At the Maestros gig, Gary Barret (The Bootleg King) spent the whole gig trying to avoid us so we wouldn't ruin his bootleg recording – no joy ha! When The Fire Engines had fizzled out, they morphed into Win who achieved surprise chart action with 'You've Got The Power' (Tennents Lager Advert) 7-inch single. Josef K were the other Edinburgh band who used to cook up a storm as a riveting live act. By the time they released their one and only album 'The Only Fun In Town' on Postcard Records the momentum had gone and their original fire had fizzled out. Main songwriter Paul Haig then went solo and took off on a ghost rider experimental trip and still records to this day, his own obtuse kinda sounds. THANK FUCK FOR CREATION RECORDS! This was a genuine record label that actually cared about music and the bands that recorded for the label. The pop charts of 1983 going into 1984 sucked a big one and it was time to take a subway train, deep down into the underground to recapture some of that psychedelic punk madness in all its fucked up, drugged up, freaking glory. Creation was governed by three very different voidoid characters: Alan McGee (the manic one), Joe Foster (the psychedelic one) and Dick Green (the sensible one). These guys weren't yer typical record biz bozos, lounging on leather recliners, twirling bits of paper and hiding out in faceless skyscrapers trying to get down with what's happening with the yoof of today. (leave that to J.S. Porter) These dudes were on a one way mission to spread the psychedelic word to a new crowd of young garage converts looking for a different kind of musical kick. Alan McGee was the top 'Creation Cowboy' who kick-started the whole Creation Records revolution. In the early 1980s McGee had left Glasgow behind and headed to The Big Smoke of Londinium to chance his luck. Finding himself at a creative dead-end he cadged a £1,000 bank loan and began to run his first club venture. McGee's philosophy at the time was why burst yer arse working in a job you detest (aka British Rail) when you can be making the same amount of money creating something you really enjoy such as putting on bands and running a club, at a healthy profit. This now infamous club was called 'The Living Room' which even spawned a shambolic live album recorded there called 'Alive In The Living Room'. With entrance fee at £2 a pop and the joint jammed with 150 sweaty, heaving bodies, grooving to the indie garage punky pop groove, just how could you fail? Early gigs there comprised of The Membranes, The Television Personalities and Primal Scream's first ever gig-supporting The Jasmine Minks on this particular occasion.

With some leftover profits and fast running out of interesting bands to promote, McGee then decided to start up a record label called Creation Records, named after an obscure pop art beat combo called Creation funnily enough! They must've dug this band bigstyle coz McGee, Joe and Dick then formed their own group named after one of their mesmerising 45s, called 'Biff Bang Pow' (Wonder what they thought of Boney M's attempt at Creation's 'Painter Man'?)

The early releases on Creation Records were The Legend – '73 in 83' (flogged at record fair), Revolving Paint Dream – 'Flowers In The Sky' (Andrew Innes's first band), The Jasmine Minks – 'Think' and 'Where The Traffic Goes' (Aberdonian mod pop), The Loft – 'Why Does It Rain?' and 'Up The Hill And Down The Slope' (should've been a hit single) and The Pastels with two early guitar pop gems in 'Something's Going On' and 'A Million Tears' (with the class 'Baby Honey' on the 12-inch b-side). If I may say so, not a bad collection of 7-inch records to kickstart a record label! These early releases mainly operated on a sell 3,000 records, break even operation and any leftover profits then were pumped back into the next batch of new releases. Their 'Creation Compilations' were also a smart move to introduce a band, with their unique sound, in trying to capture that new hungry beat audience out there, wanting an instant raw, snappy record to blast out on yer hi-fi to.

By this time, Farringdon's answer to an indie Phil Spector, Joe Foster, was beginning to sprinkle his magic fucking fairy dust all over the new Creation releases in his own idiosyncratic style, ie turn the dials up to maximum levels till they hit red and let the mayhem ensue. Previous to being the self-acclaimed 'Pied Piper Of Creation Records' Joe Foster had been bass player in one of punk's first independent racketeers to press up their own 7-inch records – The Television Personalities with the 'Part Time Punks' EP. I still possess a copy of this prized artefact (in my punky coffin record box) and you can viddy straight away how Joe carried the d-i-y concept of the 7-inch record inna clear plastic bag idea that all early Creation Records came in, from this early TVPs release. In creating 'The Part Time Punks' EP it took them all of four hours to create and all for a measly fee of £22.50 for total costs. Back then in 1978, 7-inch records cost 75p a go and with each record costing 14p to concoct, this left a healthy profit of 61p each for every record sold. Not a bad piece of savvy business acumen applied there! Speaking to Joe recently over a hot brew in the West End, he spouted an interesting tale of how this defining piece of vinyl first appeared alchemically. Dan Treacy (main wordsmith) lived in a tower block near the main drag of superhip Kings Road. Living on the edge of all the punky goings on, he had firsthand knowledge of the burgeoning punk rock scene exploding before his perceptive eyes observing all the punkoid peacocks strutting up and down, in their overpriced 'Boy' and 'Sex' outfits that only trendy suburbanite fashionistas could really afford. – I always thought it was more fun to create your own d-i-y take on fashion personally! With observations fermenting in his fertile brain Dan Treacy proceeded to pen an all time sarcy punk classic that still raises a smile to this very day. Joe Foster at that point in time lived in bohemian Fitzrovia, bang central in London, between Euston and Bloomsbury districts. He left the TVPs in 1983 due to the usual swindling management goings on that were endemic in those days in the shark-infested waters of the music business. Rifling through my record box the other day I came across a TVPs flexi disc 'A Picture Of Dorian Gray' which I'd forgotten about – now whatever happened to those floppy perspex plastic discs?

With McGee in full on, hyper Loog Oldham mode, hyping and talking up every single release, and Joe spreading the 'fairy dust', it was left to Dick to pay the bills and keep a beady eye on the bookkeeping in amongst all the helter skelter feverish happenings taking place in the Creation office.

We'll come back to Creation Records later in the book, now let's catch up with the gig scene in Glasgow in 1984. In March myself, Bob G and Beattie blagged a ticket to hit Queen Margaret Uni to check out the latest competition in the jingle jangle pop stakes. The Smiths were the latest 60s influenced group to appear with an 80s accent on classic pop tunes with a twist. I had already snaffled up their 12-inch damaged pop ditty 'This Handsome Man' and totally dug it. It possessed a superb Byrdsian singing groove, with Morrissey's angelic choir boy voice soaring over the top. Watching The Smiths perform, with the crowd going apeshit for Morrissey's flowery antics, I just couldn't get into it and succumb to their clean cut, well produced sparkling sound. It was all a bit too polished for my liking. You could tell these guys were gonna go far with their songs and Johnny Marr's excellent guitar playing with Morrissey a sure fire hit in indie bedroom walls all over the UK and let's face it how could they really fail to shine in the 1984 blando pop scene charts? I much preferred listening to The Smiths on record, as I found Morrissey's foppish stage antics a tad annoying on the big stage but the student masses were lapping it up bigstyle in their over the top ecstatic delirium. Love the lyrics, love the songs, love the picture sleeves but heavens knows I might just be a miserable git…..

A couple of weeks later me and Bob G found ourselves innna half empty venue in Edinburgh called Coasters on a nothing to do weekday night, to catch Julian Cope live onstage. I'd been previously in this venue many times over the years when it was called Clouds and I got to see up close some superb intimate in yer face gigs there: The Ruts! Siousxie And The Banshees! Adam And The Ants! Gang Of Four! The Doomed and The Mekons. Me and Bob G had been massive Teardrop Explodes fanatics from the late 1970s onwards, when they'd produced excellent pop nuggets such as 'Sleeping Gas', 'Bouncing Babies', 'When I Dream', 'Treason' and 'Reward'. Whenever I hear 'When I Dream' I am still instantly transported to the basement of '23rd Precinct Records' when I heard that knockout track for the first time. The Teardrop Explodes' second album 'Wilder' for me contains the unsurpassable toppermost of the poppermost instant sitar drenched pop classic in 'Passionate Friend- - it just doesn't get any better than that single for pure pop perfection (well ok – Abba's S.O.S.). By 1984 The Namdam (madman backwards) was on a one man psychedelic trip and had just recently released 'The World Shut Your Mouth' album that contained (to my well tuned lugholes) two instant gems in 'Head Hang Low' and the current single of the lp – 'Greatness And Perfection' with ba! ba! ba! ba! harmonies to kill for. It seemed with this recent release, Julian Cope had shrugged off his Smash Hits teenybop fans and by the looks of the sparse turnout at that night's gig it was strictly hardcore heads attending only plus Fish (out of Marillion). Was he a secret Copehead admirer or did he just drop in to catch some groupie action? Also in attendance were Frank (barracuda) McGurl and Derek (soft boy) Lee – two solid gone garage heads who travelled all the way from Cumbernauld zombie town to catch some crazy, swirling' psyched out Namdam action. These two notorious acid heads could even outdrug Keef Richards in his more glorious, debauched wasted moments.

If my fried memory serves me right The Copehead mostly performed the recent 'World Shut Your Mouth' lp along with a sensation of Teardrops tunes but the one song that sticks out in my memory is 'Pussyface' which Julian battered out on a piano – superb!

There was also another gig happening in town that night and we just about managed to drag our carcasses to Buster Brown's nightspot in time to catch Mark E Smith and his latest chick Brix Smith, hoover up a couple of nasty lines of shit hot speed (by the sounds of it) before they hit the stage for the night's Fall gig. We just weren't in the mood for these guys one little bit after the joyous Julian Cope gig. I think we just spent the whole gig slightly inebriated by this stage, heckling and shouting at Brix – 'Yankee Go Home' ha! Oh the joys of being young, cocky and not giving a flying fuck!!!

The REM gig in Nite Moves, Glasgow in April was a bit of a trip into the unknown. We'd only read about these guys in the NME and hadn't seen any video footage of them in action yet. By the time that they'd played Nite Moves the 'Murmur' album had been released and contained some dynamic Byrdsian type action in 'Radio Free Europe' and 'Talk About The Passion' which had created a bit of a garage buzz here in the good ol' UK. 'Reckoning', the new album just released to coincide with their short UK tour, for me personally, contains two of my all time fave rave REM tunes in 'So Central (I'm Sorry)' and the super grooving, harmonic 'Don't Go Back To Rocksville'. For this particular gig Beattie dug deep into his culture bunker and dragged out this overlarge grey military coat that would've been more suited to Freddie Starr impersonations, instead of insisting that it would suit me better than him – good wan! I felt a real berk in it if truth be told when I first tried it on and when the bouncer quipped at the entrance to Nite Moves "I ain't seen a jacket like that since Sergeant Peppers days" all my fears were confirmed. It was that big – it was wearing me! Once you stepped inside the venue, you could feel the sense of excitement building up, with the feeling that you were gonna be witness to one real special occasion. The joint was rocking with the anticipation of getting to see a band who were as massive Byrds fans as ourselves and fellow kindred spirits of the Rickenbacker god. The crown assembled made up an eclectic mix of younger garage heads mixed in with the older, greyer garage cats. The place was absolutely rammed downstairs so we took up a good spot on the balcony to catch 'em. At one point, some technical sounds appeared (Dino at the desk again?) so we started shouting out for some garage sounds. "Hey! what about 'Fire Engine' by The Elevators or give us a blast of The Standells – 'Barracuda'?" And you know what? They started to play 'em, jamming away till the techy problems were sorted out. It was totally spontaneous and amazing to watch, these guys synced in to the same fuzzed out jangle wavelength as ourselves. REM played for nearly two whole hours, with Michael Stipe's vocals at times reminding me of a young Roky Erickson and for one blessed spring night out in Glasgow, they belonged to us. I've still yet to see a band in their early days, play a 2-hour long set in a small intimate club setting and get away with it! They were a true class act to remember, all the way from Georgia USA and went down an absolute storm in Sauchiehall Street for one night only. Watching REM live, you knew that these deep down south cats were gonna take over the world at some point. They were already college radio darlings and the music press lapped them up bigstyle and you sensed that it would only be a matter of time before the rest of the public caught on. It would take precisely 7 years actually, when the world dominating 'Out Of Time' was released and stormed the pop charts – at last it was automatic for the people!

One night in June 84 myself, Bob G and Beattie found ourselves in a no-man's joint called The Heathery Bar in Wishaw to check out The Television Personalities do their pop art guitar thang. This was one helluva strange town for a music venue, situated right on the edge of a motorway roundabout. The whole gig itself is now one hazy blur of a memory, no wacky intro from Dan Treacy this time. "Hi! We're The Electric Golliwogs and we're a psychedelic band"! Two things stick out for me from that particular night. Meeting

Duglas Bandit and dancing to The Doors! Duglas (The Bellshill Dandy) was in a group at the time called The Pretty Flowers along with one Frances McKee and along with Bob G we had a good rap with him about music, life and the cosmos. By the end of the night, we were all in a merry mood so one of us forra daft laugh requested the dj play The Doors – 'The End'. The dj shot back – "I'll play it but only if yous dance to it". We asked for it and we got it – and we danced to it! It must've been the longest 10 minutes out on a dancefloor in my life! We were masochists of the floor and we just about got away with it – I think…..After that stunt we should've gotta round of applause but by the time we had finished boogying, the place had practically emptied out and didn't the kids just love it!

In November that year The Jesus And Mary Chain finally got round to releasing their first single 'Upside Down' paired with the inspired choice of b-side, the Syd Barrett penned 'Vegetable Man'. This was the record that detonated Creation Records! Within months it had sold around 50,000 platters inna blitzkrieg of vinyl buying intensity. It finally came to a stop at No 2 in the superhip Indie Charts, I wonder who stopped them from getting to No 1 as there was no Joe Dolce type novelty acts going down in those charts. With a major bragging review article in the NME and heavy rotation on John Peel they suddenly found themselves on a rocket to Russia ride. The Creation office descended into a frenzied packaging state of flurry desperately trying to cope with the eager demands of a new found, delirious The Jesus And Mary Chain audience who were all revved up and ready to throw everything at the band (and that's including bottles and chairs). Before the year was out they'd played a raucous set at Plymouth Ziggy's and stormed London's ICA venue in a drunken, shambolic rampage of sound. By this time McGee had taken on full time manager duties and turned into their megamouth 'Creation Cowboy' wheeling and dealing, in his element and suddenly working for British Rail was but a distant memory now fading fast. At the end of November The Jesus And Mary Chain embarked on a short tour of Germany, with Bob G back on the drumstool again. He sent me a typical sicko postcard with a Nazi standing at a bombed out Berlin Wall with the scrawled message –

"Today your love, tomorrow the world Ja! Ja! Ja! The Jesus And Mary Chain on tour".

When he came back from that tour I'd noticed a definite change appearing in him, what with all the press build up, tv exposure and record release hype, which seemed to be taking a tight grip on his ego. For the upcoming December gigs (in the back of the tour van) all of a sudden it was all compact mirrors and lipstick holders a go-go! Steady on dude, only The New York Dolls could pull off that stunt and get away with it. Drop the lippy!

THE MOST HATED BAND IN GLASGOW

When you think of Bearsden and punk rock you don't normally associate the two together. The former is a sweet suburbia area of Glasgow and the latter an abrasive, anarchic blast of musical mayhem with a hefty dose of attitude. Bizarre but true I once saw Crass play at a hall in Bearsden sometime around May 1979. The gig turned a bit crazed near the end of Crass's set due to the toilet being trashed and then the local beat cops appearing, turning the atmosphere even more volatile. The rozzers then took to the streets cruising about Bearsden picking up any punky looking dude walking about and then jailing them. Boy! Were we glad to get outta that place that night! (I nearly wandered off the script there!) It was at the annual Bearsden Punk Rock Festival in 1981 that The Pastels played their first ever gig. They only rehearsed two songs, were rank rotten and managed to blitz their way through cover versions of Buzzcocks' – '16 Again' and Subway Sect's – 'Don't Split Up'. Would love to have heard a bootleg recording of that one! By the next year in 1982 when I first clapped eyes on them at Nite Moves (supporting Strawberry Switchblade) they'd gotta rough setlist together comprised of their first 2 singles 'Heaven's Above' and "I Wonder Why' along with 'Jenny Braithwaite' and various other tunes of warped romance. The Pastels certainly looked and sounded different at the times producing feelings of utter disgust and revulsion at their supposed stroppiness and tweeness when it came to their songs and image which muso, macho rock bands detested with a passion and which I perversely dug! Stephen McRobbie was the main vocalist/songwriter along with his every trusty guitarslinger, Brian Superstar at his loyal side. Peter Callaghan was their original bassist but apparently got thrown out for being a crap bass player!!! Peter then took up being the resident singer in his own band called Peter And The Raindrops who were once described as being like 'spastics on speed' in one live gig review. Peter to this day still possesses the original Pastels demo cassette tape and at a current rock and pop memorabilia auction site, this prized artefact would now earn him a pretty penny or two in his pocket. Flicking through several fanzines of that crucial pre-Creation times, it's kinda funny to read about Stephen Pastel's influences back then; he dislikes The Young Ones, Coronation Street and Monty Python but loves Polystyrene and Kenneth Williams. I like a dude with a black sense of humour! Around that post Postcard Records and pre Creation time there were a surprising amount of idiosyncratic bands out on the live circuit flying under the radar and kicking up a storm: James King And The Lone Wolves! The Primevals! Sophisticated Boom Boom! Edith And The Ladies and not forgetting Strawberry Switchblade. For every one of those maverick rockin' freakoids you had to suffer and avoid April Showers! Del Amitri! Friends Again and The French Impressionists (so west end it hurts…..) From 1982 onwards to 1984 there was a veritable explosion of incisive, creative and extremely colourful collection of underground fanzines cooked up by a gang of uber charismatic characters all urging people to get off their lardy arses and start up their own gigs, club nights, bands and record labels. It was a supremely fertile time for d-i-y fanzines and some of the most intoxicating and thought-provoking were Deadbeat! Communication Blur! Pure Popcorn! Action Action! Juniper Beri Beri! Bombs Away Batman and my own personal favourite Slow Dazzle, which ran for 6 action-packed numbers before calling it quits at the end of 1984. All of a sudden, a whole new flurry of old bands suddenly appered again ripe for rediscovery: The Modern Lovers! Swell Maps! Subway Sect! The Raincoats! Metal Urbain and not forgetting the unofficial anthem of that time, Patrick Fitzgerald's sublime 'Safety Pin In My Heart' – the perfect crossover record!

Chris Davidson was the main man responsible for all 6 issues of the Slow Dazzle fanzine which were all xeroxed, printed and flogged before Creation Records had really exploded onto the music scene. His fanzines contained a thoroughly readable, myriad selection of footy, politics, travel, book reviews, gig happenings and record selections that were simply breathtaking in their kaleidoscopic vision of unknown pleasures and delights. It was in the No 6 edition of Slow Dazzle that The Jesus And Mary Chain achieved their first ever front cover, that also came with an excellent, bitchin' Creation Records article and last minute gig review of The Creation Records showcase night at The Venue in October 1984. What other fanzine could provide informative articles on Kurt Vonnegut! Neil Young! John Peel! A Certain Ratio and Pat Nevin all in the same edition! This Greenock garagehead knew his psychedelic onions and at the end of the year Chris was the chief promoter who organised Primal Scream's second live gig. The bill contained Primal Scream, The Pastels and Buba And The Shop Assistants and it took place in Gigi's which was soon to be renamed Daddy Warbucks in the next year. Douglas (Hart) was still hanging out with the Primals gang and got roped in for the night to man the turntables along with Chris pumping out a non-stop mix of primal, garage street punk for the jangle heads that appeared on this freezin' ass December night. Sometimes forra warped laugh Douglas likes to fling on The Bluebells 'Young At Heart' just to get a reaction and people debating – "Is he playing that for a joke?" I've still got the ultra green luminescent A4 poster from the gig that captures a pop art image of Captain Scarlet in all his supermarionation pomp and all for £2 pop kids (the entry fee that is…..) For Primal Scream's second gig, the crowd had expanded like wildfire as the word of mouth and poster splattering did its job in pulling inna healthy crowd on a cold ass December night. By the time we hit the stage, Dungo and Beattie were well pissed and for the sheer hell of it and experience – I popped a tab of acid. All I can say is that by the time we crawled onstage to play, Bob G was notta happy bunny! The whole set totally collapsed in a shambolic mess of drunken bass and guitar with my tambourine being bashed to an invisible beat in my head only. There was only one way to go after that and that was to blast out 'Belsen Was A Gas' to end the night on a memorable high. It was the definitive highlight to the abortion of a set and there endeth our second ever gig to a mixed, bemused crowd of onlookers. I was that gonesville, hypnotized by the wall of mirrors onstage throwing distorted shapes that I couldn't find a way offstage so I had to step down from the front of the stage and make a fast exit to the dressing room!

Our third and final gig to end 1984 with was in enemy territory, a one hour jaunt down the autobahn to Auld Reekie (Edinburgh) to support The Pastels once more at a venue called The Waterloo Bar, near Calton Hill. Gotta feeling that The Shop Assistants provided a gig hand in promoting this particular gig – tanx dudes and dudettes! It was the week before Christmas on a Baltic Thursday night but we still managed to pull a decent crowd of music lovers through the indie pop grapevine. This gig was memorable for the fact we covered P.I.L.'s 'Albatross' off their 'Metal Box' album. It was still early experimental days for The Primals, a tad unsure of our own pop catalogue and it was a bit of a throwback to Primal Scream's embryonic year when it was just Bob G, Beattie and a drum machine. 'Albatross' was an epic song, a true avant garage construction penned by the whole Public Image gang and I think we just about managed to pull off a decent version complete with my obtuse tambourine fills. At one point in the gig, Tam's hi-hat legs gave way, so for the rest of the gig, I had to keep one Chelsea boot on the base so that it wouldn't collapse in a shambling heap. Oh the joys of being in a band with transferrable tambourine skills!

TOP 20 TURNTABLE SOUNDS – 1984

1. The Cramps – The Most Exultant Potentate Of Love
2. Julian Cope – Greatness And Perfection
3. REM – Central Rain (I'm Sorry)
4. Pink Floyd – Astronomy Domine
5. Wire – The 115th
6. The Jesus And Mary Chain – Upside Down
7. Love – My Little Red Book
8. Clay Allison – Fell From The Sun
9. Panther Burns – Tina The Go-Go Queen
10. The Byrds – All I Really Want To Do
11. Felt – Penelope Tree
12. Subway Sect – Nobody's Scared
13. The Seeds – Did He Die
14. Orange Juice – What Presence
15. Chocolate Watchband – Sweet Young Thing
16. The Loft – Up The Hill And Down The Slope
17. 13th Floor Elevators – You're Gonna Miss Me
18. The Pastels – I Wonder Why
19. Shangri Las – Past, Present And The Future
20. The Gun Club – Sex Beat

LONDON CALLING JANGLE HEADS

Before we hit London I've got the small matter of another gig we played (before we set off for The Big Black Smoke) to spout on about.

Our first gig of 1985 was in a small basement called Lucifers Glasgow. It is now known as The Sub Club, top electronic dance hangout in town. I've always dug basement clubs as they're conducive to providing a subterranean frisson of mystery, especially when you're heading down the staircase and you can hear the music pumping out – it sends slivery shivers up yer spine!

Support band for the night was a rare outing from The Original Mixed Up Kid, a neat nod to Mott freaks, and this was to be our first official gig as headliners this time so drop the drinks and the acid before the gig guys!

The A4 poster advertising the gig was in glorious, shocking pink with an image (pilfered from my horror book) of a chick with a spike sticking out of the back of her head and chosen by Bob G. That boy sure possessed one helluva stay stick sense of humour at times! For 1985 Primal Scream acquired a new rhythm guitarist called Paul Harte to beef up the sound and to give The Primals a punchier kick in the live gig setting. Harte was a total Sex Pistols and Velvets fanatic who possessed a certain striking image complete with a Steve Severin mode of fashion – 1960s style. For the Lucifer's gig we managed to pull in a near packed crowd in the sweat ass hellfire basement club, with not one cover version in sight this time! It was all killer and no filler and with new garage recruit Harte on rhythm, we produced a more dynamic, tighter set.

After the gig, to unleash some of that leftover pent up stage energy, I like to cut loose on the dancefloor and when the dj suddenly put on a brand new musical biscuit, ie The Velvets – 'Beginning To See The Light' I pounced on the floor and let rip some rockin' dance moves, to get rid of the onstage demons. This gig was also memorable for the fact that I'd gotten my sister Sadie and her pal in on the guest list. If you're family start coming to yer gigs, you must be doing something right as musically, we had zero musical tastes in common. My sister was a Top 20 pop devotee and Wham daft – strictly for young guns of a certain age only. All aboard the bottom liner bus – destination Londinium!

I hadn't been down in London since the late punkerama 1970s searching for daytime adventures and night-time thrills. London to me possessed an edgy, dangerous atmosphere of the unknown. A really queer city populated by dapper gents and eccentric hobos dotted about the streets and subways. I saw my first transvestite down The Kings Road in 1978 and it totally blew my 17-year-old mind at the time – a 6 ft tall dude inna beard with a dress and high heels – Holy Quentin Crisp! When the Primals gang arrived in early '85, the squatting scene was still in full throttle but instead of dossing down in one of these offbeat establishments, we found ourselves being holed up in Tottenham and the dangerous, gritty back streets of Peckham. Dave The Driver lived in Peckham and McGee was shacked up in skankin Tottenham. There were now 6 garage heads to accommodate so we had to be split up into two gangs of 3. One night, hanging out in McGee's living room he started telling us this super scary tale concerning the dark end of his street. Apparently there was a brazen gang of robbers on the loose, who took to flying through people's windows feet first (Errol Flynn swashbuckling style) and then robbing the people of all their worldly goods. Watta fucking warped fucked up story that was to behold, before you dropped off to dreamland for yer kip – tanx Alan ha!

The reason we were down in London was to record our first single for Creation Records, the a-side 'All Fall Down' and the b-side 'It Happens'. Primal Scream were a bit late out of the starting blocks when it came to releasing their first record. The Loft! Jasmine Minks! The Jesus And Mary Chain and The Pastels had all previously recorded on Creation and at last it was now our turn to produce some pop magic. The production duties fell to that Fitzrovian dandy of the indieworld, Joe Foster. Previous to this recording, Joe had decided to trump all the wannabe feedback bandwagonesque jumpers by creating his own chaotic cash-in disc called 'I'll Follow You Down' under the alias of Slaughter Joe. On that very same day, using the same equipment, he also cut 'Don't Slip Up' by East Kilbride's teenage upstarts Meat Whiplash. Joe's philosophy at the time was, there was no time to do the standing still as the current music establishment looked like the proverbial cow's arse – always behind! Over another brew, Joe told me when he first clocked eyes on Primal Scream he remembers us as this weird band of people with a gang like mentality that reminded him of Dexy's Midnight Runners in attitude. For some reason for the recording session, Beattie hadn't brought down his own guitar so he had to borrow Joe's 12-string one, so that he could create some beautiful ringing harmonics. For the picture sleeve design of the 'All Fall Down' 7-inch record, the front cover was an obscure black and white photograph of everyone's favourite French chanteuse at the time, Francoise Hardy complete with a band shot photo on the reverse sleeve. For some unexplained reason now lost in the ether, I didn't appear on the back sleeve or play tambourine on the recording?!?! Maybe my services weren't acquired at that moment in time for some garagehead band poses or tambourine bashing? This record would be the 17th release on Creation Records and in time I would have my 5 minutes of glory. 'All Fall Down' was released in May and initially sold around 3,000 hard vinyl copies without any radio play and only some fanzine exposure. Looking at that week's NMEs single releases in May 1985 about the only 2 decent releases were Nick Cave's 'Tupelo' and Vic Godard's bouncy 'Holiday Hymn' 45 – it was all Chaka Khan! Don Henley! Jeff Beck! Osibisa and Chewy Raccoon – fuck me gently but slowly as I reach for my razor blade.....In the Indie Charts there appeared only 2 Creation singles: The Jesus And Mary Chain – 'Upside Down' (freefalling fast now) and Slaughter Joe's 'I'll Follow You Down' which was planted at No. 27.

If you head onto YouTube now, you'll find that 'All Fall Down' has been viewed by 55,000 hits and the b-side 'It Happens' a healthy 31,000 indie viewings. 'It Happens' also popped up on the Creation sampler later that year called 'Different For Domeheads' alongside 2 other gems in the The Loft's 'Why Does The Rain' and The Pastels' sublime 12-inch epic 'Baby Honey' – worth snaffling for these 3 records alone. 'All Fall Down' is a neat first single but live I've always preferred 'It Happens' with its uptempo, snappy whiplash beat which according to Julian Cope on first hearing it, declared it as 'crucial'. Now the Namdam – has got good taste!

Meanwhile one day in London during the recording of 'All Fall Down', sitting about the Creation offices, shooting the breeze with David Swift (NME writer) he casually dropped this little nugget "Who wants to come along with me to The Whistle Test at the Beeb to see The Ramones cut it live in the studio?" Rewind that record again. 'Watch The Ramones live in the flesh, upfront in an intimate setting'. In no time at all 6 Glaswegian pinheads were stalking the bare, empty corridors of the BBC, with not one security monkey in sight or a pass being flashed. It was so goddamn lax and within moments we were bang in the studio, waiting patiently for 'The Brudders' to explode onstage for our very own entertainment. This tv performance was around the time of the 'Too Tough To Die' album promotional tour and Marky Ramone (the drummer) at this point had just been replaced by another gum snapping, Lewis leather clad rocker called Richie Ramone. I'd also noticed that Dee Dee (bassist) had shorn his famous moptop barnet for a more spikier cut. Was this his way of rebelling against The Ramones straightjacket image of sneakers, biker jacket and shaggy long hair? In the Beeb studio, they blitzkrieged bopped their way through 'Mama's Boys', Chasing The Night' and the Dee Dee vocalized 'Warthog'. As soon as The Brudders finished their set, we darted straight over to Dee Dee, who was now sprawled out, lying down on the stage, having a breather. I think we took him by surprise, spouting Glaswegian gibberish ten to the dozen that totally bamboozled ol' Dee Dee. His actual words to us were "Can you guys slow down a gear – I can't make out a word that you's are saying?" Ha! And this from a delinquent tuffy from the gutter streets of Queens, New York City. It was bleeding hilarious! In the hot seat being interviewed by one of the Whistle Test bozos was that one and only camped out former Buzzcock – Pete Shelley. This was now turning into one helluva punkarama treat for us ol' punk diehards in the raw. Out of the corner of my star spangled eyes, I could spy Johnny Ramone listening avidly to what Pete Shelley was spouting. We didn't dare bug him, as he seemed real aloof and did not look the small talk kinda guy so we just gave him a wide body swerve.

Later on that night The Ramones were all revved up and ready to go to hit The Lyceum stage for some teenage lobotomy punky thrills. The whole Primals gang had managed to blag our way onto the guest list and out of the lot of us, only Bob G had previously caught em live, at The Apollo. How I missed seeing The Ramones live at The Apollo is still a 3-pipe mystery to this day?!?! Onstage these cretin hoppers did not disappoint. Blasting their way through their usual 30 songs in one hour set, blowing our acid eater brains out on a road to ruin of Ramones classic after classic with the new 'Too Tough To Die' tracks blending in with ease amongst 'Commando', 'Blitzkreig Bop', 'I Wanna Be Sedated' along with a rip roaring 'Pinhead' for the encore (the official Ramones anthem) that had their roadies donning their freakish pinhead costumes, complete with those crazed 'We Accept You' placards sending the assembled cretin hordes crazy, howlin at the moon.

As the gig came to an end, the word was out that we were invited to the Ramones aftershow party at The Embassy Club. This was the same joint that featured in The Great Rock 'N' Roll Swindle, with The Black Arabs belting out a funkyfied version of 'Anarchy In The UK'. Threading our way through London's mean streets by now in a pissed up rebellious mood someone cracked "There's a helluva lot of Union Jacks flying about here – I dare someone to torch one?" Quicker than you could say 'butcher's apron', Tam had scrambled up the greasy pole with one zippo lighter at the ready. With the flag now blazing away, laughing our heads off and clapping Tam for his daredevil antic, someone spotted a wee local nyaff (weedy dude) scampering away shouting at us "I'll get the police onto you's for this act of treason". The penny then dropped that setting a Union Jack flag alight in conservative Londinium out on the streets was tantamount to being beheaded in the Tower of London for our unpatriotic behaviour. This thought quickly sobered us up and as we got to the end of the street, we spied a couple of coppers up ahead, so we split up into twos to throw them off our scent. With our angelic masks now on, we managed to give them the slip apart from Beattie getting hauled over and questioned –"No Sir! Yes Sir!" – phew that was a close shave. We were then one step from the gutter and just a kiss away from the jail guitar doors! It reminded me of a story about Salvador Dali who once as a protest against the fascist Franco government, took to burning the Spanish national flag at art college in those heady political days of the Spanish Civil War.

After splitting off the main drag and finally coming across The Embassy Club, we got inside to find out that The Ramones were a no-show! About the only dudes we recognised from our piss stained eyes were Andy Kershaw and one Jeffrey Lee Pierce, (The Gun Club) who we had a particular rockin bone to pick with. He'd previously been venting off in the music papers about how crap Creation Records were especially The Jesus And Mary Chain. We then sidled up to him, circled him and began to interrogate him about his slagging comments. In no time at all he'd backtracked all his derogatory statements, quoting the old usual "I never said that, I was misquoted" – bollocks Jeffrey! Since we were all merry and massive Gun Club fans, we forgave him and split, to bug someone else.

All in all it had been a night to remember and an incredible unreal day, meeting The Ramones, seeing The Ramones and nearly spending a night in the clink! Gimme! Gimme! Shock Treatment!

PASTELS A GO-GO!

Come April a whole gang of The Primals and mates piled through on a train to catch The Pastels at some unknown venue in Edinburgh. In those embryonic days, there appeared to be a common appreciation society forming between the two bands in playing on the same stages and turning up at other gigs to support each other. At the gig, Stephen dedicated a song to me at the end of the gig – "This one's for Joogs – 'Suicide!'" as he knew I was a massive Suicide freak, good touch Mr Pastel. It was around this time that they'd released 'A Million Tears' which possessed the Velvets-like epic groove of 'Baby Honey' tucked away on the 12-inch b-side. Come early June and The Pastels had been invited to play at a CND festival of bands that comprised of Wet Wet Wet as the headlining act. We popped in, then we fucked off, before they hit the stage with their shiny, plastic soul pop groove. Luckily for us, The Pastels were on in the early evening slot so we could avoid the pop masses gathering. A week before, Stephen had invited myself and Bob G up onstage to have a rockin' blast during 'Baby Honey'. I thought to myself if The Kelvin Hall stage was good enough for The Kinks to cut a live album there, then it was good enough for us garage hombres to bust loose on it. Bob G appeared onstage, to sit down with his guitar while I produced Lux's 'mouthie' to blast out a cacophonous sound as the extended feeback outro kicked in near the end. It was a buzz to taste the big stage and getta audience reaction, no pressure, (it wasn't our band) and just let it rip!

A couple of weeks later we were back in our old haunt The Venue for a double bill of The Pastels and The Membranes. I'd been invited onstage once more to cut loose to 'Baby Honey' but this time it was suggested, for some calamitous, whip cracking action a la Gerard Malanga style. When the feedback finale came, Paul Harte and Bob G's girlfriends Louise and Karen bounced on to dance from one of the wings while I exploded onstage from the other wing to crack that whip and whip it good! According to Eugene (Kelly) and

Sean (Dickson) (as the strobe lights were sending me into an epileptic frenzy as I started to whiplash some of the crowd near the front) I nearly rendered them blind as I lashed out like a madman caught up in the cataclysmic moment. It was a low budget version of the Velvet Underground Exploding Plastic Inevitable Show without the full Warhol entourage and eye zapping projections but it was another fun gig, with the pressure off, before I was ready to hit the road with the Primals once again. But before then a new club in town was just about to open…..

SPLASH 1 CLUB

In June 1985, Splash 1 Club nights finally appeared, to breathe some much needed action, time and vision into a floundering Glasgow music scene. Initially we all got together one night to thrash out ideas on how we could bring this vision alive. At the end of the night, the new committee was down to 7 social deviant members: Grant McDougall! Billy Thompson! Derek Lowdon! Bobby Gillespie! Paul Harte! Karen Parker and Louise Maxwell. The club itself was bang central, not far from Queen Street rail station and went under the name of 'Daddy Warbucks'. I always thought it sounded kinda gansterville until I found out where the name came from – 'Little Orphan Annie' – a bleedin' kids' film! Primal Scream had already played at the same venue in October the previous year when it was called 'Gigi's' – what's with all the Hollywood monikers? I suppose it was meant to sound exotic and glamorous. It sure didn't have the same ring to it as 'The Ultratheque' that's for sure….. Speaking to Billy (Thompson) recently I hadn't realised that Derek Lowdon was the chief catalyst in jumpstarting the Splash 1 nights as he was the main guy who produced the capital dosh with the other 6 members providing lesser amounts. If only myself and Big Paul (McNeil) knew that at the time, we would've joined the other 6, come onboard and cashed in too! The Splash 1 gang made up an enterprising mix of people using their varied skills such as Bob G (printers and Creation), Karen Parker (chief cashier since she worked in a bank), Lowdy and Grant McDougall plus Billy T (enthusiastic newstart promoters) with the rest of the groundlings (plus me and Big Paul) helping out creating poster ideas and pasting them up along with concocting the cassette mixtapes.

The first band to headline was The Loft with Big Paul's band The Submarines going down in Splash 1 history as the first ever band to appear onstage on the hallowed stage albeit as the support band. The A4 poster for the gig contains a vivid orange image of Malcolm McDowall (that guy again) outta 'A Clockwork Orange' purring away in his Durango buggy, peering out menacingly with the bands names scrawled at the side. On the top of the poster 'A Splash 1 Happening' was emblazoned with the blurb 'A psychedelic garage soundtrack' and all for the princely fee of £1.50. Splattering our way up and down Woodlands Road, pasting and posting at a rapid pace, worming our way into the town, we got collared by the local beat bobby but Lowdy had a quick word in his ear and all was forgotten. That boy sure had contacts in low places! The first Splash 1 happening was a rip roaring success, so a couple of weeks later Grant, Billy and Lowdy got to promote a group of their choice: Big Flame, a kinetic, thrashy group and the total opposite of the Creation bands cutting about at the time. Support on that night came from local kinetic, thrashy band 'The Mackenzies – hi Bev! With 7 different people with 7 different tastes in music, this clash of tastes and opinions was certainly going to produce some friction baby but reflecting back now, nigh on 30 years it was the correct choice. As the word was spreading like wildfire, with Splash 1 fever taking a grip on people's psyche, an explosion of Bobby Gillespie doppelgangers mushroomed outta nowhere producing a severe case of 'Anoraksia' in the streets of 'No Mean City' (Glasgow schmucks!) All of a sudden you couldn't move in Splash 1 (and Paddy's Market) for midget like 5ft indie kids with moptops all snaffling up an abundance of old 1960s style anoraks that had been hanging around on clothes rails for years before, untouched. I've gotta admit I had too much rockin' bones in my body to purchase one of these ridiculous items of clothing, but some people surprisingly succumbed to this dose of 'anoraksia' very easily. Step forward Jim Beattie – who always claimed that his particular dose was actually a climbing cagoule – good wan! Another interesting curio that started to sprout on people's backs was the Breton stripey t-shirt thang. There is actual proof of this phenomenon existing, as I have a precious Splash 1 vhs recording of footage where you can spy Bob G and his striped cohorts in all their sartorial glory, posing and chatting away on the edge of the dancefloor. Maybe it was some sort of unconscious nod to the Velvet Underground, we'll never know for sure.....

The 'Bob G Clone Phenomena' got real strange and embarrassing at times especially when you were hanging out with the real Bob G, (who at least saw the funny side of it) and you'd spot these guys down Paddy's Market (local flea market) or hanging out at Splash 1. The whole caper even got an article in The Glasgow Herald as it gripped the whole Scottish nation. Believe it or not but even that uber trendy monthly magazine 'The Face' also got in on the whole Splash 1 shebang at the time. One of their roving reporters created a piece on the 'anoraks and tambourines' of the scene even getting Alan McGee to compile his personal Top 10 Tambourine tracks! In amongst the Shangri Las! Vic Godard! Elevators songs is the classic McGee wind-up group: Anoraks From Hell who created a catchy ditty called 'Waiting On Napalm' The article took on a humouresque tone and made out that everyone who appeared at Splash 1 Happenings all wore bleedin' anoraks and rattled a tambourine onstage – Holy Zils!

Meanwhile a psychedelic punk brew was also fermenting out in zombie town Cumbernauld. Derek Lee had known Grant, Lowdy and Billy through hanging out at gigs in Nite Moves and The Glasgow Tech. After catching some Splash 1 action himself, he felt energised to start up his own psychedelic garage club with the intention of catching the plague of satellite garage heads who couldn't make it to Splash 1 events in Glasgow. Since 'The Cumbernauld Crew' had their own special corner in Splash 1, Derek was convinced there was enough people in Cumbernauld of a garage punk persuasion, to start up his own particular monthly club. As there weren't any decent pubs with a function suite available, he struck lucky when he managed to rent out a spare room in The Village Theatre and called it 'The Roky Underground' in tribute to the unhinged genius of Roky Erickson, lead vocalist in Texan acidheads The 13th Floor Elevators. Managing to acquire a set of turntable decks (complete with flashing lights) and spreading the town crier word of mouth, Derek also hit the pasting posting trail leaving a trail of A4 posters splattered all over Cumbernauld Town Centre. The Roky Underground was an instant hit from the word go and big favourites receiving heavy rotation on the decks were Syd

Barrett! The Baraccudas! Robyn Hitchcock! The Church and The Dukes Of Stratosphear. The Village Theatre was a smaller venue than Daddy Warbucks in Glasgow but Derek still managed to cajole a plethora of bands to hit the motorway outta Glasgow such as The Honeymooners! The Faith Healers and The Submarines (that band again).

From the first night that Splash 1 exploded on the jaded Glasgow club/gig circuit, not one actual record was played in the club! For obvious reasons (probably lazy ones) we took to creating a couple of C90 cassette mixtapes which were blasted outta the sound system instead. Most people just couldn't be arsed taking turns, manning the decks, as it was too much hassle and plus the fact everyone involved just wanted to hang out, get high and have a real good time. In hindsight, probably a sound idea as, mostly everyone was tripping out of their gourds at the time or smoking their brains out. Sometimes me and Big Paul would hang out in the dj box, getting high, having a laugh and at times someone would come up and request a certain record. We just told them we hadn't the record in our box but we'd bring it along the next time. As if we were gonna remember that! in the cold harsh light of day ha! in the state we were in…..

Big cassette dancefloor shakers at the time were X Ray Spex's 'Let's Submerge', Sex Pistols – 'Satellite' and Jacky – 'White Horses' ahem! One night forra daft laugh, me and the two Pauls decided to record The Ramones – 'I Remember You' and stuck it on the end of the mixtape just to see if anyone would get up and dance to it. I took on the Joey vocals, with Big Paul on badass Dee Dee bass and Harte on Johnny guitar and dare I say it we managed to convince ourselves it was a decent version and were even more surprised at the next Splash 1 to discover people boppin' about to it, without realising it wasn't the real Ramones – it must've been real good acid cutting about on that particular sinful Sunday night!

One other record we recorded but didn't pass quality control was 'Some Velvet Morning' – the Rowland S Howard/Lydia Lunch version, with myself producing a snotty Sid Vicious version on vocals. The original by Lee Hazelwood and Nancy Sinatra was a Splash 1 anthem and was one warped, weird out waltzin' psychedelic masterpiece but a real bugger to dance to! One other record stands out as a dancefloor hit and that was Sonic Youth's – 'Death Valley 69' which was never off the cassette compilation mixtapes. Bob G was hanging out one night when we were compiling the cassettes and suggested we put on Love's – 'Live And Let Live', the fucking undanceable last epic track of the second side of 'Forever Changes' album – Holy Sunset Strip! When the record came on at the next Splash 1 gig he grabbed me up to dance and Bob G then went into his spazzed out, lolloping dance move with me trying desperately to keep up with the fractured stop/start groove. Not an easy one to pull off, especially so early in the goddamn sober evening!

For a twisted laugh Bob G and Harte decided to slap on 'Tomorrow Belongs To Me' (Cabaret soundtrack) also. It went down like the proverbial brick balloon, no floor action, just complete stunned hushed silence. People must've been thinking are these guys for real? or a buncha closet Nazis in disguise as 1960s obsessive garage heads?

Answers on a postcard please! It was also bizarrely covered by that impish Glaswegian pirate rocker Alex Harvey, who himself possessed a wicked, black humoured soul. Ooh! Ma Liddi!

OUT ON THAT ROAD 85

Just as June was coming to an end, Primal Scream set out on a short mini tour of England taking in Nottingham, Manchester, London and Plymouth. There were only two problems, Harte required a new rhythm guitar pronto and I needed one non destructible tambourine sharpish! In the middle of June Pete Shelley played a solo gig at The Glasgow College Of Building And Printing and left one guitar lighter, care of Harte who'd been reading one too many blagging stories of his guitar hero Steve Jones in his spare time. Before Pete Shelley's guitar went walkabout, he'd played a short set consisting mostly of his solo recordings with 'Homosapien' and 'Telephone Operator' being particular stand outs. He only played one Buzzcocks track (if my shot to bits memory serves me right) 'Strange Thing'. Later on in the story, karma would strike us down as payback time caught up with Beattie's guitar in Bristol…..By the time this mini tour had kickstarted I'd already smashed to smithereens quite a few lightweight tambourines onstage. The circular ones looked great in a variety of plastic colours but smashed too easily. The semi-circle ones sounded great but looked shit inna live setting. Harte still had a day job in a local bus garage and he suggested that he could build an indestructible metal tambourine in the garage workshop. Only thing was, it weighed a ton, looked great painted white but sounded crap, with the zils producing a bland jingle thud sound when slapped on the wrist. There was to be no middle ground for tambourinists. I just had to accept the situation and suffer the consequences as a live tambourine man. I then took to wearing black leather gloves to dull the pain that was now cutting deep into my aching wrists. Even a secret bit of sponge (at the point of contact of tambourine) inserted in the gloves didn't do the trick.

Most of Primal Scream at this time had adopted a modern day 60s influenced garage look that comprised of pointy Chelsea boots, black turtleneck and leather strides complete with shaggy moptop bouffant to complete the updated 1985 garagehead look. One thing all us young whipsmart sophistos had to sport were ultra tight black trousers, either of denim, suede or leather. If your breeks weren't tight enough, Beattie would whip them off quickstyle (tape in hand) and transform them from dullsville straight legs into strapping tight ass kecks in no time! There was no room for 'dan dares' in Primal Scream while out on that road, you were either a dedicated follower of garage fashion (Dungo and Tam did possess a serious white sox faux pax at one time) or you stayed in the house. Once we'd some available 'cutter' in our pockets, we'd all descend on this nifty tailors in Union Street who would create one off made to measure strides for our pleasure, for a pretty penny or two. I acquired a super suede pair that had fringes on the bottom, trying to cultivate the Arthur Lee strolling on Sunset Strip 66 look. I still don't know to this day how the leather trousers disease broke out?

We were all massive Doors freakoids and maybe somewhere deep in the subconscious cortex recesses it must've struck an impact on us all, as all of a sudden it wasn't only The Primals donning the leathers, it was McGee and The Weather Prophets and I'm sure The Jesus And Mary Chain too. If there was a battle of the leathers at the time I think The Primals would've won foot down. As we all went future mad retro daft, a strange thing happened to me as I was strutting down Byres Road in my shiny, shiny leathers. A camped up Captain Beefheart clone came up to me, waiting at the traffic lights and propositioned me to come back to his kinkoid lair. Not bleedin likely mate with those ridiculous leather lederhosen he was sporting!

Looking back I suppose the leather trousers gimmick served its purpose at the time and stuck out in amongst the 'cardy and anorak' indie scene that was quickly spreading like wildfire over the UK music scene. One piece of natty footwear we all craved was those Arthur Lee suede boots that he and The Seeds would pose about in, on the album sleeves. We just could not find anywhere to reproduce them and at that time we would've walked backwards in to the future just to thieve a pair right off their album sleeves. And talking of The Seeds and Sky Saxon, I was hooked on getting an Arab style headdress for live gig happenings to add a bit of pizzazz to my stage get up wardrobe but it wasn't to be. Even Paddy's Market couldn't conjure up that particular piece of natty headgear.

Two of the gigs on the mini tour were as support to The Jesus And Mary Chain along with their junior East Kilbride 'cousins' Meat Whiplash. It was around this point in time that The Jesus And Mary Chain star had begun to rise as they'd signed to Warner's offshoot label Blanco Y Negro at the start of the year and had already unleashed another couple of flaming 45s in 'You Trip Me Up' and 'Never Understand' which according to my finely tuned lugholes was a straight up copycat version of 'Upside Down'. By the time of the tour when we joined them, they were still receiving riotous gig reviews whereby the newly acquired squad of Mary Chain freaks now demanded a side order of riotous behaviour along with the shambolic 20 minute gig set. No pressure then lads!

First gig up was in Nottingham Rock City, a Barrowlands type size venue only without the raucous atmosphere of a pent up, crazed, Glaswegian crowd. It was a neat, clean looking city that possessed a healthy ratio of 2 girls to every guy scenario – how could we fail to score? (We did!) But we were in extremely safe hands if there was any bovver, as the bouncers employed for the night were the local chapter of The Hell's Angels. Needless to say the gig passed by without any hint of aggro from the mug punters assembled. Just after the soundcheck, ourselves, plus Meat Whiplash got stuck into a beggar's banquet feast of top notch nosh as The Mary Chain weren't big eaters (thank god!). Us and The Lash proceed to stuff our faces like a bunch of food deprived townie gannets as if we hadn't come across a decent plate of grub since we left Glasgow. Both bands were at the bottom rung of the ladder on Creation Records at the time and were mighty starvin and skinteroonie into the bargain so we were quite glad that The Mary Chain had politely declined their food rider so that we could step up, into the food party. After the non-eventful gig, we all took to the floor to shake some action and to sniff out any local talent but no takers this time. Whatever happened to that mythical 2-1 ratio? It was deadsville! Bored with the non-action out front we all headed backstage to check out the craic! The

Hell's Angels were holding court and were now in full flow cutting and choppin up copious amounts of speed offa nasty looking knife, rappin away with crazy tales, out on the highway with their hogs. I sure wouldn't have liked to have gotten on the wrong side of those greasers that's for sure, even though they were kool and talk friendly with us. It was curious to watch The Mary Chain in a live situation from the wings, stirring up the crowd into a feedback frenzy of noise – for 20 minutes! The Primals at that time were small fry. Only Bob G was known from the band at the time due to him still doubling up as The Mary Chain drummer for live gigs. It was around then that they asked Bob G if he wanted to be their full time drummer. We had heard on the garage grapevine about the whispers and rumours from the gutter press and it definitely created prickly situations at the time as the rest of us didn't really know where we stood in the group. Bob G took one look in his crystal crescent ball and decided to quit The Mary Chain once and for all so he could devote himself 100% to the Primal Scream cause.

In the tour van at times, to alleviate the on the road blues, Beattie and Bob G would get the guitars out and start jamming. Sometimes by the time we'd arrive at the next city, they'd have knocked a rough tune together that would turn into a particular favourite live or on record.

There always appeared to be something going on in Bob G's cryptic mind, the all-seeing-eye observer, constantly watching and thinking of the next step ahead as the rest of us were tearing it up, living in the moment, caught up in the eye of the musical hurricane.

Next stop Manchester – The Hacienda to be precise! The last time I was there, was in 1984 the year before freaking out to The Cramps and now here I was actually on the stage myself – who'd have thought eh? At the time, the The Hacienda was a large, steel eyed, soulless venue that lacked any kind of a genuine atmosphere.

I was real gobsmacked a couple of years later when it took off during the acid house revolution – it's amazing what a tab of ecstasy can do! Backstage I noticed Hooky hanging around, scowling at the Scottish invasion of bands that had descended in his precious domain. You could tell straight away with the vibe in The Hacienda on this charged night that there was to be no Hell's Angels taking care of business on this particular occasion. The atmosphere was certainly more volatile and prickly this time round. Meat Whiplash were first up onstage and took more than their fair share of drunken abuse and heckles in their short set, from the fired up Manc crowd. For one night only, straight down from Glasgow central came The Pastels who turned in the most exciting and together set out of all the bands assembled. They blew everyone else away, including ourselves and The Mary Chain. The buzzed out crowd seemed to energize The Pastels who tore into their wacked out songbook with a high energy set that inspired us all that night in Manchester. It was at this gig that I first donned my infamous black neckerchief mask (a Johnny Thunders tribute) to add a frisson of mystery to my tambourine persona. I also had my right hand heavily bandaged as it was in agony from the previous night's gig with the big white tambourine, tearing up my wrists bigstyle. By the time we finished our short set of about 5 songs it was time for the headline act to demolish their 20 minute set of drunken, stumblin' chaos. As soon as they set foot onstage, it was a constant barrage of bottle throwing and non-stop heckling. Watching the ensuing mayhem from the side of the stage, we decided to start throwing the plastic bottles back into the crowd for a reaction. It was bleedin' hilarious to us all these foppish indie kids venting their frustrations out onstage – oh! you hit me with a flower! The Mary Chain produced their usual metal machine shambolic mess, no structure, just howling feedback drenched ramblings a go-go. Very anti music but wears a bit thin once you've copped this gimmick a couple of times. £5 for 20 minutes of noise – popkids you knew what to expect! I also remember seeing Pete Shelley at the gig, obviously he never recognised Harte playing his stolen guitar or he would've put 2 and 2 together! Sorry Pete!

The next day we were heading for The Big Smoke aka London to play our first ever headline gig. Offstage now in the back of the van,

Tam was now holding court centrestage keeping us all amused as he went into full throttle pranksterish mode. Him and Beattie were relentless in slagging Dungo off for polishing his ol fellow's sash for the forthcoming Orange Day Parade – he just couldn't concoct an answer to the witty repartee that had the whole tour van rockin in laughter. Every service station we stopped at, Tam would load up with a collection of blagged stroke mags (Reader's Wives or Razzle anyone?) that would keep us entertained till we got to our final destination.

These magazines weren't blagged for the 'swing the big eyed rabbit' behaviour, it was strictly for the oh-so-serious reader's letters section. Tam would hold the mag in hand like a tv newsreader and in his most convincing posho accent, would proceed to read out some choice letters of kinkiness which would have the whole Primals entourage rolling about on the van floor. You always read that the drummers were the real loonballs of the band, hyper and unpredictable and when Tam wasn't keeping a tight backbeat on the drumkit, he liked to unleash his inner demons. Bonham! Scabies! Filthy! and Moonie The Loonie were his unconscious role models for his anarchic on the road hi-jinks. When Tam hit that tour van, he turned into a rocking Tasmanian devil complete with the ever growing Manitou (little devil) growing outta his neck, eating away at him. Since we had some downtime to relax and kick back (as the Yanks say) we begun to hang out in the Creation offices in Farringdon. Within minutes McGee would have us all slotting and packing all these 7 inch records into little plastic see through bags. If you've seen the recent feelgood flick 'Good Vibrations' (Belfast punk scene) of everyone in the shop helping out – you'll get the picture!

It was a great drop in halfway house wherein you might bump into a Jasmine Mink or two answering the phone or Pete Astor would drop by forra chinwag. Rumour had it at the time that even Jah Wobble would appear, in the guise of daytime delivery courier to deliver the mail to Creation offices. Must've been his wilderness years post P.I.L. before he strapped on his bass and got his solo career back on track once more. For our endeavours McGee would hand us a whack of freebie records to take away and sometimes would take us upstairs to Factory Records also (London branch) forra quick hit on their record shelves too….. Most of the records we got were crap, so we'd flog all the duffers in our local second hand record shop for much needed fast cash. The things you do for a bag of sugar eh! I probably regret selling some of the early Creation record releases as quite a few are worth a bob or two right now at record fairs, online auctions and ebay. One day at the Creation offices I got into a bit of naughty trouble when I innocently defaced a large JAMC poster that took up the whole of one wall. I gotta slap on the wrists for my troubles – sorry guys but it was probably the green eyed monster at work. Later on that same afternoon, Harte got the lightbulb idea of hitting some record shops and going on a blagging spree. I think me, Harte and Beattie were the main guilty culprits officer! It was a two fingers to the overpriced underground London record shop scene which mightily pissed us off as we had roughly only 2 shekels to rub together, between us all. It eventually turned into a competition to see who could pull off the most audacious, expensive vinyl heist. I think Beattie won the award, conjuring up a super rare Alex Chilton EP on Ork Records that included the bonkers 'Bangkok' track. Harte's prized blag was the original Velvet Underground first album complete with peel off banana – a very cheeky scoop there. My top find was a 13th Floor Elevators EP, made of up of killer cover versions which turned out to be not so rare after all but did possess a superb psyche out picture sleeve. We had concocted a whole routine, split into different sections of the shop, one to attract the shopkeeper's attention while the other 2 blaggers got down to some serious thievery. Harte was definitely top thief, cool in his straight faced demeanour until we got outside and exploded with laughter at our sheer audacity of an extremely naughty act. Reflecting back on those times now, I do feel a tinge of regret as we were stealing from independent record shops whose livelihoods we were exploiting for our own pitiful gains. Sorry dudes but if anyone's missing that obscure 13th Floor Elevators EP from their prized collection, I'll personally hand it back to ya!

Later that night at the Thames Polytechnic Union, the atmosphere was building up and by the time we took to the sober stage, we were ready to be unleashed. By this time (one year on from our 1st rehearsal) we were beginning to sound like a tight ass, snappy pop group, with some decent songs now appearing in the set such as 'Crystal Crescent', 'Subterranean', 'Aftermath' and our smoochy, love song 'I Love You' which was our attempt at a Spectorish composition. The gig was a belter and it was also our first headline gig in supercool London but the assembled crowd of jangle heads ate up every song we played. Tam said he was getting a great buzz from the back, watching the band lock into a groove which inspired him also, in driving the beat home. As a 6-piece band onstage now, the sound was more full on, with the set also taking shape and kicking up a gear in our onstage performances too, producing an exciting live act into the bargain. Today your love – tomorrow Plymouth!

By the time The Primals crew sailed into Plymouth in June 85, The Pastels and JAMC had already rocked the joints of Ziggy's nightclub (a former strip joint) in the previous year. Plymouth at the time was an intoxicating, colourful seaport town, situated on the south coast of Devon and possessed a heady potent brew of students and sailors who frequented the local university and naval college respectively. This lethal combination of assorted peoples produced an exciting cocktail of danger and rowdy behaviour any time we played Ziggy's nightclub. Maybe it had also rubbed off on their local footy team too, Plymouth Argyle (aka The Green Army) who at that time were playing in the old English 2nd division and were managed by a creative Dundonian called Davie Smith who (complete with tartan bunnett) inspired his team talks with snatches of poetry, to fire up his team to thrash the opposition – eat yer words fitter Cloughie! Walking around Plymouth you could sense an inspiring, pioneering sense in the air. It was no surprise when you dipped into its history and discovered that The Pilgrim Fathers had once departed from these very same shores to venture out into a brave new world of dangerous, unchartered territories, namely The Americas on The Mayflower in 1620. Now enter Jeff Barrett, the local Plymouthian motormouth promoter supremo. This guy would give McGee a run for his dollar with his enthralling spitfire stories of rock 'n' roll. In the early 80s Jeff promoted his 'Club Thing' nights that came complete with its own club info fanzine 'Frantic'. These guys meant business! His 'Club Thing' nights certainly provided a variety of bands to perform; try these on for a size 12: Section 25! The Loft! Nikki Sudden! Pink Industry and The Jesus And Mary Chain at the tail end of 84. Ziggy's nightclub was one hot ride, intense sweatbox that had the crowd right up tight to the stage which made for a rip roaring action packed experience – there was no room in this club for casual posing round the edges! Get into the groove and get into it now! As we lowered The Jolly Roger coming into the bay, Jeff upon clocking The Primals posse thought we were the koolest gang of guttersnipes to ever appear in Ziggy's with our defiant Glasgwegian attitude, Seedy look and poptastic tunes. Jeff was a total Dexy's Midnight Runners nut who bought into the whole 'Young Soul Rebels' gang philosophy of life – us against the world, punk soul rebel music, feet on the amplifier, with sarcastic, viper tongued Kevin Rowland on scowling vocal duties – a sweet surrender beat to die for…..

McGee and Jeff clicked straight away in their outlook on life and within the year, he departed for London to take up employment in the Creation offices producing press, tour managing and promoting gigs in amongst copious amounts of bevvying across the road from the offices in the local juice tavern. The other Plymouthian character important in the underground Plymouth scene was one James Williamson (not that Stooge), who ran an excellent record shop called Meat Whiplash (in homage to Fire Engines b-side) which was the major hangout for us garage cats whenever we blew into town, snaffling up rare rockabilly 45s to satisfy my lust for life in everything Cramps related. James possessed a warped sense of humour and every time I met him he affectionately called me 'Joogs Ramses' who was this bug eyed Egyptian prince from the original gory Z movie classic 'Blood Feast'. I must admit there was some kinda warped influence in there with 'Ramses' when I saw a clip of the vhs movie at the time ha! I've always preferred the bouncy, hyper excited Joyce Grenfell myself personally.

James Williamson by the next time we saw him had changed his name to Giles De Ray, some kinkoid De Sade influence dude that he currently worshipped. The last anyone heard of him was, he was last spotted lying about in the sun, soaking up the rays in Bangkok, Thailand – the saucy bugger.

The gig itself was real raw, guitars ringing out, tambourine being rattled to death crinkleheads with Bob G desperately trying to keep up vocally – not an easy task I can tell you.

Backstage after the show a mysterious female appeared and introduced herself to the band. She was over 30, older than us young garageheads and seemed to have been smitten by The Scream. We called her 'The Rich Bitch' as she was a real rich posho who took to hanging out at Meat Whiplash record shops and every week bought up a whole load of new independent releases. This lady pops up again later in Bristol…..As the gear was getting packed away Tam seemed to have clicked with the local star fucker (on a small scale) and asked me If I wanted to head back with him for some moral support as he was venturing into unknown territory. All I can say is that Tam certainly got some back door action that night and as I came across the lovebirds in the morning all I got was a pink dildo candle and a copy of De Sade's 'Venus In Furs' book! That's how the old rock 'n' roll pendulum swings at times! Bless my goddamn cotton socks.

SILVERFOILCITY

Before we get to Silverfoilcity in Byres Road, I have a peculiar tale to tell before I moved out of the family home in Govanhill. One afternoon someone from the local constabulary chapped our tenement door and requested how many people stayed in our family abode? When my mum asked why? The copper replied: "It is for security reasons", as the following week Prince Charles was to officiate at the opening of a new fruit shop (that was directly below us) as part of The Prince Of Wales new start up business initiative for young people. When the time came for the royal visit, my sister was babysitting a little kid called Ali, who was yer typical hyper 5 year old who liked to hang out in my bedroom, as he was fascinated by the sounds and was especially fond of gazing at the record sleeves. As the time grew nearer, marksmen started to appear on the opposite tenement, poised to snipe, any would-be anti-royal assassin. For some punky fun (since it was a special royal occasion) I decided to put on The Sex Pistols – 'Bollocks' album to give the ever growing collection of royal stargazers gathered down below our 1st floor window, some musical entertainment to accompany this joyous, historical event. I opened up my sash window just as the royal entourage appeared and just as The Prince stepped out of the car, I put the needle down on 'God Save The Queen' which proceed to blare out a raging, diatribe of loathing, directed at the royal dynasty. At that moment, Prince Charles for one split second looked up, with his accompanying minders at his side frantically signalling up to us tenement dwellers, to turn the music down, without realising what the record was preaching! It was at this point that little Ali then grabbed 'The Bollocks' album sleeve, went to the window and started to jump about and wave his arms in the air much to the utter bemusement of the royal masses down below. As a matter of principle (to the disgust of fellow family members) I refused to turn the music down. It was nothing personal on The Prince himself, it was just a show of contempt for what he represented that I disagreed with. They live in the unreal world of Buckingham Palace cut off from the real world. I resent paying taxes in contributing to the lavish lifestyle of these unelected scroungers of society. Turf the whole lot of them out into the street, strip them of their privileges and make them sign on the dole at Hackney Job Centre for a year to give them a dose of reality check! And if you go chasing rabbits.....

I was born in 1961 (pre Beatlemania) and lived in the West End district of Whiteinch, Glasgow until 1966. Our family then decamped to the Southside working class tenement infested area of Govanhill, Glasgow. I then spent my teenage years growing up in this exhilarating urban jungle and when 1977 came around (when the two 7s clash) I just couldn't wait to leave school in June that same year, to bust out at full throttle and unleash that inner rebel, that had been simmering away for the last couple of years. In spring of 1977 one record came along and provided this life changing creative catalyst – 'God Save The Queen' by The Sex Pistols. Discovering this crucial record was the pivotal moment in my life, that set me on an unconscious journey into a new enthralling subculture of sounds. It was during the blazing hot summer of 77 that I mostly started to hang out in Graffiti Records on Queen Street, as it produced a mouth watering collection of ultra vivid punky record sleeves on display that defied you to buy them and spew them up, on your hi-fi record player. The Buzzcocks! The Jam! The Stranglers and The Sex Pistols were my own personal favourites of the punk rock explosion that had suddenly gripped my feverish imagination.

As soon as I turned sweet 16 in September, I began my first job as a punkawallah floor boy in the local Gorbals upholstery factory. This event coincided perfectly with receiving my first wage packet (weekly brown poke envelope). I went straight to The Apollo box office and purchased a ticket for The Stranglers (my virgin punk gig) and after seeing them live, it confirmed to myself that there was no way back to being Joe Nobody again in the dullsville straight world. Now fast forward to 1985 – ZOOOMM!!

Come the summer of 85 (aged 23) I had outgrown the double bed and the area. It had gotten a tad weird by then as I was dropping the acid bomb at a fast and furious pace, when I still shared a double bedroom with 2 brothers, who were certainly on a different trip to myself at the time! One particular night, totally gonzoid on a microdot, my mum rushed into the room shouting, "We've killed it! Finally killed it!" Frank (my brother) had apparently slug-gunned this mouse who had been scurrying about the house for the last few days! I never even gotta chance to ask if he was called Gerald!

All this family drama was going on to a backdrop of bleedin Jimmy Shand blaring out of my maw's kitchen radio and I decided that it was now definitely time to depart the family home once and for all…..

About the only person in the house who seemed to be mourning my departure, for pastures unchartered, was my wee Irish maw. She always said "The wrong one's leaving". I don't know if she meant my 2 lazy brothers or my 2 messy sisters? For the next couple of years (apart from being on the road) I would return religiously every Thursday back to Govanhill, to catch up with the family goss, some moonshine washing line behaviour and to catch up with a week's load of daily papers to read.

Govanhill in 1985 was still a working class area made up predominantly of Irish and Asian dynasties with a sprinkling of bedsitter arty craftys knocking around on the fringes. All the local pubs were your typical laddish citizen zombie bars with a hefty quota of Irish pubs scattered around the area also. You certainly didn't catch many moptop garageheads struttin up and down Allison Street with their bootheels wandering that's for sure Roky! The everyday people fashion of the times for males was strictly footy/casual gear complete with curly perms, taches, trainers and mullets a plenty. I definitely felt like 'the timewarp kid' who'd been beamed down from another 1960s alien planet that had suddenly gone off course and had crashed with a psychedelic bang in the here and now. By the time I'd left home, most of my mates and school muckers had buggered off to high rise living in either the Gorbals, Toryglen or Castlemilk area of the Southside. I was to be the first of the family to move out and seek an independent life of my own, free from the claustrophobic hassles of family living, with all 7 of us living under the same, sweaty roof all our lives. Right time, right place for a move! It felt good to be liberated. For me personally it was a trip into the unknown world of sharing a flat with the two Pauls – Big Paul McNeil and Paul Harte, who were a couple of years younger than me and actually had a day job. I'd only known these guys from hanging out in the Griffin and tripping out with them occasionally but it's only till you start living under the same roof with people that you truly get to know them – the good and the bad habits.

Around this time, it also seemed as if half the music loving crowd in The Griffin had also decided to up sticks from the satellite towns and move to the ultra trendy hipshaking West End of Glasgow. It made for a refreshing move, a ned free zone in the haughty atmosphere of bohemian normality. The place definitely required some south side action into the area, with a new shot of raw energy and dynamism to blow away the coolness of Byres Road. The pub scene in Byres Road was non-existent and pretentious into the bargain but it did possess some excellent cheap and cheerful charity shops where you could still pick up a neat album for a £1 and a book for a paltry 50p until the charitable vultures spread their wings and then turned charity into a greed fuelled business of overpriced, crap items. Lucky for us vinyl freaks there were a couple of ace record shops around to satisfy our lust for obscure records namely Echo Records (run by the scary Freak Brothers combo) and the record store up the 1st floor in De Courcey's Arcade. West End living certainly provided a more flamboyant mix of curio shops than Govanhill's same old fabric and fruit shops!

I went from one tenement block to another and our particular flat was situated directly above the local fish 'n' chip shop, near The University Café, bottom end of Byres Road. (1 special fish and a pickle please!)

Rumour had it that when Sheena Easton first left Bellshill to have a shot at the big time, she lived inna tenement flat in Byres Road above a chippie! I still don't know to this day if that was a curse or not…..

Since the 2 Pauls were working and shared the rent, they took a room each and I got lumbered with the kitchen which I instantly transformed into Silverfoilcity. What started off as a greasy, grubby kitchen was quickly transformed into a self made silver palace overnight. My bed (mattress on the floor) was in the recess area and straight away I set about creating a mini Warholian slice of Factory life. I covered the whole recess in strips of silverfoil, bought up in cheap bulk from the local supermarket. To give it that decadent West End flavour, I added some black chiffon curtains for privacy, from all the frenzied tea making going on outside. As a nod to the Cramped trash art aesthetic, I then hung a black top hat on one wall, a black whip on the other with an African female mask in the middle wall to cultivate a kinky, voodoo bordello look. I'm sure at one point, a silver suited picture of Billy Fury suddenly appeared also, to blend into the environs of Silverfoilcity.

It was the perfect time to leave our family abodes behind as we moved in on the Friday and had a flat warming party on the Saturday with a Primal Scream gig on the Sunday at Splash 1 also, to look forward to. It was all go-go-go! We tried to jazz up the bathroom but the attempt at Bronx style graffiti on the walls didn't quite work out, with no sign of a tupac of toilet roll and heaven forbid not a pair of toilet curtains or blind to be had. Sorry ladies but these guys had a lot to learn living together, even a rat would've walked outta that joint backwards just to escape the bad funk in the bathroom.

On the Saturday afternoon, there was a knock on the door and there stood to our surprise, Debbie and Tina, the two pleasure seeking Manchester groupies, who arrived just in time to catch the party on the Saturday and The Primals on the Sunday. God knows how they found our address? Word of mouth sure was a powerful tool back then before the world of social media and moby phones took over the universe. These girls about town cut a dashing 1960s indie look and were extremely knowledgeable about what was happening in the clubs and the current music scene. They mentioned this band from Manchester that everyone was flipping out about called The Stone Roses. According to Tina they'd seen us live and were inspired by the whole Primal Scream package – the look, the gear, the attitude. It maybe took The Stone Roses a while to stamp their own identity on their music at the time and get into their own flared up sound, inspiring a whole new craze a couple of years later, but they did…..

Debbie was the first chick to crash out in Silverfoilcity, spending most of the night chewing my fingernails for some strange unknown reason?!?! The recess could only take a single mattress so there wasn't much room for acrobatic bedroom manoeuvres and as the party wound down we just fell asleep in a narcotic haze. The following night at Splash 1, Bob G told me to watch out for Debbie and not to get too smitten and carried away, as earlier at the club she had propositioned him and he rejected her, as he was going steady with his current chick Karen. Exit Debbie – the vanishing girl! That's got to be a first ever, a groupie sleeping with the tambourinist, to get to the lead singer!

The Splash 3 Happening was the first time that I'd clapped eyes on The Soup Dragons and I'm a sure shot that somewhere along the line that night, one of The Soupies guitar amps got stage damaged by Beattie which caused a bit of the ol friction again baby. Primal Scream didn't really have much respect for amplifiers and microphones – they were there to be used and abused.

Hanging out in The Action House, Byres Road the next day, Bob G dropped in to hang out. Big Paul was at work and Harte had the rare day off. As we were gassing away, we felt in a mischievous mood so Harte got hold of a collection of stroke mags and started to artfully arrange them all over Big Paul's wall. Then Harte dropped his strides and proceeded to lay down some 'brown cables' on a piece of newspaper. He then smeared it all over the porno pics on the wall (filth on filth) and then Bob G joined in with some shaving foam which he sprayed, mixing the textures up and outta nowhere, I concocted a couple of cardboard poles to complete the picture. I'm sure Yoko Ono would have a name for it – 'spontaneous conceptual art' but one thing we never reckoned was the fact that Big Paul wouldn't be back for a couple of days – oh shit! After the first day, his room really began to honk and all we could do was get the air freshener into action and to open all his windows to air the joint. By the third day me and Harte were beginning to regret what we had done and we both made a pact not to be around when he finally came home. When we finally got back to The Action House, Big Paul was there and totally disgusted with our antics and wanted nothing to do with our twisted, sick minds. At first he wanted to molicate both of us but eventually settled for "I'll get my revenge on yous one day when yous least expect it" – fair enough!

Our next door neighbours (across the landing) were Billy Thompson and Grant McDougall, fellow pals from The Griffin, and them living next door provided much needed breathing space when things tended to get real hectic next door in The Action House. Grant and Billy, like ourselves, were obsessive musique idiotes supreme and their pad would provide an oasis of calm over the next couple of years. Billy was the giggling electronics boffin constantly tinkering away in his bedroom while Grant was the smoking, tokin Wire freak who had a certain thing or two for Cosey Fanni Tutti, the Throbbing Gristle chick. Our gaff maybe didn't possess a tv, radio, phone or shower curtain but we did have 3 master blaster stereos to keep us amused. Whenever I woke up, I would lie in Silverfoilcity for a minute and think "What record will wake me up today for a blast?" it always had to be a rocker, to blow away those afternoon cobwebs either The Sex Pistols – 'I Wanna Be Me' or The Rolling Stones – 'Start Me Up'. This didn't sit too well with the guy frying the chips down below so the deal was "Turn it down or no free pickle with yer chips next time" – done deal! Talking of blasting out the sounds. One night we decided to try out a 'Wall of Sound' experiment on the hi-fi's. I had 3 copies of The Ronettes 'Baby I Love You' and dished them out and right on cue, we dropped the needle on the record, to produce one symphonic, glorious pop moment that reverberated throughout the whole flat, close and street in sensurround sound. Sod yer Brookside! If there was a tv programme worth watching we'd invade next door to watch it but within minutes the tv set would fade into the background as Grant got the spliffs rolling and out would come the Throbbing Gristle, Wire lp's to take us all into another dimension.

After a few weeks of living in Silverfoilcity I came to be known as 'The Boy In The Kitchen' whenever Harry The Landlord would pay us his monthly visit to see how things were going. I was supposed to be the guy who was to keep the flat tidy, hoover and clean the dishes but there always seemed to be one more record to play that was just that little bit more important.....I never even had blinds or curtains in my kitchen abode either – a definite case of serious voyeuristic curtain aversion going down in our particular flat that's for sure! Harte's chick Louise once made a brave attempt to gentrify the bathroom but by the next day, normal service had resumed once more. Hovering between the 2 flats, there was also a constant swapping of reading material being passed around to devour. The most thumbed paperback cutting about was 'Beyond Belief', a book about The Moors Murderers – Ian Brady and Myra Hindley. This enthralling book sent a cold chill through everyone who ever read it, in its sheer page-turning horrific details of their diabolic child crimes in the 1960s. We hadn't even clicked that The Smiths had named their band after one of the characters in the book, who finally found the courage to report Ian Brady and Myra Hindley to the local Manchester police.

The other book that gripped our feverish minds was 'Helter Skelter' about the infamous 'Manson Murders' of the late 1960s in America. Again this book was another superbly researched, gripping story that was written by the prosecuting attorney Vincent Bugliosi himself. This tale had you hooked right from the start straight through to the horrific, cataclysmic ending.

Since I was jobless and had loads of free time to kill, I would sometimes wander down Otago Lane and browse through the musty book racks of Voltaire's Book Shop. I managed to pick up 2 excellent books in one raid – 'Uptight' – The Velvet Underground Story and 'Edie – The Life and Times of A Warhol Superstar'. I became utterly obsessed with these 2 engrossing biographies and these were 2 books that never left my bookcase to pass around, they were that precious to me. 'Uptight' for me is a revelation, in stark raving monochrome and for me personally, is the ultimate book about The Velvets that encapsulates perfectly, that seedy, creative New York underground freakshow vibe. At that time in 1985 (it's funny to look back on Andy Warhol now) he was still an underground figure who still hadn't crossed over to the overground yet. Nowadays you can't move for Warholian artefacts in museums and High Street shops, though I still wouldn't mind a triptych of Liz Taylor, Marilyn Monroe and Liza Minnelli in all their pop art technicolour glory on my wall…..

The Edie Segwich biography was one interesting, absorbing disturbing rollercoaster ride of a book. Edie was the Twiggyesque little rich American kid who, once she moved to the glittering lights of New York City, proceeded to live off her parents' monthly cheque to lord it up as a burgeoning Warhol Superstar but once the money ran out and the drugs kicked in, she crashed and burned and was eventually discarded from The Factory inner circle of hipness. In her later life, Edie was constantly checking herself in and out of sanatoriums, at times receiving ect shocks to the brain. Along with her serious drug habit, it all proved too much for 'The Girl Of 65' who finally succumbed to an early death of drug poisoning in the early 1970s. Speed! Madness and Flying Saucers pretty much summed up her chaotically charged lifestyle. Ciao! Manhattan – read it and weep.

WHORING IT FOR THE MEDIA

And a big hello to the world of music media. Apart from a couple of gig reviews and fanzine interviews, it was about this time that Primal Scream branched out and burrowed their way in, in to the mindset of the insatiable music press of the day, to spread the garage pop word to the masses (well NME, Zigzag and Melody Maker). Our first real bit of press was a half-piece page interview in Zigzag with Bob G and Beattie the main mouthpieces for the band. At the time there was a varied selection of music mags that you could try and put your philosophy over to such as Sounds! NME! Melody Maker! Record Mirror and Smash Hits. In August of 85 Primal Scream conducted their first major article and photograph in the NME. The picture was a striking image of 6 Glaswegian garageheads squeezed into a church doorway, adopting a myriad of striking poses for the camera. Bang central was Dungo with Bob G and Beattie either side of him, pouting away for all their worth, in their leather strides. I'm situated, left front, sitting down and I'm wearing my favourite psychedelic top, with a finger at my lip, in tribute to an Elevators pic of Tommy Hall on the 'Easter Everywhere' album. Bottom right you had Harte, sitting down, grinning away with a natty beret on his napper and behind him, pulling a defiant, menacing stare in to the lens is Tam, with his legs coiled up around Harte. This photo screamed "We're coming to get you popkids". The interview was a decent enough spread and intro to the band, emphasising that with enough airplay, record company push and popism tunes, Primal Scream would like to break out of the indie ghetto and attack the mainstream Top Twenty with pure pop. Get the Picture!

The next major article featured a few weeks later in the Melody Maker with a half-page spread and photograph accompanied by the humorous caption of PRIMAL THERAPY'. Hogging the front cover was the shaggy haired Robert Smith out of The Cure, and if he and Siouxsie can cut across to the mainstream with their Gothic inspired imagery and unusual subject matter for mainstream pop…..well!

Strange to observe that there weren't any Creation records in the indie charts at the time but they had a 'Cassette Chart' that featured those long forgotten positive punkers Brigandage and Blood And Roses in it. At Number 1 in the real Top 20, you had Madonna with 'Into The Groove' and also at Number 2 with 'Holiday'. Now that's where Primal Scream wanted to be – hanging out backstage with 'The Queen Of Pop' in the TOTPs studio, swapping tips with the material girl on how to make it bigstyle! In that same Melody Maker edition they conducted a feature on The Paisley Underground scene, happening in the USA. Whatever happened to The Dream Syndicate! Green on Red! The Rain Parade and The Three O'Clock? The Bangles were the only band out of that scene to appear out of the psychedelic haze and to storm the charts with a piss poor ballad called 'Eternal Flame' that hogged the Number 1 spot for what felt like years. To tell ya the tongues of truth – I never really dug any of them! Back to the Primals piece. The main caption 'Primal Therapy' captures perfectly the essence of 6 very different personalities thrown together, trying to create some kinda updated 1980s pop magic. The photograph was shot around the same time as the NME article on the same day but it doesn't quite capture the dynamic pose of the NME feature. It seems at the time the press just couldn't get their head round the fact that our lead singer could also be the drummer in another band, and a more successful one at that…..

SPLASH 1 REVISITED

For the Splash 5 Happening, The promoters decided to experiment for one night only. No bands, just music – bad idea! By then most people who frequented it, went along to check out the latest band from the underground and the cassette sounds blaring out on the dancefloor, was a neat bonus for the night. The night resulted in a half-empty discotheque, lacking any real tension, anticipation or buzz. It just didn't seem as exciting, playing music non-stop for 4 hours from 8 till midnight.

Having two bands on each time, broke up the night and created a more intoxicating, charged atmosphere that people looked forward to. Running a club on a Sunday night may seem in hindsight a non-starter but I never heard anyone complain that they had to catch the last train or bus home, to get up for college or work in the morning.

Splash 1 club nights contained a healthy mix of new hungry youths on the scene, along with a good dose of original punkoids from the late 1970s – a real trans generational mix of dolites, students and workers all united under the same roof for some dancefloor action.

Before the Splash 6 Happening with The Jasmine Minks, the whole Primals posse plus The Submarines (all 14 bodies) found ourselves in the back of a transit van bound for ghost town Liverpool one August Saturday afternoon. As the driver opened the back door the whole lot of us practically fell out, in a drunken narcotic haze at his feet. Taking a walk around Liverpool back then was a strange town experience. The place was total deadsville for a Saturday night, a very eerie weird out feeling that carried itself into the gig venue for the night. Support band for the night was The Tractors, a local band who received a greater reception than The Primals and The Submarines put together! The Liverpool crowd didn't dig us one little bit, a lot of heckles and jeers and all round bad vibes. Not a pleasurable gig to remember in The Mardi Gras if I recall correctly.

For the Splash 6 gig, those Aberdonian-born London based power poppers The Jasmine Minks were in town as headliners. I still have great memories of the whole squad of them taking over Big Paul's front bedroom and storming their way through a full blown rehearsal complete with blaring trumpets and amplifiers blasting the windows out. I've still got a rare Splash 6 vhs tape of The Jasmine's onstage, playing to a packed out audience of eager Creation heads of that particular night.

Splash 7 Happening was also a memorable occasion if only for the fact that about 20 bodies must've crashed out at The Action House that weekend coinciding with the arrival of The Weather Prophets. There was that many people, Billy and Grant next door had to take the overflow from our extremely crowded house. Up from London for the occasion came NME scribe David Swiff, his chick and her pal Jo, the dark-haired beauty from Redhill, who I had the hots for, at the time. Also appearing was a dude we named 'The Crusher', who was built like the proverbial brick shithouse, with bullet shaped head completing his mean appearance. I think he may have been The Jasmine's roadie up for the gig?!?! We also later found out it was The Crusher's first time ever on an acid trip too – Holy Garbageman! It was on the Saturday night before The Prophets gig that the whole squad of us met up in The Studio One bar in Byres Road and popped a microdot (apart from David, his chick and Jo) to catch the acid fried double bill of 'Altered States' and 'Bladerunner'. Just that name 'Altered States' just about sums up the night perfectly! By the time we got to The Grosvenor, we were all in our own private Idaho orbit and just flopped out in the first 2 rows in the cinema, stoned to the bone! There was no seat available for me so I just crashed on the cinema floor. At one point during 'Bladerunner', The Crusher went to the toilet and I then nabbed his seat – notta good idea! When he arrived back (with a confused, dementoid look on his fizzog) he took one look at me, picked me up (like a scene out of The Mummy) and then threw me to the ground – ouch! This guy was seriously unhinged now as the acid had taken a real stranglehold on his brain machine. I stayed well clear of The Crusher from then on, as he was beginning to turn into a real mean looking bastirt.

Watching 'Altered States' on the big screen, I turned around at one point and came across a whole row of popping eyes, hypnotized, mouths gaping, staring intensely at the screen. All of a sudden we weren't watching the film, we were inside the film, along with William Hurt in the flotation tank, experiencing every goddamn freakin incident he was going through. Boy! Were we stoned immaculate! Ken Russell! Give that man a round of applause..... As the double bill ended, we'd all decided that we'd had enough acid visuals for the night and that it was time to head back to Silverfoilcity to blast out some sounds to keep us elevated on the trip. By this time The Crusher had fallen asleep and as I nudged him awake out of his drug-induced stupor, he stood up (looking perplexed) and then proceeded to walk straight bang into the cinema screen as the credits rolled on by, head first, thinking it was the exit for some strange, unfathomable reason?!?! By this stage The Crusher had entered cabbageland so we invited him back to our flat (along with the other 20 bodies) to continue the night. Once there, Harte plucked out this ace Velvets cassette bootleg and stuck it on. It sounded real raw power and intense and seemed to have revived our musical ears as we all sat about in Silverfoilcity tripping out of our tiny, fried minds. The Crusher at this point was sitting at the table, silent like, digging the sounds moving his hand up and down and I looked over and shouted out "Check out The Crusher, he looks as though he's having a J. Arthur Rank to The Velvets" and at this point everyone then exploded into shards of lysergic laughter. It had been a strange vibe up till then, as Jo had come into the kitchen and tried to strike up a sensible conversation but everyone was too wiped, to hold one together so she gave up, sat there and started to seriously read a book and just about then, Stew baby then proceeded to perform this ridiculous impersonation of a straight faced newsreader. He then started to take down his trousers, now sitting in his underpants besides Jo, who was still casually trying to read her book. I think eventually she just gave up and crashed out on the hall floor with a blanket. It was that kinda night in The Action House, a lot of frazzled, whacked out pulsating heads digging the right here, right now vibe. There's a real kool piece of Splash 1 footage of around then of everyone out on the floor going ape to X-Ray Spex with Jo appearing out of nowhere for a few brief seconds, looking into the soul of the camera, a second of your life captured for a brief moment in time amongst the madness of the night.....

Next up for the Splash 8 Happening were The June Brides who, all of a sudden were everyone's favourite pet indie band that everyone adored. Again on the Splash 1 vhs tape, there's a couple of rare live pieces of footage of The June Brides in all their shining, punky pop glory to a packed out Sunday night crowd of pleasure seekers. By September the word was out that there was a new club to be seen and heard in town. Even Pat Nevin showed his Chelsea face now and again, checking out the band scene and in particular digging the Creation type bands. It was mighty unusual for a footy player of that time to have rare good tastes in alternative sounds, it was mostly all U2 and Simple Minds and that was stretching it.....

Meanwhile back at The Roky Underground Batcave, it was time to pile into the back of that transit van once more and show some brotherly support to The Submarines who were headlining there. With the Glaswegian contingent in tow, we all descended on The Village Theatre for a guid garage punk night out in The Nauld. Only one small matter – Derek's turntables had packed in!

Luckily for us Billy had brought along various cassette tapes, then someone produced an old cassette player and the next you know it's blaring out of a guitar amp – voila! One instant, spontaneous psychedelic punky party later.

One gig that was promoted there at Daddy Warbucks but not under the Splash 1 Happening banner was The Jesus And Mary Chain gig in early October, with The Pastels as support. I think this was a homecoming warm up gig before their debut album 'Psychocandy' got unleashed in November. Their newly acquired army of youthful feedback fans and old 77 punks were still turning up in the hope of having a white riot of their own. The Pastels, support for the night, were either on too early or I had a mild chemical imbalance of the mind (probably the later). By the time The Mary Chain were set to perform, the joint was heaving and tightly packed so me and Big Paul took up our positions on a couple of chairs up the back, ready for the kamikaze fun to begin, as we went into full on critical, switched on mode!

At this point in their career, due to the previous riotous gig happenings, The Jesus And Mary Chain took to hiring a buncha monkey men goons at the front of the stage to keep the baying hordes at arm's length in case they tore strips of The Reid brothers onstage. From our vantage point at the back, it looked fucking hilarious! I just couldn't take the scenario seriously, where was the chicken wire dudes? This was no Clash at The Apollo in 78, no Doors in Texas in 68 and certainly no Gene Vincent gig in Japan in the late 1950s. I'd been to a couple of genuinely scary, dangerous adrenalin fuelled gigs in Glasgow either involving The Clash or The Cramps which were thrilling and exciting in their sheer anything could happen wildness but this was strictly second division stuff going on here – a buncha pissed up, cardy wearing indie kids trying to live up to the NME's portrait, of how a Jesus And Mary Chain audience should perform – oh you're so vicious! Outside at the end of the gig, William Reid was being heckled and in frustration started lashing out at black bin bags lying around venting off. It was one helluva tight straightjacket that they had gotten themselves into and it needed loosening – quick!

LOVE AT HUMAN PSYCHEDELIC VELOCITY GIRL

'Velocity Girl' was constructed and created in a recording studio, down a back lane in Shawlands, Glasgow in one speedy fuelled session in October along with the stinging punk instrumental 'Spirea X'. These 2 tracks were the chosen b-sides to 'Crystal Crescent' which was the a-side for Primal Screams' second record release on Creation Records. Little did we realise at the time when we recorded 'Velocity Girl' that it would go on to be everyone's favourite early Primal Scream track.

For me, it still sounds like a timeless piece of sparkling pop beauty – all 1 minute 26 seconds of it. Bob G's asthmatic yearning vocal, Beattie's urgent ringing guitar, my slamming tambourine beat, Harte's solid rhythmic backing, Dungo's tuneful bassline and Tam's ultra snappy backbeat – it was a winner all the way daddio! When 'Crystal Crescent' was released in December 85, everyone instantly flipped it over for the bittersweet b-side that everyone was raving about. It would go on to be an underground indie classic in 1986, even entering John Peel's Festive Fifty at Number 4 that year. 'Spirea X' the other track on the 12-inch b-side was all guitars blazing with Beattie cutting loose and unleashing his inner Steve Jones. We even cheekily sneaked a sample out of 'A Clockwork Orange' at the end of the disc without anyone even noticing ha! The joys of those innocent, carefree pre-sampling not getting caught years. The a-side 'Crystal Crescent' was recorded in a studio in St John's Wood in London and turned out to be an expensive, over-produced record complete with a tacked on horn section in the middle. The front picture sleeve consisted of a still photograph from an obscure arty crafty short film called 'Meshes In The Afternoon' starring Maya Deyen. For the back sleeve Creation used a live picture of myself, complete with maskie, brandishing my gigantor white tambourine. Both images perfectly captured that wistful, jingle jangle joy of the music inside the picture sleeves. This was definitely my Andy Warhol 15 minutes of fame time. The back sleeve photo was one from a live gig in Edinburgh's Hoochie Koochie Club, October 85 and was shot by the perceptive eye of one Dick Green. The gig was also recorded live on video at the time and you can actually spot Dick near the front, snapping away at Primal Scream onstage. The quality of the vhs tape is still of a reasonable watchable quality and just recently I transferred it on to a digital cd for posterity. The gig was also memorable for myself wearing my Johnny Thunders style maskie and as the gig goes on I proceed to get more pished with every tambourine beat, swaying about, with a sober Harte shooting me glowering looks of disgust. I really didn't give a flying fuck as I was getting pissed and having a real good time, digging The Primals beat, playing up to the crowd.

When the NME put 'Velocity Girl' on its free C86 giveaway cassette in 1986, the song seemed to have taken on a new lease of life of its own, with Peelie constantly airing it on his night-time slot on a weekly basis. A band from Washington in the mid 90s were so inspired by the track that they even named themselves 'Velocity Girl', producing their own yankee indie spin on velvet guitar pop. They seemed to have disappeared as quickly as they appeared! I was also quite surprised to find out that James Dean Bradfield (out of The Manics) used to busk 'Velocity Girl' out on the gutter streets of Cardiff during their early days. I always thought that it would be more to Nicky Wire's dressed to kill indie tastes? When The Manics finally got round to covering 'Velocity Girl' on their 'Australia' cd ep, my ears pricked up and I bought a copy. I couldn't believe how weak their version sounded, it was a total wimp out! These are the same guys who've written such anthemic classics such as 'Faster!' 'Motorcycle Emptiness' and 'If You Tolerate This' but made such a lethargic hash of 'Velocity Girl'. Stick to the originals valley boys! Having a swatch on YouTube, typing in 'Velocity Girl', I was surprised to find that it has now achieved a stupendous 250,000 hits, a quarter of a million viewings – not bad for a song on a b-side that initially only sold around 3,000 copies in 85…..The a-side 'Crystal Crescent' has only achieved a paltry 16,000 hits – that tells you all you need to know really. If 'Velocity Girl' was stretched out to 3 minutes, was on a major record label, with a decent video and the whole marketing shebang behind it – it would've soared straight into the Top 20, no danger. I suppose in hindsight you could say that about a lot of rediscovered records nowadays with the first Velvet Underground album now reaching over a million sales but back in 1967 when it was released, it barely sold a thousand hard copies.

Around the same time that we recorded 'Crystal Crescent' in London, we also managed to squeeze in our first John Peel session in the Maida Vale studios. This happened to be the recording where I was sent to Coventry (ie studio hall) by that belligerent old Mott boffin Dale Griffin, for supposedly playing my tambourine out of time and interrupting the session. We recorded 4 songs for the session but we never got to meet John Peel himself in person, I suppose he was hiding out in Peel Acres at the time…..The four recorded songs were 'Aftermath', 'Subterranean', 'I Love You' and 'Crystal Crescent'. I actually prefer the 2 rawer versions of 'Aftermath' and 'I Love You' on this session compared to the overproduced, superslick versions that eventually appeared on 'Sonic Flower Groove' a couple of years later. These versions are to my ears, more natural and unadorned and are full of the joys of life at that time, December 1985, just before the dawn of a new year beckoned. That first John Peel session has now achieved a reasonably healthy 15,000 viewings on YouTube so far. Some songs just sound great on radio sessions and when they take them into an expensive recording studio they just proceed to bore the arse off it with total overproduction overload…..

SPLASH 1 KICKS UP A GEAR

In late November 85, Felt were the latest band to grace the Splash 10 Happening at Daddy Warbucks. They'd just recently signed to Creation Records on the back of The Jesus And Mary Chain rollercoaster bandwagon. Before they joined Creation, Felt had already been infiltrating our musical palette with their impressive catalogue of strange, ethereal, classical slabs of majestic pop. Big Paul and Grant were grade one fans, especially of the beautific guitar genius Maurice Deebank, whose inventive fretwork particularly stood out amongst your usual shambling indie platters. Their inventive album titles alone, make your eyes stuff with wonder: 'Crumbling The Antiseptic Beauty', 'The Splendour Of Fear' and 'The Strange Idols Pattern'. These albums were totally different from their 7-inch singles releases which I devoured on every new release. 'Penelope Tree', 'Sunlight Bathed The Golden Glow' and 'Primitive Painters' which were superb, enchanting vinyl treasures to behold in your record collection. The latter single had Grangemouth's finest otherworldly chanteuse Liz Fraser (of Cocteau Twins) adorning the song, with Lawrence's sweet tones accompanying the duet. 'Primitive Painters' to this day, still sends a tingle down your shivering spine in its sheer utter decadent way. As Felt signed to Creation, Maurice Deebank departed and Martin Duffy then magically appeared, to take up organ duties to flesh out their new departure in sound. This new groove was to be found on the jangle tastic 'Ballad Of The Band' release which was sparkling pop music at its grooviest. After their Splash 10 appearance, we managed to put up a couple of Felt dudes in our halfway house, to save them costs in staying in seedy, overpriced hotels. One memory sticks out from them staying at our pad and that is wakening up on the Monday morning, stepping into the hall and finding one of the Felt guys lying flat out cold with Harte's swastika flag wrapped round him as a blanket! That teutonic nasty flag and the Felt dude under it, just didn't go together..... Herr Harte must've whipped it off his wall the night before, as we had a severe shortage of blankets back then and there was no such thing as a duvet then also in 85 tenementland.

The Splash 11 Happening in December 85 were Wire. Now this was a major scoop for everyone involved at Splash 1 as Wire had just got back together again as the original 4 man 'beat combo'. Between 1981, when they split up, till now they had mostly been involved in various solo projects and once reformed again, they defiantly announced that they wouldn't be playing any songs off their first 3 albums 'Pink Flag', 'Chairs Missing' and '154'. By fuck! These dudes only danced to their own tune! No '115th' to be played here, which was their ultimate pop moment of '154' album. For our masochistic pleasure for one night only they should've hired 'The Ex Lion Tamers', as support (who were a Wire covers band) who only actually played the first 3 albums live – confused? you will be! Grant the promoter for this Splash 11 Happening, was in his element, as he was a fanatic Wire diehard and pulled out all the stops to make the gig an unforgettable experience. On this frozen ass December night, the place was packed to the rafters for as well as the regular Splash 1 devotees there, a whole load of other Wire fanatics turned up too. As far as I know, it was the first time on Scottish soil for Wire. In 1979 I was all set for catching them at The Apollo supporting Roxy Music but they pulled out of the British section of the European tour and we got lumbered instead with bleedin Annie Lennox and The Tourists – major disappointment! At some of the Splash 1 gigs Jim Lambie could be seen brandishing a film camera (Warhol style) to capture the moments for posterity but I've never ever seen any live footage of this one off gig either online or on a bootleg video tape. I don't know what the 500 bodies expected when they turned up as Wire stuck to their guns and proceeded to pummel the audience with an electronically charged, guitar blazing set. They were being cheered raucously after every number but sadly no 'Lowdown', 'Mannequin', 'French Film Blurred' or 'Our Swimmer' to satisfy the Wired masses. Grant's neebor pal Billy remembers the gig clearly as he was the only sober person about on the night (so he says!) as Grant and Karen (the cashier) were on another trip altogether, so Billy was entrusted with the gig takings and surprised himself the next morning, when he awakened, to find the money bag still lying there beside him. I've still gotta A4 poster of the Wire gig in bold lurid pink lettering with a green border. That's the thing with the Splash 1 posters, they all came in glorious eye popping colours of burnt orange, glowing greens, vivid blues and bucolic purples to attract people's attention. Every design was pinched and collaged, nothing was sacred in those times – Edie Sedgwick! Richard Hell! Andy Warhol! Captain Scarlet and even Hitler Youths were all homage and pasted. Sometimes good guys don't wear white.....

The promoters at the time had also tried unsuccessfully to capture The The and Julian Cope but for some reason, they just couldn't squeeze us in. Major pity, as both bands would've gone down a provocative storm as at that time, they were creatively on fire producing such excellent albums as The The's – 'Soul Mining' along with Julian Cope's mind twisting 'Fried' lp.

MEANWHILE BACK AT SILVERFOILCITY

Guy Fawkes night on November 5th came at the right time for us budding pyromaniacs in the Action House. We had noticed that there was a whole lotta old brown, teaky furniture taking up too much cupboard space so we decided to hold a bonfire 'out the back' and torch the lot! The cupboard was rammed to the gills, full of that old 'granny furniture' from the 50s, which is probably worth a vintage mint nowadays but at that particular time in 1985 us young garage cats didn't quite dig the vintage furniture scene. Chairs, wardrobes, tables, dressers and sideboards all got the Guy Fawkes treatment, much to the utter disgust of the neighbourly curtain twitchers who looked on in horror aghast. We then decided to brighten up bonfire night a tad more by bringing down some Roman Candles and then proceeded to aim them at all the peacenik neighbours – bullseye! We still possessed that naughty street streak in our southside make up – the haughty West End crowd didn't go in for pyrotechnics or come to think of it, the burning of old vintage furniture! I'm surprised to this day that no one actually called the fire brigade – Nobody spoil our fun! I always wondered what Harry The Landlord's reaction would've been, when he went to his cupboard and discovered all his old furniture was missing? I never stayed long enough to find out thank god!

Since I was a bit of a lazy sod in the mornings, as soon as I woke up in the afternoon, I would head to The University Café for my late breakfast of 2 gammon rolls. Back then it still had the rickety old seats and formica table combo with everyone's favourite snack of peas and vinegar on the faded menu card. It was the best café around in The West End at the time, before they all turned into gastro poncified over priced joints, that were way off your low budget lifestyle league.

If I'd had a late night before, it was more than likely that I was up to the wee small hours, creating my 'Trash Books' – a collection of 6 volumes. I started them in 1982 out of sheer creative boredom to charge up the brain and to spew forth my vivid imagination. The 'Trash Books' were a kaleidoscopic mix of collage, gig reviews, paper headlines and album lists. It's amazing what you can concoct with a pair of scissors, a scalpel, pritt stick, felt tip pens, old magazines and current music papers! By 1985, these books had turned into full blown psychedelic jabberwocky scrapbooks that only made sense to me. Obviously some of them were created under the influence of lsd and when you visualize some of them right now in the cold clear light of day (nearly 30 years later) there's a lot of insane acid babble going down in those pages, accompanying the cut up visuals.

In amongst the 6 volumes of 'Trash Books' which I completed are several reviews, posters and articles in regards to Primal Scream which I have either collaged or defaced, depending on my mood at the current time. At one point, I even started to scrawl down the lyrics of certain favourite tunes, which was no mean feat, as I had to instantly stop/start the record to catch the sometimes indecipherable lyric. All I need to do nowadays is punch in Scott Walker – 'Plastic Palace People' in Google and up pops the lyric in seconds.

Whenever Big Paul would split to his parents midweek, myself and Harte would get some serious record sessions on the go. One dude who we shared a common bond with, was that dirty ass, drugged out punk from the dingy backstreets of Queens, New York, with the fuck you attitude and sleazy swagger that took Keef Richards debauched, decadent lifestyle that one step beyond – Johnny Thunders Ya Bas! I first got into him when The Old Tart (Dougie J) gave me a copy of Johnny Thunders And The Heartbreakers – 'Live At Max's Kansas City' album. It was so raw and alive, encased with killer riffs and real street trash vocals. This guy touched your inner rock 'n' roll soul in an instant, like no other guitar god around. This rock 'n' roll saviour for me, left the whole Clapton! Beck! Townsend! Santana guitar army, jerking into their guitar cases. Playing his pink vinyl 12-inch of 'You Can't Put Your Arms Around A Memory' once again, I then flip it over to the b-side 'I'm Hurting' and lose myself in one of the truly great gut wrenching guitar breaks of all time, exploding in one pent up, smacked out orgasm with killer lyrics to die for about the big break up! I bet even Bob Dylan would cut off his right arm to write a double a-side that good – Get off the phone! L.A.M.F.

Harte's sound system was more dynamic for playing the record sessions, so we mostly tended to hang out in his bare minimalist room – swastika flag draped, guitar/amp plugged in and humongous amount of vinyl goodies lying around. He was real good at seeking out real vinyl gems, cratedigging amongst the dross, was Herr Harte. There was one compilation album he discovered that had 4 super rare Richard Hell cuts on it that no one had heard before (well 2). It was a dodgy comp showcase for Shake Records who had earlier released The Neon Boys tracks 'That's All I Know Right Now' in a blistering, twin guitar assault on the speakers that literally explodes! The other superb find on the album was an unreleased Richard Hell song called 'Don't Die' which possesses an unusual, syncopated, jerky rhythm that for me is one of his finest compositions. I think every available copy of that compilation was snaffled up pronto, just to hear those rare Richard Hell tracks from the mid 1970s punk period of New York.

ANN MARGRET IS THE SEXIEST MOTHERFUCKER TO EVER HIT OUR TELEVISION SCREENS – FACT!

Well that was the conclusion that me and Harte came to, one night watching her shake her tush in 'Viva Las Vega' which also starred Elvis The Pelvis. We all dug Brigitte Bardot! Francoise Hardy! Marianne Faithfull! Anita Pallenberg and Sophia Loren with a passion but for the sheer wow factor – Ann Margret took some thrashing! This Swedish born pussycat could act, sing and dance – triple class, Hollywood style! Her hottest feverish flicks were 'The Cincinatti Kid', 'Carnal Knowledge', 'Murderers Row', 'The Pleasure Seekers' and her ultimate action painted sexiest – 'The

Swinger' from 1966. In the 1970s they even gave Ann Margret her own all singing, all dancing, hip shaking tv programme, riding atop a motorbike in one show and bizarrely introducing The Bay City Rollers singing 'Saturday Night' in another. Ann Margret was one helluva foxy lady to behold and don't even mention her writhing about, on phallic styled cushions, covered in baked beans in 'Tommy'. There endeth 1985 on a high…..

TOP 20 TURNTABLE SOUNDS – 1985

1. Tim Buckley – Phantasmagoria In Two
2. Sly And The Family Stone – Running Away
3. The Barracudas – I Wish It Could Be 1965 Again
4. Sonic Youth – Death Valley 69
5. Nancy Sinatra And Lee Hazelwood – Some Velvet Morning
6. Primal Scream – Velocity Girl
7. The Ramones – I Wanna Be Sedated
8. Scott Walker – Plastic Palace People
9. Gene Clark – Because of You
10. Big Star – Kangaroo
11. The Misunderstood – I Can Take You To The Sun
12. Pretty Things – Honey I Need
13. Neon Boys – That's All I Know Right Now
14. Sex Pistols – Satellite
15. X Ray Spex – Let's Submerge
16. The Cramps – Strychnine
17. Electric Prunes – Get Me To The World On Time
18. The Seeds – No Escape
19. 13th Floor Elevators – Slip Inside This House
20. Jacky – White Horses

Live Edinburgh gig circa '85 top and the tamby man taking front page position.

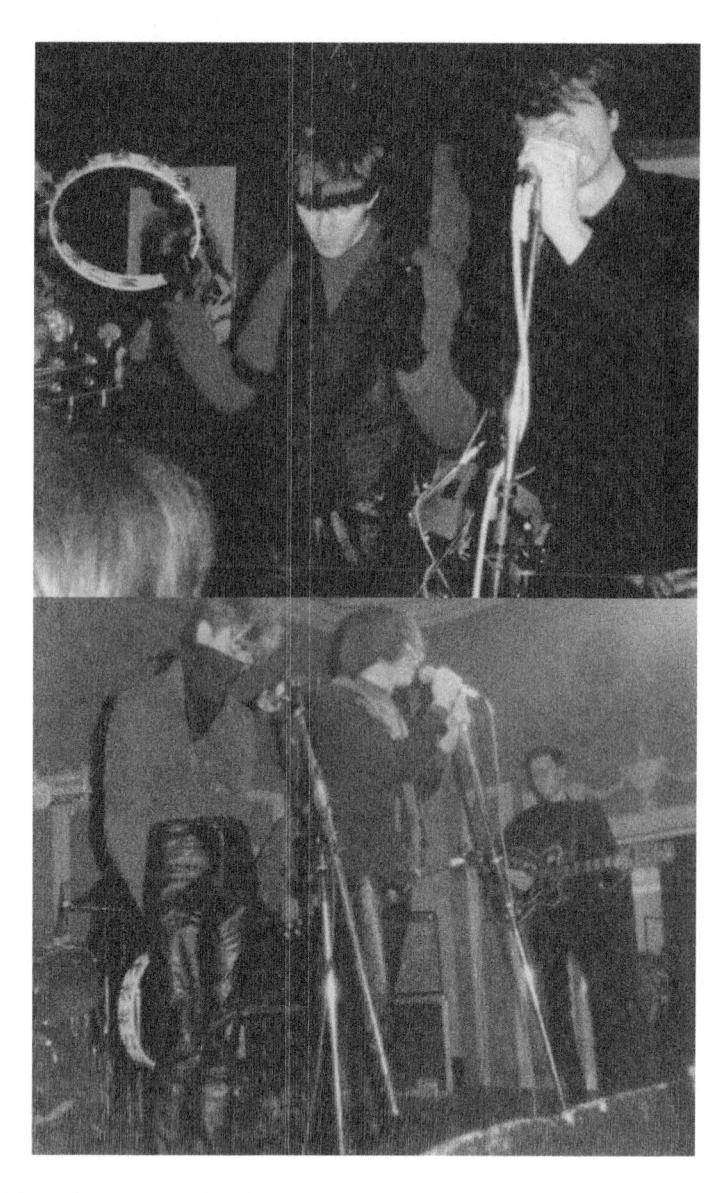

Two live shots of Primals in action with London Clarendon Ballroom June 1986 at bottom.

Kicking back in 'Silverfoil City' in the Action House.

Dungo hanging out in the Creation office, Farringdon, meanwhile meet Joyce X – 'Nice As Fuck'.

London Harp Club Feb. 1986 – one minute rattling that tambourine onstage, the next chewing on bottles backstage after lasting all of 15 minutes…

Convex mirror meets 'Mr Tambourine Man'. Photograph courtesy of Grant MacDougall.

Primal Scream promo pic circa '85.

Primal Scream hoist The Jolly Rodger at Plymouth Ziggy's November 1985 and Primal Scream blast it up at Glasgow Splash May 1986.

1st Splash/Happening with The Loft at Daddy Warbucks June 1985 and Primal Scream's 1st headlining gig at Glasgow Lucifers Feb. 1985.

'Mr Tambourine Man' gets his Warholian 5 minutes of fame on the back sleeve of the 'Crystal Crescent /Velocity Girl' 45 single and then fast forward to June 1987 for the 12 in Gentle Tuesday single.

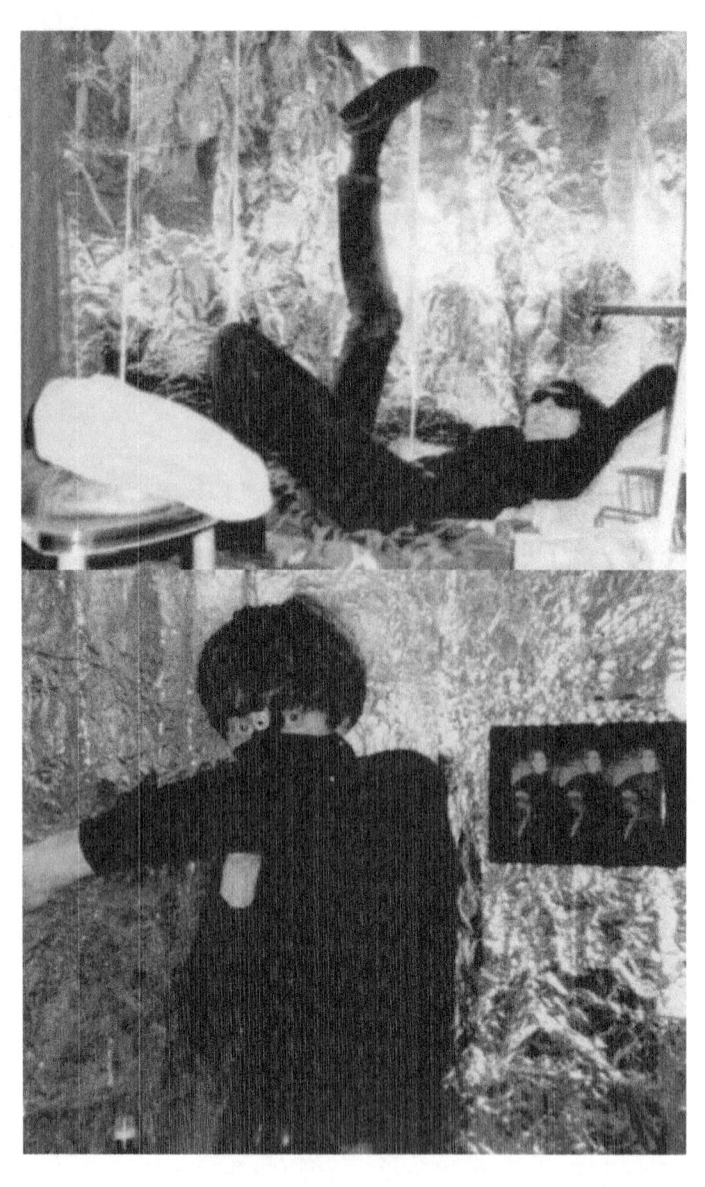

Martin St John shooting it up in Silverfoil City and kicking it up in style in his tenement recess…

My last ever Primal Scream gig at London ULU 26th June 1987 – r.i.p. Mr Tambourine Man and London ICA live photo from summer 1986 during NME's 'Cool In The Spool' week of gigs. Photograph courtesy of Craig Steptoe.

Tambourine case and white metal tambourine conceived and built by Paul Harte with front cover designed by Bobby Gillespie. Note: in tamby case one mouth organ blagged straight from the mouth of Lux Interior on a sweat-filled gorehound gig in Leeds circa early 1984.

OUT ON THAT ROAD 86

It was time to get on board that rockin' train once more – London calling for the ICA gig on January 1st. As we're all sitting about in McGee's gaff in Tottenham, as loose as a goose and not really feeling the Hogmanay spirit, Dave (out of The Prophets) phoned to let us know that he was having a squat party to celebrate the New Year! This phone call energized us and as soon as we arrived there, we were drinking, chatting and swinging from the rafters in no time, like there was no tomorrow – a real tonic for the troops! Most people in bands, living in London seemed to be involved in the squat scene at the time. The only downfall to this fuck the rent, bills, freestyle way of living was if the sleazy landlord appeared, with a couple of mean heavies and a crowbar, to take care of their business. Case of, hands up guvnor, I'll put my trousers on and split at once – till you found another empty, vacant house to doss in. Even Joe Strummer was still slumming it up in squats in London in the 80s even though The Clash were on a major record label at the time. After the Hogmanay party, I found myself crashing out in another squat, this time in Islington, in Dave's (bass player out of The Prophets) shack. His gaff was really minimalist with dodgy squeaking floorboards, a broken bicycle and a big fuck off Union Jack bedspread that I had to sleep under! Oh! The catholic shame of it! If only my brothers had clocked me that night, I would've been branded a traitor and knee-capped on the spot – ouch! I innocently like to associate the Union Jack as a symbol of the pop-art 60s a la The Who instead of all the sectarian hatred that it's normally associated with. Lucky Dave never appeared with a camera – instant blackmail corner! By January 1st 1986, Primal Scream had only played once in London before, so playing the hallowed grounds of the ICA Gallery in The Pall Mall was a definite step up in gear. The place was steeped in history and importance and over the years early Pink Floyd, The Clash and just recently The Jesus And Mary Chain, had all ripped up the joint, producing high energy, chaotic gigs. The gig that Primal Scream found themselves playing at, was a C86 NME

Showcase for raw, upcoming gallus and reckless bands, currently bubbling under the independent radar. The NME gave away a free C86 Cassette mixtape, which contained 'Velocity Girl' and this track in particular seemed to have caused a stir among the more discerning pop enthusiast in the indie subculture. The other band sharing a stage with us, were those intense Irish ranters Microdisney who produced the classic album title of 'I Hate All You South African Bastards'. There was to be no compromise on these guys' parts that's for sure.....For our gig, Primal Scream were gushingly introduced by that bedsit disco queen Tracey Thorn herself, as her current favourite pop group and that seemed to have set the tone then, for an excellent, thrilling night as all the psychedelic stars aligned as one, in a wholly communion of singing ringing guitars, tambourine on the beat and even Bob G's voice, soaring angelically, in the groove with the rest of the band. The sound onstage was crystal crescent clear and harmonically in sync with the historical surroundings. The frenzied audience was not your typical transparent London crowd of blasé hipsters. They produced a pulsating atmosphere, cheering and stomping their approval from the first to the very last number, with 'Velocity Girl' rousing the biggest cheer of the ecstatic night in the big black smoke. One reviewer at the gig apparently overhead a fan gasp "It's like.....will they? won't they? – it's sexual!!" Interesting viewpoint of a hyper excited Primals fan caught up in the early throes of Screamadelicamania! Onstage the sound, surge of the crowd and the sense of power felt galvanising and at that moment in time, gave you a small snippet of what real fame would encase, if the Primals ever achieved a Top 20 chart hit and got to be covered in peanut butter all over the smeared and sticky pages of Smash Hits! Just as the night couldn't get any higher for sheer adrenalin thrills, Jo popped up backstage for some flirty fun and next you know I'd wangled Joe Foster's house keys off him and found ourselves on a night bus to Dalston. Only thing with this little cosy arrangement was the fact that her mate had to come along with us too, as she had missed the last train home and had nowhere to crash. They say 3 is a crowd and it certainly rung true that night. As me and Jo bunked down, ready to bring in 1986 with a bang, you couldn't help but notice, her mate sitting up the back of the living room, trying to read a book nonchalantly as we got down to the old 'sewing machine act'…..

There was a real shocker in store in February when Paul Harte suddenly announced that he was leaving Primal Scream, after just one crazy, guitar rhythmic year! Harte's departure was a real jolt and took everyone in the band by surprise, including himself probably?!?! Harte did possess indecisive periods of self doubt at times and this, along with his neurotic way of thinking culminated in his decision to leave Primal Scream, just as they were building up a momentum in the music press and radio.

Harte was an excellent rhythm guitar player and brought a certain El Pistoleros attitude and look to The Primals for one year only….. Within weeks he was instantly replaced by Stewart May aka The Brat, who was pinched from The Submarines complete with his Brian Jones teardrop guitar! He had barley strapped on the guitar, when he was transported straight away to The Hellfire studios to get him in to the Primals jangle groove pronto, as there were a couple of important London gigs looming on the horizon once more. Stewart was totally different in looks and personality to Harte. He was a good couple of years younger than the rest of us and possessed a twitchy, quizzical demeanour and was the first of the band to break out of the south side circle, as he was currently living then in the tragically hip West End of Glasgow at the time, in early 86. Once The Brat boarded that tour bus he was instantly an easy target for the south side banter merchants ala Dungo, Beattie and Tam who were merciless in their cruel, caustic putdowns of Stewart's upbringings. "I bet you've never saw a row of condemned tenements in your puff!" was one classic slagging of the southside crew. First gig up was in The Harp Club, a real nowwheresville venue in eerie New Cross, London. The gig was set up as a 'Creation Records Package Night' with Primal Scream headlining along with The Weather Prophets and possibly The Bodines as the support acts? After relentless late nights of intense rehearsals to break in The Brat and an arse enduring 7 hour epic van journey we only lasted onstage – all of

15 fucked up, shambolic minutes! Bob G threw the mike stand down and produced a prima donna strop, muttering something about his voice cutting up. It was a complete shambles, in front of a packed, eager crowd of Primals fans who had queued all day in the freezing cold and certainly deserved to be treated better than this display of contempt! The place was run by heavy, mean Irish barracuda types and I'm surprised they never visited us backstage with their shooters, to tell us to get our pissin' Scottish asses back on that stage. Welcome to the big, bad, unpredictable, anything could happen world of pop Stewart! I was well pissed off with Bob G's reaction as the rest of the band were cooking (including The Brat) and as you had a stroll about the New Cross area during the day you could sense the feeling of real anticipation in the air plus the fact that everyone had made a real special effort to get to the gig as it was bleedin' Piccadilly outside in the streets and the surrounding area permeated a strange ghost town aura also. The night was a complete sell out and there was a great buzz in the gig venue and to walk off after 15 minutes was a feckin disgrace! If that had happened to my favourite band The Cramps I would've stormed the box office and demanded my hard earned cash back! I believed in giving it your all, up on that stage (even with technical problems to conquer) for that brief moment onstage, no wimp out to the fans – deliver the goods that you're paid to perform for. I have a couple of live shots of The Primals backstage and there's one picture that tells it all, of Dungo chewing on a beer bottle with a pensive looking Bob G and Beattie in da shadowy background, looking on despondently.

From the sweaty confines of The Harp Club to the sumptuous setting of The Town And Country Club in Kentish Town. This time as support act to Colourfield in front of a pissed up Friday night crowd of a 2,000 strong band of noisy followers of ex Special frontman Terry Hall and his new band. This was to be The Brat's next baptism of fire. I was a massive fan of Terry Hall in The Specials, not so keen on The Funboy Three and still to be convinced of his new Colourfield project. A gang of us had gone to see Colourfield at The Queen Margaret Uni in Glasgow and left unimpressed with a set that was too polished and slick, that 80s pop sheen disease had struck again. The highlight of their set was a cover version of ? And The Mysterians 'I Can't Get Enough Of You Baby' which satisfied our 60s garage lust but that was it. Apparently Terry Hall dug The Primals and had requested us as support act for the night so I suppose he had good tastes in support bands. Listening to Bananarama's version of The Sex Pistols 'No Feelings' I wondered did Terry Hall have a say in choosing that cover for them? as he always had that punky demeanour about him, with a healthy dose of sarcasm on the side. Onstage all I seem to remember is looking up at the balcony and all the twinkling red lights of the lamps up in 'the gods' as we churned out a decent set, to an appreciative, drunken crowd of 'Cockney Red' revellers. By the time Colourfield had come onstage, their fans had taken to singing, football style, their appreciation of Terry Hall (ardent Man Utd fan) and had created an intoxicating atmosphere of joviality and fun as the night went on.

It was around this weekend that me, Bob G and The Brat got caught up in a scary incident one night in Peckham, as we were staying in Dave The Driver's pad for the weekend. Feeling peckish in Peckham, we decided to hit the local burger joint for a bite to eat. Straight away The Brat picked up bad vibes, as some shady youths sitting down, were apparently giving us some serious eyeballing and glowering looks. We just laughed it off and told The Brat not to be so paranoid. Bob G was in his tailored crombie, leather strides and flashing the ol wallet. As we left and turned into razor blade alley (aka Dave's multi-storey pad) we heard a shout of "Hey you!" I looked around sharpish, saw the two shady youths fae the burger joint with a blade and then shouted "Run!" Me and The Brat were off our marks in a royal flash but Bob G just stood there, rooted to the spot, and never caught on that they were looking for his wallet of easy cash! By the time we had gotten to Dave's landing and looked over, they had split and fled the scene. We then waited, as a shattered and confused Bob G appeared on the scene up the stairs. He said all his money was gone, as he had to hand over his wallet, as they had a knife brandished at his throat. Obviously Bob G's wallet coming out in the burger joint was the green light for these thieving opportunists of the night. The incident got reported to the local copshop but that was the last we heard of it. It certainly gave us all a wake-up call that we were in unknown territory and strictly out of our comfort zones. At least in Glasgow you know the dodgy areas and give them a wide berth but here in this dangerous bad part of town, you don't realize how nasty it can get until something happens to you personally. You live and learn – only fools and horses eh!

It was also around this period in Londinium that we also completed our second John Peel Radio 1 session again at Maida Vale Studios. The 3 songs plucked out for this recording were 'Tomorrow Ends Today', 'Leaves' and 'Bewitched And Bewildered'. This latter tune for me personally, is one of the most enchanting pop songs that Primal Scream ever cut live in a recording studio and it never even made it onto the 'Sonic Flower Groove' album, for some unfathomable reason. It was a one-off gem, recorded spontaneously on the spot and possessed a cool, mellow mid-paced groove accompanied by a joyous piece of piano tinkling. Dungo was on ivory duties and created a beautiful melody to die for in the chorus. Having a YouTube swatch at the session, I'm surprise that it has only attracted a paltry 3,000 viewings – a poor show as 'Bewitched And Bewildered' is a stone cold pop classic.

Continuing on our gigging jaunt, we come to Brighton, which turned into a real staunch, hardcore stronghold for Primal Scream over the coming years. Brighton is a bohemian seaside town (not many around) that is situated on the south coast of sunny England and is only a half hour jaunt on the train to swinging London. It is populated by a creative, rebellious mix of arty vultures, music lovers, theatre luvvies and a high percentage of gays which certainly provides a unique, hedonistic environment. Brighton is also famous for the 2 films that were shot on location there: 'Brighton Rock' in 1947 and 'Quadrophenia' in 1979 and this film for me is still the greatest teenage movie ever created in these isles about being young, stylish and fucked up, all to a shit kicking soundtrack of 1960s tunes. Visiting Brighton recently you can still have some 'spot the locations fun' of Quadrophenia action scenes, such as the backstreet shagging lane, the café rumble and the kipping arches of the mods and bikers. Somehow I just can't quite picture the first choice role for the main role John Lydon as 'Jimmy The Mod' due to his association with the punkoid Sex Pistols. Phil Daniels was born to play that role and completely nails the part of the character with his intense pill popping, gum chewing, tight suited, guyliner wearing act as main protagonist 'Jimmy The Mod'.

Lucky for us by the time we arrived at The Twang Club there was no sign of that proto psychotic 'Pinkie Brown' either, stalking the noirish backstreets of a bitter cold, snow laden Brighton on this electric Saturday night. As we descended into the subterranean basement, before we hit the stage, we could pick up the vibes that the crowd were up for a Saturday night pop party. When we hit the stage around 11, it was a wild and feverish atmosphere that enveloped us with everyone jam packed up against the stage, swaying and falling about at our Chelsea boots. The sound was raw and alive with chiming guitars cranked to the max, vocals turned down, Tam on the whiplash beat and me upfront whirling like a crazed tambourine devil, playing up to the hyped up crowd. It was one of those glorious nights where you just didn't want the gig to end, definitely one of my all time favourite Primal Scream gigs to date and one I cherish to this day still, in my fuzzy timewarp box of memories.

Outside the venue, packing our gear away, chatting to some fans, out of nowhere a giant snowball fight appeared of epic proportions, with everyone joining in, pissed out of their friendly minds and merry as hell! Brighton you were a gas, gas, gas!

One of The Primals' prime places to play in Bonnie Scotland was in the Inverclyde district – Gourock and Greenock to be precise. Like their grittier cousin further down the Clyde, Glasgow, they made their name as shipping towns initially along with a burgeoning cruise ship craze that is now taking precedent in 2015. Our first gig was in a nightclub called Gourock Janies and was promoted by Paul Barr and Sheer Taft and was also an under 18 event. According to Sheer Taft, our requested rider consisted of bottles of cola and an assortment of sandwiches – not my kind of rider for sure! What about the 'Earl Grey' teabags and 'Breakaways' biscuits dudes? During the soundcheck, we rattled through a few Love cover versions to satisfy the teenarama Gourock masses assembled whose insatiable lust for obscure 1960s garage punk matched ours perfectly. It was at this particular gig that a teen Primals fan was seen wearing a customized shirt that had the back sleeve of 'Crystal Crescent' printed on it, another 5 minutes of fame for myself ha! Since it was an under 18s event, the gig attracted a youthful crowd of fans who created a passionate response apart from one overenthusiastic kid, who volleyed a few gobs of spit at Bob G's direction. I don't think he realized that Bob G wasn't the drummer in The Mary Chain anymore – eject! I got someone to snap some photos of the gig and there's a real funny one of The Brat looking sideways at Dungo but in between them is a blow up photograph of a screaming baby on the wall. The Brat meets The Brat onstage, in downtown Gourock. The stage is so low, with the crowd packed in real close to the action, that you don't even see the Brat's guitar onstage. He looks like a guy who's just wandered onstage in a confused state of mind.

Whenever we played Aberdeen, Edinburgh or even Glasgow, we never received the adulation that we got whenever we blasted in to play in the Inverclyde region – made from girders! It was an eventful 3 days as on the Friday, we ventured once more to Liverpool and made it back in time on the Sunday to catch The Cramps at The Barrowlands. The Liverpool gig at Krackers (class 80s disco name) was more memorable for the poster than the actual gig. It was designed in a Russian constructivist mode and was a striking poster concept and real unusual at the time, and sad to report, that I sold this item only last year at an auction site, which I instantly regret straight away now. Jayne Casey sure had a real kool eye for design!

The Cramps hadn't played in Glasgow since 1981 when I was bodily thrown out of Strathclyde Uni due to some over-exuberant, stroboscopic crowd surfing behaviour on my part. Five years later they were ready to rumble at The Barrowlands. They had just released their first album since 'Psychedelic Jungle' proper – 'A

Date With Elvis' (not including their mini masterpiece 'The Smell Of Female' album a couple of years earlier). By 1986 The Cramps were the biggest and greatest underground cult band in the world and had recently acquired a bass player for the first time in their rockin bones history – one Fur Dixon, the gum chewing, fishnet stocking wearing, foxy lady complete with Mohican haircut who sure gave Poison Ivy a run for her fishnet stockings onstage, as a living, rockin bedazzling entity. I don't think Poison Ivy's onstage scowls were for show this time! Fur got right into the skin of The Cramps and was exciting eye candy to watch, as she sent the assembled Gorehounds crazy on this insane, bug eyed Sunday night. The place was rammed to the max and even though it was the 10th time that I'd caught The Cramps live, they still sent an electric charge through my body when they exploded onstage to rip through most of 'A Date With Elvis' with a healthy smattering of tracks from 'Songs The Lord Taught Us' and 'Smell Of Female' also. Only The Cramps could come up with a song title of 'Can Your Pussy Do The Dog' and at one point it very nearly gatecrashed the Top 40 suckers. Now that would've been a sight to cherish forever – The Cramps tearing it up in a TOTPs recording studio alongside 'The Purple Imp' himself Prince…..

ENTER JOYCE X – THERE'S A GIRL IN MY SOUP

Joyce X entered my life around the start of late January 1986, according to my well informed diary from back then. I'd previously noticed her in The Griffin, an ever present face on the scene, along with her Airdrieonian buddies Kate and Jean in tow. One night over a few half pints and Joyce X's favourite straw sipping snakebite tipple, we arranged to meet up the following week. By that time, both of us had separate pads in the West End. We agreed to meet at Joyce X's pad in Hillhead Street as she had cooked up a spaghetti bolognese to devour. It was only years later, that I found out that it was her sister Elaine, who actually made the meal – Joyce X was no Fanny Delia Craddock Smith!

At the time of January 1986, Joyce X had a shaggy bright orange hairdo complete with a slightly gothic mode of attire. Within 6 months, she suddenly transformed into a Bardotesque blonde. I think my Brigitte Bardot obsession at the time, must've rubbed off on her! As the weeks rolled on by, we began to hang out on a more frequent basis with each other, switching between our flats as the moods took us. We tended to spend more time in Silverfoilcity as that was more geared up to a freewheeling lsd experience. It was still a strange feeling at times, living as 'the boy in the kitchen' (for privacy reasons) coz at any given time during the old 'in out sessions' and acid trip outs, any one of the Pauls could suddenly appear to make a quick brew or heaven forbid do the dishes! There was no gentleman's knock on the door agreement in this house! Joyce X at the time was a couple of years younger than me and possessed a feisty, headstrong personality and took no shit from no one, especially from other people's girlfriends. I think she preferred guy's company to other female ones, as guys were less bitchy and more up for a daft, crazy laugh at life. Louise and Karen, would hang out in The Action House frequently, getting up to silly, girlish pranks that kept us all amused but Joyce X had her bullshit detector screwed on tight and didn't particularly forge any close friendships with both Louise and Karen as she viewed them as too bitchy and girly. Joyce X was an individual ladette before her time, who could outdrink and outdrug the best of them – including myself, which wasn't that hard! (half can Dan!) In Silverfoilcity my eating habits left a lot to be desired and my feeble attempts at cooking up a serious meal. In the house, I was also known as 'The Ratatouille Kid' as I practically lived on the stuff on a nightly basis, as the tins were dirt cheap to buy. If I was feeling slightly flush, I would treat myself to a waffles, beans, tuna and mayo gourmet, which sounds pretty revolting on paper but prepared the right way, was a bedsitterland cheapo classic, bit of nosh. Harte introduced me to another low budget food treat. One bag of cheap macaroni and one tin of Campbell's condensed tomato soup – an instant supper classic in a flash. Joyce X's sister Elaine also introduced us to the delights of an Italian recipe that soon turned into an instant favourite (cos it lasted 4 days) Messerti, a pasta dish invented by Elaine's own foodie imagination. This delicacy comprises of Campbell's condensed mushroom and tomato soup, mushrooms, mince and an onion thrown into the stew, accompanied by a bed of penne pasta – Gordon Ramsay! Eat your macaroni! I think there was some sorta Andy Warhol subliminal thing going on in our kitchen, what with all the Campbell's soup tins that we bought up and lived on, on a weekly basis! The Pop Art maestro would've been proud of us all…..When we were real penniless and skinteroonie, me and Joyce X would launch daring 'Bonnie and Clyde' shopping raids at the local supermarket for the prized Menu Master meals that were way out of our affordable price zone. This was the late 1980s, before cctv cameras had really kicked in and security staff had been employed. There was such an organisation as the thievery corporation of secret store detectives but they didn't seem to exist back then in Byres Road.

We must've been pasta crazy in The Action House, as Bob G and Dungo once appeared to compete in a spaghetti competition to see who could produce the most delicious pasta meal. I think we definitely took the pasta obsession just a tad too far there.....

One night forra change, Joyce X invited me over and Dungo and Peter (McShane) also toddled along, to drop some acid for some serious eyeball kicks. Looking at Dungo coming up on his tab, he had the look of a guy who hadn't tripped out many times, as he proceeded to literally melt into Joyce X's couch, he was that ripped. Someone had brought along a bizarre 'Alice In Wonderland' adult porno video which was a strange choice of movie to watch out of your tree and especially with Joyce X present but it didn't bother her too much, as we all got the hyper, manic, giggles watching this fantasist, freakoid flick as Alice went on a liberated, kinkoid journey of a very sexual Wonderland, for our hilarious pleasure. Later on in the trip we all decided to head outside forra midnight stroll through Kelvingrove Park and to try and catch a burger stall as the munchies were beginning to kick in also. At one point we all stopped at the entrance to this dark tunnel in the park, then someone dared someone to walk through it to the other end. We were all spooked out at the thought of disappearing down a black hole or being attacked by a 'jakie' who'd skippered down there for the night. The silly things you got up to back then as decent people, got up for work in the morning tut! tut!

One other moment sticks out in the memory box. Someone spotted a hedgehog, parked at the side of a pavement, curled into a spiky, little ball, sheltering from the big, bad urban world. This sent us all into raptures of wonderment as we couldn't quite believe that this spiky creature of the night, was all alone, out in the cold ass streets of no mean city, instead of hiding away in some secret spot of shrubbery, somewhere in the park.

Back in the real world, things were getting a bit tricky on the love front. I was still in contact with Jo, who phoned to let me know that she was heading to Glasgow for a short visit with some of her friends. How could I refuse her access, one last time in Silverfoilcity? I don't think Joyce X was too happy with the arrangement but it was still early days of our affair, nothing concrete and I was still a free man, who didn't want a serious commitment at the time due to the gigging Primal Scream juggernaut that was pretty relentless at the time. When Jo arrived in Glasgow, she was surprised to find that I was still blasting out Big Star's 'Sister Lovers' album on a regular basis. Jo just laughed and thought it was so last year's discovery. I was definitely stuck in a warped groove in Silverfoilcity! PS Burgers and acid don't go!

Did someone just mention, get your leather strides on boy, there's a Dutch tour coming up real soon.....

HI JINKS IN HOLLAND

Creation Records had decided to set up a 5 date mini tour of Dutch cities along with our constant hombres on the gigging highway, The Weather Prophets in early Arpil 86. The 5 lucky cities were Den Hague! Amsterdam! Eindhoven! Deventer and Gronenverg (where the dickens were those last 2?)

    The thing you noticed travelling around Holland was that it was a real compact country, easy to get to each town and not too dullsville for us dudes in the back of the tour van. Our first gig was in some forgettable club in Den Hague. This was the gig where someone got permission to video us onstage. Looking back at the replay, at one point the sound cut out onstage, real amateurish like and then everyone turns round to The Brat to give him daggers, as if to say "Did you pull the plug?" He was the real whipping boy of the band at the time if anything went wrong, even if it didn't have anything to do with him. I would love a swatch at this video now, just to see how bad we really were on that first night of the tour. It was during this tour that Primal Scream started to introduce a couple of tasty garage covers to liven up the proceedings as most of the Dutch crowd hadn't heard our atmospheric vibrations live before (unless they'd been in Camden High Street after one of our London gigs and picked up a bootleg tape). Van Morrison's 'Gloria' gotta good ol blasting in Den Hague. Our version was more in The Shadows of the Knight mode, a mid pace garage groover chugging away with Bob G rappin a whole load of garage gobbledygook over the top to a Dutch crowd of bemused horizontal onlookers. Pass The Dutchie on the left hand side dudes! Once offstage, we heard a dj was blasting out some tunes in the basement so we all headed down and demanded that he play some rockin Ramones right now, so we could release some of that pent up gig steam off. As we were jumping about like half crazed, loopy chimpanzees, someone grabbed a chair and launched it on to the dancefloor, totally lost in The Brudders beat as we released one big garage orgasm explosion of destructive energy.

Packing away our gear for the night, someone got into a spat with the local road crew and a few beer bottles got launched back and forth forra while. There was no human physical damage done, just a frustrated release of tension due to the onstage technical difficulties that happened and also as a deadbeat reaction towards the comatose Dutch audience.

Next stop was that undisputed, hedonistic capital of sex, dope and not rock 'n' roll – Amsterdam. We got to The Dam early afternoon and since we had a couple of hours to kill till soundcheck time, we took off on a back street wander to check out the sex, vinyl, joke shops to keep us amused. Walking around you couldn't help but notice that this city had more than its fair share of pretty girls everywhere, strolling about. It felt like a real youthful city with a liberating, cosmopolitan vibe to it, drawing you into its clandestine universe. Going into our first sex shop, outside we were like a buncha giggling schoolboys, daring each other to go in until we all drifted inside, playing with toys and peering into the seedy slot machines. Through an empty back room we came across this humungous red leather settee that wouldn't have looked outta place on a New York Dolls album sleeve. Next door was the joke shop and for some goofy photo opportunities, we put all these nonsensical giant papier mache masks on our heads, even Bob G got into the silly act, posing with one, in his crombie and leathers. Word had got out that The Cramps also happened to be in town playing a gig at The Paradiso (instant karma) so we got Jeff (Barrett – Tour Manager) to stick all our names down on the guest list.

Our gig venue for the night was The Milky Way, which was a lot smaller than The Paradiso and provided a more intimate atmosphere. Hanging out in a café a wee while later sipping a tea (not that kind) Bob G looked out the window and just casually said "Joogs! Lux and Ivy have just passed us!" By the time he got to Ivy, I had bolted out of the café and proceeded to stalk them until they stopped at this camera shop. I then approached Ivy forra chat but gotta frosty reception off her so I then moved on to Lux and started up a bit of conflab with him as he looked more approachable. I told him that I'd seen them a few times live in Glasgow including the infamous Glasgow Apollo gig in 79 when as the support act, they blew the main headliners The Police to smithereens. Lux remembered them well, smiling away as I went in to full on reminiscer mode. I told him about Primal Scream and Creation but this drew a blank with him. I asked his permission to snap a couple of photos of them, unposed as they eyed up some 3d cameras in the window. I'm kicking myself now that I never took a group photo of them (with me included) but I was so hyper excited at meeting Lux and Ivy that all rational thought processes had evaporated by this point. Going to viddy The Cramps later, had given Primal Scream an extra thrill and buzz and since we knew that they'd be on around 9, we volunteered to go on first at The Milky Way gig, so that we could catch their full set later. The venue itself was a quirky set up with 2 rows of seating set at an angle facing the stage, with a standing area in the middle – those surreal, wacky Dutch!

Apart from The Harp Bar fiasco, this must've been the quickest Primals gig in history, as soon as I hit the last tambourine beat, we all flew out the back door exit, following that blazing neon cross sign all the way to The Paradiso. When we arrived there, we could already hear The Cramps onstage and this gave us all an exhilarating rush, so the whole gang of Primals charged through the stalls doors and proceeded to push and elbow our way through the toking Dam hipcats until we got to the front of the stage. This was the most compelling, pulsating, sexiest rock 'n' roll show in town – show some respect you's bunch of lifeless doped up stiffs and shake some goddamn action you fucking automatons!

Within minutes, I was once again possessed by the Cramped-up beat, kissing the pvc boots of Lux as we took up position stage front for the rest of the gig. For the rest of The Primals, it had been their first occasion that they'd caught The Cramps live and they suddenly realized that when it came to providing sheer solid gone rock 'n' roll entertainment, The Cramps were way out on their own stratosphere. I always wondered how it looked from their onstage perspective, these 6 rockin loonballs bulldozing their way through the Dam zombies and charging towards them, grabbing at Lux and shouting and yelling like a bunch of crazed maniacs high on adrenalin? As the gig ended, we headed back to The Milky Way to pack our gear away. A couple of Grant's mates lived in Amsterdam and since we had gotten them on the guest list, one of them gave me a tab and I then talked them into letting me go forra ride on one of their white bicycles forra lark. As this was happening, Beattie had gotten into some verbals with some deadhead hanging around and the next you know this dude launched a beer bottle, which then proceeded to bounce off the van roof and then skelp Beattie right on the napper! He then hit the deck in full dramatic Laurence Olivier style as Tam and Dungo then set off after this guy, running and screaming that they were gonna mollocate him if they caught up with him. Then I started circling Beattie on the ground with my bike like a vulture and then I proceeded to laugh my head off at the whole ridiculousness of the situation, as the acid kicked in slightly. The bottle barely grazed Beattie's head but he fell down as if he'd been shot by a platoon of soldiers!

Next stop Eindhoven! I'd only every heard of this place through the local footy team, PSV Eindhoven. To us jangleheads, it was just another concrete jungle of a city. This was the gig where we covered the One Way Street garage anthem 'We All Love Peanut Butter'. It was a simple garage, guitar riff with me and Bob G chanting away that we all dug peanut butter! Like the hell I did! It was strictly for Yanks tastes back in the 1960s but through the years I grew to love the crunchy peanut butter type – yummy, yummy, yummy! Eindhoven was also memorable for meeting up with a delectable, supermodel blonde chick who was way out of my tantalising league but for some reason, she liked to talk to me and possessed an easy going, friendly manner. She actually said that she thought me and Bob G had some groovy kind of love thing going on between us as we kept giving it sideway glances and easy smiles on the stage. Everyone was well jealous that this foxy blonde had attached herself to me and not the usual lead singers or lead guitarists – it was real funny to observe. Even the normally horizontal Weather Prophets were salivating at the mouth at this sultry Catherine Deneuve temptress. It sure blew them out of their vegetative, smoky haze for a little while. After the gig, Reena took a few of us to some Eindhoven nightclub forra few late night refreshments and then it was back to the hotel, to kip down for the night. I got the feeling that Reena had a boyfriend at the time, who was probably at the club and that she just wanted to hang out with a band for some innocent kicks – it was strictly hands off – no hanky panky! I was shacked up in Beattie's room for the night but the jealous sod had locked me out so I chapped up Dungo who let us in. Into the night, we just crashed out on the floor, cuddling up and chatting away until we fell asleep. Reena was a classy, intelligent chick who by the next day had disappeared once more back on to the streets of Eindhoven – there went another vanishing girl!

Our next destination was meant to be Deventer but either the gig was cancelled or my memory box was. I can't remember a thing about the town or gig.

The last port of call on our short Dutch tour was a town called Gronenverg. This gig was more memorable for the tomfoolery and delinquent behaviour that went on, back at the hotel, after the gig. I had gotten completely puggled on the gig rider and was practically at the collapsed comatose stage by the time we touched down at the hotel later. I'd puked up in my room, and was flat out in a semi-conscious state and all I can total recall was the rest of the Primals gang lifting me up and dragging me like a battering ram, into the lift, then in to the foyer then back up again, where I was dumped in my bed once more. Then a fire extinguisher fight broke out that had everyone covered in foam, rolling about the floor, in fits of giggles at the rock hi-jinks that were going down. As far as I can remember, no tv sets got launched out the windows down below – gardyloo! (Watch out!) I think that might've been the same night that Jeff (our tour manager) got severely sloshed too as he ended up losing all the tour money, all 4 nights of it straight down the river Dam! One thing I'll say about the Dutch, they know how to treat a band fairly, no hassles with the gig money, a good tasty meal for your troubles and friendly vibes all round, unlike certain promoters back in Blighty.

Arriving back at Glasgow Airport, straight from Amsterdam, we'd barely set a Chelsea foot down on the tarmac when we were questioned and then frogmarched by a couple of security blockheads, who took us into their cubby hole office and proceeded to interrogate us. Where had we been? Where had we been staying? Did we have anything to declare? Looking back at the incident, we must've stuck out like the proverbial social deviants – shagged out moptops, dark shades, manky leathers and some half pissed exuberant behaviour going down. Every stinkin one of us were told to drop the leather strides (apart from Beattie?!?!) so that airport security could have a peep up our ronson lighters for any stolen, hidden contraband. By then after nearly a week on the road, we couldn't have really given a shit, as we were feeling really scuzzy, manky and tired by this point. We also needed a real good hosing down, just to get rid of the past weeks debauched, sordid dirt from our persons and if security wanted to dig deep – be my guest. We had nothing to declare but our battered psychedelic souls officer! Thank God, no one stupidly attempted to bring any drugs back with them as we would've ended up on Scotland Today at 6 and then locked up in Bar-L for our sins. At one point the security were even squeezing out all the shaving foam containers and then they started on Bob G's prized shirt, ripping open his collars as they had found something jaggy in it?!?! It was no 'Midnight Express' scenario but it was a serious enough shakedown that attempted to strip you of your dignity but by then we were well past the point of caring and all we wanted was our beds badly, to sleep off the fatigue and to banish the comedown tour blues to kingdom come…..

SILENT SPRING

The mini Dutch tour had totally brain drained us all and I was just glad to get back to normality and Silverfoilcity once more, to recharge the life batteries and just to hang out in the flat and next door, at Grant and Billy's. Being on the road, stuck in a never ending soul stabbing minibus gets real claustrophobic at times, in turn creating frissons of friction, as you can imagine with 6 impulsive, extreme personalities, also thrown into the mix. Lucky for me, the next gig wasn't until a week or two away, in Sheffield Leadmill of all the places. This gig was memorable forra couple of reasons.

Primal Scream required a van driver, so Lowdy put us in contact with some random dude from Mount Vernon who was available for some Saturday night driving action. He brought along 2 of his mates for support – Dennis Little and Drew Mulhollland. I was really surprised to see Denny Little in the back of the van as I hadn't clocked eyes on him, since I left Holy Cross primary school back in the mid 1970s. I hadn't met his mate Drew Mulholland before but 10 years after I'd left The Primals, I would hook up with Drew once again, this time on theremin and tambourine duties as part of The Mount Vernon Arts Lab experience (I'll get to the full story of this episode later on in the 'Aftermath' section of the book). Again the gig itself was pretty non-eventful but I do recall having a couple of clinches, after the set, with a local Sheffield honey who dug The Primals. The next you know, you're back in the sodden transit van, motorway city bound, through the wee small hours. A funny thing happened when we stopped off, halfway, at a greasy café. I met an old mate called 'Lanny', that I hadn't seen since the late 1970s punky years in Glasgow. Over a hot brew, we had a right good chinwag on how both of us came to be in this godforsaken joint in the middle of the night ha! Was there someone up there pulling our strings…..

On the Sunday it just happened to be the latest Splash 12th Happening, a real wildcard choice this time, straight out of the leftfield – 23 Skidoo. It didn't seem like a 4-month gap since the last Splash gig with Wire in December 85 but it was. Grant and Lowdy and Billy were ardent fans of this band and it was a real shot in the dark how they would go down, among the regular Splash heads but they triumphed in style intoxicating the packed crowd, who witnessed this enigmatic band in concert. It was a refreshing change to get away from guitar orientated bands for a while and to savour a different kind of music, to stretch the musical boundaries of your perception. I'd already been bombarded with the Skidoo sound in Grant and Billy's and to my ears they were mesmerising in an uptown, funky electronic style especially the classic 'Fuck You G.I.' track (which Grant played non-stop in his camouflage kit) and 'Coup', a superlative 12-inch piece of electronic funk heaven which The Chemical Brothers ripped off years later, snatching the bassy intro, for their 'Block Rocking Beats' single. 'Coup' was that snappy and way ahead of the synthetic, electronic funk sound, it took the electronic dance crowd a couple of years at least, to catch up with it. According to Sheer Taft, who was also at the gig, he thought that "23 Skidoo were from another planet" and they probably were – Planet Skidoo – anyone up for a bit of pornobass?

Next on the Primal Scream schedule was another couple of gigs: Nottingham Garage and The Manchester Boardwalk. For the Nottingham gig, Felt joined us as the support act. It's funny to think that I seem to remember incidents and events before and after a gig but not much of the gig itself unless it was out of this world. In 1986 Felt had released 2 albums on Creation. Check out these wondrous, mysterious titles once more: 'Forever Breathes The Lonely Word' and deep breath now 'Let The Snakes Crinkle Their heads To Death'. Lawrence certainly surpassed himself on that album title there – wow! These unforgettable lp titles must've come straight out of 'The Poetry Of Life' and not 'The Book Of The Dead'. Since me and Bob G couldn't be arsed going back up to Glasgow after the gig and then coming back down again on the Saturday for the Manchester gig, we decided to crash at Lawrence's sweet suburban pad in a leafy part of Birmingham. Lawrence certainly lived in his own peculiar, enigmatic bubble looking around his abode. His flat was totally spotless! It was also the first flat I'd been in, that had an actual prop up wall bed, that you put away when you've had your sleep in it. Walking about, I also noticed that he had a hidden cache of stroke mags tucked away in the kitchen cupboard covered in a polythene bag. Lawrence also had an OCD thing going on, about flushing the toilet at all times and to keep the toilet seat down every time you used his convenience. There was certainly none of that neat freak behaviour going down in The Action House, up the road with us – the opposite really. Hanging out with Lawrence and getting to know him on a different level, he struck me as a unique individual, with a child like, truthful innocence about him, who, sadly found it a real effort to form any kind of lasting female relationship due to his crippling shyness at times and his uneasy feeling of awkwardness in unknown company. It was a real pleasure to get to know the man behind those fantastical, exquisite album titles and the music that breathed inside of them.

The next day me and Bob G were whisked away in another tour van, this time driven by a new driver that Creation had found – Josh The Driver! Next stop – Manchester Boardwalk club for the Saturday night gig happening. In Glasgow, Josh had picked up the rest of The Primals posse and even had time to swing by The Action House and borrow Big Paul's 3-seater couch for the back of the tour van, as it fitted perfectly in to its new surroundings along with the usual amps, guitars, drums and tambourine case and not forgetting the 'carry oot' of beers. Upfront hugging the front window action was Tam, Beattie, The Brat and Josh The Driver while me, Bob G and Dungo took up residence in the back on the 3-seater couch. Out of nowhere came a shout of "Josh! You're heading the wrong way." The driver (then in a panic) decided to perform a 45 degree turn at the wheel (as he's cruising about 60mph) and the next thing we know, we're doing a triple cartwheel stunt on the motorway, being tossed about like a tumble dryer in full automatic spin mode as all the kit, couch and us 3 in the back, went into full tilt a whirl upside down mode, getting completely soaked in beer into the bargain.

On the last of the somersaults The Brat pipes up "I don't' wanna die!" as a fearful, dreaded silence grips us all, as the tour van now scarily, skids along the bank of the motorway until it eventually crashes into an embankment, finally at last coming to its never ending horrific journey.

When the van was sliding and skidding upside down it felt like a real horrorshow dream, that had come alive in an all too real situation. All I could think to myself was "Please roof, don't give way now or we will all be decapitated". We very nearly were knocking on heaven's door and boy were we relieved when the van finally ground to a halt! Myself and Bob G seemed to have copped the full weight of the damage as I could feel a girder embedded in my knee and when I looked over at him, he had a guitar amp lying on his body. Big Paul's 3-seater couch was a total write off, it was that fatal a crash. (Big Paul was not a happy bunny when we told him about the trashed couch when we got home). Like a scene out of 'The Plague Of Zombies' we all started to stumble outta the van and out of nowhere, some sicko got out of his car and took a couple of photos of us and the wreckage and then fucked off quickstyle. By god, there are some seriously twisted ghouls out there who are even more warped than us it seems!

Luckily for us, a doctor also happened to be passing the accident scene (as they do) and stopped and phoned for an ambulance. At this point, I was lying on the grassy verge nursing my wounds, lying outstretched, totally shell-shocked with a blanket wrapped around me when Dungo appeared, pulled the blanket right over me and then proceeded to do a Nazi-style salute! Even in near death, these dudes in the band possessed a stay sick sense of humour – thanks guys! I suppose at that point, we all required a touch of humour in our life as we were very nearly all gone daddy goners! Everyone upfront in the van along with Dungo and Josh were all punky dory, injury wise. Me and Bob G took the full brunt of the accident by the looks of things. Speaking to Tam about the incident recently, he said before the crash had happened, we'd just fuelled up at the garage and all he could think of was "Please don't explode or we'll all be blown to tiny pieces of flesh". The upfront windscreen had totally caved in and lucky for them, they were all strapped in (big boy) so they managed to escape unharmed from the crash. A traffic cop appeared and spoke to Beattie and all he could mutter was "At least none of you's died". Thanks for that sympathetic touch PC Plod. When the ambulance came, me and Bob G entered it in a fragile way, still inna deep sense of shock with our injuries. I couldn't help but stare out at the tinted windows and think to myself, how lucky we really were to get out alive, survive and not combust into human flames. Lying there felt like an out of body experience, a slow motion revelation in unreal time. I just kept staring at my gaping leg wound, that had cut right through my leather strides and looking at it, as if it was kind of moving around. It was cut to the bone but since I was still inna trance like state, I never felt much pain. Thank god my leathers were made of strong material or the leg injury could've been a lot worse than it was. After getting stitched up and heading back to the hotel to recuperate, we received a phone call to tell us, that the gig in Manchester was still on – believe it or not…..The promoter had completely sold the gig out and in the big bad world of rock 'n' roll, life is cheap, the show must go on!

The soundcheck was a total blur as the adrenalin then started to kick in as we got a new surge of electric energy, playing the instruments onstage once more. A guy I knew from Glasgow was gonna be at the gig but he brought a mate along who hadn't gotta ticket so a deal was struck. In exchange for a precious guest list spot I would receive a gram of speed to ease my aching leg and soul. It was actually a god send as it numbed the aching pain in my leg and seemed to have then smashed blocked me out of my trance like stupor which I was still in at the time. The Bodines were the other band playing that night and there was meant to be another support act too but apparently the lead singer had gotten the jail the night before!

Hobbling onto the stage, zombie like, a massive cheer went up through the amped up crowd of Creation diehards who'd obviously heard through the garage grapevine of our accident earlier in the afternoon. I would love to hear a bootleg tape of this particular gig as I can't remember a damn song we played. Hanging out backstage after the gig, supergroupie Tina appeared and invited me, Dungo and The Brat back to her Hobbit like abode to continue some late night drinking. As the night wore on, Tina disappeared into the bedroom and a short while later reappeared and said "Which one of you's wants to sleep in here?" A coin was quickly tossed and I won – Holy Ecstasy! Since I was still a bit fragile like and stitched up, the leather strides stayed on, it was strictly girl on top action. It's amazing what a car crash and a gram of speed can do to your sex life! What a Way To Die…..

The next night we were back in Glasgow to play Splash 13 Happening, with The Submarines as support, as 450 sweaty bodies were crammed into Daddy Warbucks to witness a very lethargic Primal Scream gig. The car crash aftershock trauma had just kicked in and I just didn't wanna be on a stage that night with nearly a 1,000 peepers staring us down. I hadn't even told my family or Joyce about the van crash. Joyce only found out through her flatmate Diane, who was seeing Stewart (aka The Brat) at the time. Everyone else in the band had phoned home but I didn't wanna make a big song and dance about it.

My family to this day still don't realise, that one of their brood could've been wiped out for good on May 3 1986. This cat sure had more than 9 lives, purr!

For this gig, this was to be the last time The Submarines played under that name before they morphed into The Compass Flow, a Janice Long session and oblivion. The Submarines had released only one record to date – 'Grey Skies Blue' on Jeff Barrett's Head Records which was a kool 60s inspired jangler. Big Paul has fuzzy fond memories of playing there and hanging out there. He wasn't involved in any of the shenanigans of the club as he preferred to get high, listen to the sounds and chat up the chicks. He felt that his personal more commercial tastes in music were looked down upon with a disdainful sneer by the Splash 1 committee a la The Beatles and Neil Young, in the cliquey, close knit scene that was developing at that point in time.

To tell you the truth, I was feeling fed up with the whole scene myself and you sensed that Splash 1 was losing its unique, distinctive flavour and turning into just another regular indie club, with everyone turning up with the same uniform clobber indie chic look, with their shades just perched perfectly, inna dark nightclub setting on a shitting Sunday night.

The Splash 1 committee produced a real scoop for Splash 14 Happening – Sonic Youth, were the latest appointed band to grace the Daddy Warbucks stage. I gotta sneaky feeling that Bob G had a major hand in pulling this gig off as he and McGee were talking buddies of Thurston Moore at the time, the main guitar shredder and vocalist of Sonic Youth. The other group members were Kim Gordon (foxy bassist with ace cheekbones), Lee Renaldo (intense guitar shredder no. 2) and Steve Shelley (yer typical drummer). These New York based no wave, noise dudes had been around since early 1981 and had already released a couple of culty art rockin albums in 'Confusion In Sex' and 'Bad Moon Rising'. The name Sonic Youth came about through a bastard amalgamation of Sonic outta Fred 'Sonic' Smith (of The MC5) and Youth out of Big Youth, top ranking rockers.

Thank fuck we never got lumbered with their original choice band names of 'Male Bonding' or 'Red Milk'! Their current album release in May 86 'Evol' contained the more accessible pop noise of 'Starpower' which came in a tasty 12-inch silver sleeve, which also had a groovetastic cover of that beast of the night, Kim Fowley's 'Bubblegum' on the b-side. In 1984 Sonic Youth released their masterpiece single 'Death Valley 69' which for some strange reason was a massive dancefloor hit at Splash 1?!?! Great song but a helluva weird out beat to dance to.

The support band for Sonic Youth was 'The Hanging Shed' – straight outta Cumbernauld for one gig only and who'd arrived with a 4-song set that had just been cooked up the night before at rehearsals. Billy Kerr (guitarist) had just recently bought a gleaming new Japanese black semi-acoustic guitar and Lee Renaldo took a particular shine to it during the soundchecks and asked Billy if he could borrow it for a number or two – "be my guest", said Billy. Little did he know that when Lee strapped it on for 'Death Valley 69', that he would proceed to batter the guitar strings to oblivion with a set of drumsticks that left Billy's new pride and joy guitar, lying at the side of the stage, in a battered confused state of wreckage! At one point during the gig, a heckler shouted "Fuck off!" and an angry Thurston Moore snarled back "Don't tell me to fuck off – I've travelled 3,000 miles to be here", classic putdown, with heckler, egg on face – piss off! Also at the gig as a punter was Sheer Taft, who was that pished that he actually fell asleep, leaning against a pillar – standing up! Now that's got to be a first ha! It was certainly a gig to remember, as I had a clear view of the stage action to the side, on a wipe out microdot, that made Sonic Youth sound even more deranged and to this day I'm still convinced they left stage to Ciccone Youth's 'Into The The Groovey' on a constant looped up tape but then again.....I noticed between songs that they had a tape of recorded white noise, in between songs, and swapping instruments around. Sonic Youth were a fresh blast and totally unique at the time. I caught Sonic Youth a couple of times live over the years since, at The Bay 63 Club in London and at The Barrowlands but nothing can beat that Splash 1 gig, on a packed, sweaty spring night in an exuberant, intimate club setting.

By the summer of June 86, Splash 1 Happenings had grounded to a terminal halt. Splash 15 had The Weather Prophets gracing the Daddy Warbucks stage for their 2nd and last appearance. Splash 16 was the final happening and The Pastels were the chosen band to go out in a rock 'n' pop glory as the last band to play on the Splash 1 stage.

It was also around this time, with everyone living around The West End at the time, that we started epic footy games in Kelvingrove Park, accompanied by a gaggle of groupies, perched on the hill, cheering on every goal we scored and missed .....The Primal Scream select team comprised of us, the 2 Pauls, Jim Lambie and Bill and John (The Clouds). Now you'd think that this bunch of jinkin misfits would create real damage on the pitch but we were up against the Bellshill mob of assorted Soup Dragons, BMX Bandits and pre-Teenage Fanny's. We had Beattie in goals for us and a chick on the hill on clockwatch duties. The first game we got screwed 9 – 7 but for the return match, we managed to scramble a 8 – 8 each draw but only after some skulduggery involving the stopwatch from our friend on the hill. Beattie had let slip a goal right through his legs just as the game ended and victory for The Bellshill select but the chick ref had already blown for full time, supposedly, before they scored their last goal, so it ended up a 8 – 8 draw ha! Stick to making music Primals – we were way out of shape sunshine!

After the game, packing up, someone spotted a pregnant kitty near one of the trees and the next you know, we've re-housed this expectant tabby cat in one of the spare cupboards back at The Action House. By the time I'd woken up on the Monday afternoon, I had about 7 hyper furry kittens scuttling about and climbing up the curtains in Silverfoilcity. We eventually had to give the whole litter away plus the tabby. There was just too much kitty action going down for us dudes who were constantly out and about and never had the time to care for all the abandoned moggies, in our house. I'm sure Grant and Billy next door copped one or two of the furs and Louise took one home with her also. I was staying at Joyce X's pad more and more around this point, up in her lair at Hillhead Street. One night kipping there a strange dream-like thing happened that spooked us right out and sent a shiver through yer rockin bones. I was awoken in the middle of the night with all these flashing lights going up the staircase in a silent, sinister manner (Joyce X lived in a da basement). It was a flurry of firemen, charging up, who once they gained entry to the neighbour above us, kicked in his front door. No one came to us and explained what was going on. It was like a nightmare dream come alive. The next day we got talking to another neighbour above us and according to them, the guy above us had apparently committed suicide in the bath, to wait for it – Art

Garfunkel's 'Bright Eyes' spinning round endlessly on his turntable?!?! The mystery was solved at last and it gave us a weird feeling to behold, that as you were in slumberland, someone above (only separated by a slab of concrete ceiling) was ending his life in dramatic fashion – poor sod.

In May, Primal Scream had recorded their 3rd BBC radio session, this time for the bubbly Janice Long. (It also got repeated on Muriel Gray's radio programme). The 4 chosen tracks were 'Silent Spring', 'Fever Claw', 'Velocity Girl' and 'Imperial'. For once I actually prefer the versions of 'Imperial' and 'Silent Scream' which popped up on the 1987 album release 'Sonic Flower Groove'. Those versions for me have more of a developed kick to them, producing an exciting punchy, jangling beat that surpasses the radio session ones. 'Fever Claw' never ever got released in any form at all which is a cryin shame as its got a fine jaunty groove to it and was a gas to play live, to get the jingling Primal heads nodding. The judge and jury are still out on the extended version of 'Velocity Girl'. I personally prefer the short and snappy original but Tam digs it! I just thought it was a half-arsed attempt to extend it, to appease the fans – your call! It must've been a new concept back then – other dj's borrowing sessions, as my battered tape copy has Muriel Gray introducing the songs on her radio show! All I can say is thank fuck, it never got passed on to Jimmy Savile and Jonathan King – I'd be scarred for an eternity pop pickers!

GET BACK IN THAT VAN JANGLE HEAD!

By the time we were set to rev up on the autobahn blues trail once more, all thoughts of our near death van experience had been banished to the outer reaches of our delicate minds. Josh The Driver had been given the ejector button treatment and trusty Dave Evans was once more at the wheel as he wheeched us all over England on a couple of mini tours a go go, to keep the Primal Scream bandwagon buzzing. Our first gig up was at Bristol Tropics, a bad vibes club on the edgy bad part of town, tucked away in the St Paul's district, a notorious darklands at that time. We'd already picked up some nasty vibes earlier as we were strolling about in the May sunshine. Some random Bristolians started to give Bob G and Dungo some verbals calling them "a pair of pooftahs". They were mightily offended at this jape as they strutted about in their crombies and leathers and thought themselves to be the height of sartorial splendour. The gig was being promoted by some inexperienced, wetrag indie cat, who found himself in way too deep as the club was run by some real, dour faced rastassholes with serious attitude problems. Packing up at the end of the gig, these rasta thugs blagged Beattie's prized 12-string guitar and they wouldn't let us back into the building to try and locate it. Boy! Were we glad to see the back of that joint! We then blitzkrieged our way through gigs at Brighton Zap Club – London Bay 63 – Portsmouth Poly and finally Bath Moles Club. Apart from the Bristol gig, it was a non-eventful tour, with not much rock 'n' roll shenanigans going on. For that mini tour, we'd been put on a £5 a day gig rider thing to tide us over for snacks and beers. Back then a fiver went a long way in your back pocket. A gig ticket cost £2.50 and a beer at a quid each – cheap night out all round.

One tour ended in May and another began in mid-June. I was quickly turning into a perplexed gig rat on a wheel and required some artificial energy fast to awaken me out of this relentless stage stupor. The Clarendon Ballroom in Hammersmith, London was first up on the June gig schedule. In the 1920s this Art Deco pleasure palace was thee place to be seen, for London's dandies of the night as they swallowed their oysters and gulped down their Guinness. It was an eye-catching edifice of a building but by the time we rolled into the venue, it had taken on the appearance of a down-at-heel tramp, in a faded grandeur style. Also on the bill for this particular gig were The Blue Aeroplanes – The Close Lobsters and The Submarines, all the way from Glasgow in a claustrophobic, non-air-conditioned nightmare of a tour van. We arrived half pished and dishevelled, just in time to catch the soundcheck. The gig venue was a large empty, barren ballroom crying out for some sort of thought pictures projections and psychedelic lights to inject some kind of atmosphere into the place. Once the soundcheck was over Bob G had decided to go forra wander about, in his usual wasted, ripped jeans lolloping style, only to get stopped by a local rozzer who mistook him for a downbeat jakie, lost on the vagrant streets of Londinium. I wonder did those arcane sus laws still exist back in the late 1980s as I know for a fact they still existed in the late 70s, as practically every punk and rasta felt the heavy hand (and boot) of the law coming down on them, for just hanging around and not actually causing any real hassle – SPG cuntoids!

Joyce X (The Speed Queen) had decided to come down for this London gig, armed with a batch of amphetamine sulphate that nearly blew my head, clean right off! That 'Lou Reed' sure packed an explosive punch and by the time I hit the stage, I must've sniffed about half a gram due to the waiting around. It was a real long day with 3 support bands on before us and to alleviate the hanging around blues, the speed produced a much needed kick to blow them away. By the time I hit the stage, I was completely and elegantly wasted outta my eyeballs. I just kept banging my tamby and saying to myself "This is not happening!" I had left planet earth at this point of time, no way out, just further in to downersville, clutching at the gates of hell! Lucky for myself, I had my Johnny T maskie on, as I couldn't have handled being face naked, with all those peepers critically watching your every step – it certainly provided a neat cover up. One gig reviewer quoted "Primal Scream will be magnificent – eventually". How prophetic that quote turned out to be, but not on this night…..Heading home later after the gig, I was spiralling further into pukesville as the speed was still charging through my whole system with my pop up eyeball demeanour giving ol Marty Feldman's a good run for his money. We were Peckham bound, myself, Joyce X and Dave The Driver and I had to keep getting out of the van, to be sick on the sidewalk as I was still speed freakin' outta my box and ready to combust at any moment. It looked real amusing to Dave and Joyce X as they followed me, like a pair of kerb crawlers, real slow as I continued my pukey journey on foot with them shouting yells of encouragement such as "You'll be alright – I've seen you in worse states" and "Nearly there now!" I even burst out laughing at one point, at the whole ridiculous situation of the set up. As I lay in Dave's bedroom with a bad dose of sleep deprivation, I couldn't help but stare at this giant size mirror beside the bed, a mirror of my mind that kept me awake all night with my fractured thoughts. I was in a real no-man's land between sanity and insanity on this never ending speed trip – 100% mindsnapping mind powder that I'd sworn to never touch ever again – stick to the hallucinogenic world acid head! I was still feeling queasy the next day on the bus, to catch up with the rest of the gang in town and as we got up to depart I spewed up one final 'technicolour yawn' all the way down the bus stairs, to the befuddled look of other passengers on the bus! Joyce X took some photos of the gig and I don't look particularly ill on the outside but on the inside I felt like the return of the dead incarnate on that stage. Joyce X should never have left home!

The next memorable gig was in a low rent dive of a pub called 'The Hidden Bay' in Leeds. I'd been to Leeds once before in 1980 for 'The Futurama Festival' at The Queen's Hall and even then the place possessed an intimidating, fiery atmosphere to it. Tonight's gig just happened to coincide with England playing in a World Cup game and they were showing it in this laddish boozer with Primal Scream as the support act to the main course entertainment of World Cup football. The promoter was a nice enough guy, chatty and friendly to us but must've lost a fortune at the door as he was too scared to ask anyone for any money for the night's gig. In between all the shouting and yelling of the assembled footy crowd (plus a couple of brave Primals fans) we managed to bulldoze our way through a decent set of tracks with Bob G in a sarcy, cutting mood, firing out shards of verbal abuse in the direction of the English footy fans, who were getting more pished and loud as the game went on. Needless to say we bombed but England won! Outside, packing our kit away, a big 'stushie' broke out amongst the inebriated fans inside and we all just looked at each other and said in our best John Wayne drawl – "Let's get the hell out of here!"

Riding to Oxford a couple of days later, you could smell the money permeating in the air in this 'town and gown' joint and it made us self conscious working class oiks a tad uncomfortable to say the least. This place reeked of snooty ass, privileged ponces riding about on their bohemian bikes, cycling to their haughty cobblestoned places of education. The Primals gang were strictly non academic townies, rebels without a degree, with a large proletarian girder on our leather clad shoulder who could sense the feeling of antagonism before we even got to the soundcheck at St Paul's Art Centre. Before we arrived there, some childish hi-jinks were going on in the back of the tour van, rolling down the windows, with a volley of verbals being directed at all the 'Hooray Henrys' and 'Henriettas' cutting about on their bicycles with a thoroughly pissed off disdainful look on their fizzog as if to say "Who unleashed this uncouth mob of slum bred tykes on our oh so precious town". True to form at the gig, the bad vibes continued as a bunch of pissed up, pompous indie heads assembled that we just didn't connect with, at any level at all. Before we came on, they were heckling and shouting at us but we hurtled the abuse straight back at them through the sidestage curtains. We then took our time backstage, keeping them waiting even longer – you pay for your £2 – now listen to this! We tune because we care fuckers! Once onstage, we powered our way (with destructive energy firing up our bones) through a set that included 'Velocity Girl', 'Imperial', 'I Love You', 'Subterranean' and 'Bewitched And Bewildered' (without the piano). Even though the crowd and sound hassles bedevilled us, we still produced an exciting, raw, joyful set in the face of complete detestation. We played and we conquered. Time to split from this poncefied town! You could now see why Paul Weller wrote 'Eton Rifles'…..Tally Ho! Oxford.

Next gig up on the itinerary was the return visit to The ICA in London in July at another NME promoted event, this time called 'Cool In The Spool' NME 86 Live. It must've been another free cassette tape giveaway promotion as it turned into a mini festival and ran for a complete week of gigs with a fair smattering of Scottish groups dotted about, also on the bill. On the Monday night you had the triple header of The Soup Dragons – The Shop Assistants and The Close Lobsters. On Thursday night you had The McKenzies at the bottom of the bill looking up at joint headliners Bogshed and Age Of Chance. On Friday The Pastels were second on the bill to The Mighty Lemon Drops and on the Wednesday Primal Scream headlined a bill that also included The Wedding Present and The Servants as the jangling support acts. The Wednesday of July 23rd, fell bang right in the middle of another pomped up Royal Wedding shindig that was being played out on the Union Jack bedecked streets of Londinium. The soon to be named 'The Duchess of Pork' Sarah Ferguson (the ultimate socialite chancer) was getting hitched to Prince Andrew, not a million miles away from our gig venue at The ICA, off The Pall Mall. The soon to be Royal couple had apparently met at the occasional polo match and also at the Royal enclosure of Royal Ascot – now there's a surprise! I didn't think it was at a Dr Feelgood gig at The George Robey…..Out on the streets, we literally had to battle our way through the jingoistic, Rule Britannia masses to get to the venue – get yer wee shitey flags outta my face – we've gotta soundcheck to attend to! 500 million people worldwide were turning into this Royal pageantry of false smiles, gormless tourists and glorious sunshine but for us 6 Glaswegian garage heads, we frankly couldn't have given a damn mam! This was one guest list that we didn't fancy blagging into unless for a jest I borrowed a pair of Zoom! shades complete with blonde wig and pretended to be fecking Elton John in all his regal glory! The gig itself was another glorious, triumphant victory, as we rampaged and swaggered through a 15-song set that included 2 ramped up encores to satisfy the salacious appreciation of an excellently tuned in crowd (Oxford take note you plebs!) There was nothing grubby or shambolic about our set now, it was a full throttle, no messing, run through of popism crowd-pleasers such as 'Imperial', 'Fever Claw', 'Leaves' and 'Velocity Girl'. It felt special and we could've played all night long as crowd and band connected for an engrossing night of musical pleasures as once again we descended up and down the rocking ramp (Kiss style) to never ending tumultuous cheers. My own personal playing was described thus by one reviewer "As the tambourine quivers through the air," which put me on cloud 9 once more and more again. I'm sure at one point towards the end of the gig I spotted The Prince and Fergie, sneaking into the venue, just straight after their first waltz.....It was that kinda night in London.

Meanwhile back up the road, there were a couple of local gigs to attend to. In Edinburgh we played at a venue called 'The Mission', just off The Cowgate and this gig is memorable for one fact only! Bobby Gillespie booting a ventriloquist dummy right off the stage and hitting his girlfriend Karen full pelt in the face – ouch! The dummy itself was part of the support act's 'toys' and deserved a good boot into the bargain for just being there, in the first place!
One week later we found ourselves in gritty Greenock for a gig at The UFO Club, promoted by Sheer Taft and his garage hombres. Since they had cheap access to a local printers, they managed to print up a couple of large monochrome posters (ie about 10) that consisted of a pixelated live action shot of me and Bob G onstage. It was a bewitching image, with me rattling my tambourine and Bob G clutching on to the mike stand. I possessed one of these posters for years but through hard times I've had to auction it off to the highest bidder, at a music related auction. Luckily Chris (Davidson) has still kept a rare copy for posterity!

Heading into autumn now on our merry go round of gigs, the tour van draws up outside 'Burberry's' in Birmingham. I wondered as we arrived did this venue used to be the infamous 'Barbarellas' nightclub? I'm sure some old Brummie punk will enlighten me in due course….. Support band for this mini tour were Pop Will Eat Itself (or PWEI for short) and for one date only – The Sea Urchins. By this time in C86 indieland a whole crop of these anoraks and tamby bands had sprouted up all over the joint – Talulah Gosh! The Razorcuts! The Servants and The Clouds (sorry guys). I always felt that Primal Scream were totally different from these particular groups especially when it came to the songs, the look and the attitude. Maybe it was the blissful jingle guitar pop sound that the music writers connected us with and then lumped us all together as C86 bands – total lazy journalism at its worst!

Primal Scream had the character and the songs, to back up our outlook and vision and the will to escape from the bondage of the shambling C86 scene. As one Brummie music reviewer noted, he visualized that Primal Scream were going to be the first CD indie group.

Our new tour buddies the Poppies were a breath of fresh air compared with our laid back Creation cousins The Weather Prophets. This boisterous, energetic gang of grebos came from The Black Country, formed in Stourbridge and produced a lively, monolithic garage beat and were a fun band to watch live. They really stuck out in the indie underground with their biker come Stooges dress mode with lashings of attitude to go with it. I liked them as a bunch of guys to hang out with also plus the fact they liked to have some fun with their rock 'n' roll and never took life too seriously. Talking to their main mouthpiece at the time, one Clint Mansell, you'd never have guessed that this geezer would one day in the future, enter the world of composing film soundtracks forra living! The other chatty guy in the band was Graham Bentley, who once he quite PWEI, started up his own idiosyncratic group of sampled beat merchants called Bentley's Rhythm Aces. It was a strange set up for a band, as the chief songwriter for The Poppies was the quiet, introspective drummer (a first) and not the guitarist, bassist or vocalist. Time to hit that road! From one B to another – Barrow In Furness to be precise! For me this was the strangest looking town that the Primals gang had ever set foot in so far, on the gig trail. It was set in Cumbria, gateway to the Lake District and possessed a strong working class vibe to the place complete with cobbled streets and steel town centre with an abundance of charity shops to discover – a real life L.S. Lowry painting come to life. In 1886 Barrow In Furness comprised of the largest steelworks industry in the world, which mostly consisted of the building of navy vessels and submarines. And here's me thinking that Glasgow held that title! It's an impressive fact for a town, that no one had really heard of (including myself) up till that point. At one point it claimed to be the Number 1 capital of blue collar working class Britain and its other Number 1 title was as the least happiest place to live in, in Britain. It think I can spot the connection there, especially when you view Barrow in Furness for the first time. The locals spoke in a Barrovian accent which comprised of a melting pot mix of Lancashire dialect, with a sensation of the Geordie and the Glasgwegian accent thrown in, due to the nearby migrant workforce – talk about an explosive, dynamic mix. Its most famous resident born there was that ever smiling, slightly annoying Liverpool skipper – Emlyn Hughes and here's me thinking all along he's a bleedin Scouser! It was against this surreal backdrop that The Primals and The Poppies found themselves performing at The Barrow In Furness Football And Social Club one Wednesday night. On first viewings inside, the Social Club conjured up visions of Peter Kay's 'Phoenix Nights' tv programme what with the coloured tape stage background along with the obligatory formica table and hard woodened backed chairs. At any time you were half expecting that Wheeltapper of yore Colin Crompton to appear – Order! Order! Cant' really remember much about the gig but after we played, the promoter invited both bands to a post party soiree at their gaff.

At one point, sitting gassing with Graham (PWEI) this local chick appeared, sat down and started to chat to us. She told us that by day she was a labourer but by night she flowered up in to being a beautician! Hellzapoppin! This perfectly summed up our visit to Barrow In Furness. It was as if we'd been transported into a kooky episode of The Avengers and were feeling a bit unsettled, a queer feeling of not being really there, it's all an L.S. Lowry dream! One day I swore I would visit this town once again, just to convince myself that it was not a hallucination at work!

Whoever set up this crazy zigzag tour must've been sticking pins in that map of England. Next up was Middlesborough in the North East this time and it just made me think of one of their native sons Chris Rea's recordings – a miserable and depressing place with no distinct atmosphere – a real road to hell! The venue itself was a large town hall edifice that was much too grand and big for both The Primals and The Poppies at that stage in their careers. On a great night you might pull in 100 to 500 bodies but this cavernous joint held around 1,000 punters at a push. It resulted in a near empty, soulless gig that neither band enjoyed or could be inspired with. The only highlight was being treated forra curry in the local Indian restaurant after the gig. This was turning out to be one city scraped, low budget tour, as, once again, we all spent the night crashed out in the promoter's house. Our room for the night comprised of 2 old pissing mattresses squeezed together with the 7 assembled bodies (including driver) all huddled up, farting like crazy with the rank smell of dirty socks permeating the air like a smelly patchouli oil goth. I don't think we got much sleep that night as the on the road banter kicked in to keep us all amused into the wee small hours. The Poppies never even gotta whiff of our luxurious surrounds as there was no room at the inn for their posse so they ended up kipping down in their tour van for the night. Staying in Yorkshire, our next destination was the city of York with 'The Duchess Of York' bar our latest stop. You could pick up the good vibes as soon as you completed your soundcheck. This gig went down a storm with the local crowd (compared to the previous gigs) as they packed the place out and provided an upbeat, infectious atmosphere that totally energized both bands. For this particular night's accommodation, we were to be put up at a sprawling, suburban house, care of the friendly, helpful promoter. As we got there, ourselves and The Poppies just dumped our kit in the large hall and then went into one of the rooms to sink a few beers into the night as the owners and their friends gathered in an adjoining room smoking their brains out.

Feeling restless and boisterous, both bands went back into the hall, got their instruments out, plugged in and then proceeded to blast out a couple of raw versions of The Stones 'Satisfaction' and The Stooges 'I Wanna Be your Dog' that snapped the dudes next door outta their purple haze funk. They then all suddenly appeared, snapping away with their cameras like crazy as a fox as both bands raised merry hell, jamming it up forra punky party in good ol York City.

Before we all bedded down on the mattress in the early hours of Saturday morning, someone had discovered a secret stash of home brew in the kitchen. Some prankster (Dungo?) had locked me, Tam and The Brat in our bedroom, so we got hold of a screwdriver and proceeded to silently take the whole door off its hinges! In the still of the night, with everyone snoring away by now, we went on a creepy crawl kitchen raid and took a few bottles of potent home brew up to our bedroom and drunk them dry till we fell asleep in a drunken stupor. When we got the wake-up call in the afternoon the owner appeared upstairs to find one bedroom door off its hinges, lotsa empty beer bottles and 3 pissed up Glaswegians nursing extreme hangovers. I think eventually the owners were finally glad to see the back of us all so that they could get back to their cosy, smoked out suburban idyllic life!

The next you know, we're zig-zagging through the bucolic countryside of deepest England, as Dave The Driver put the foot down on the accelerator, bound for Wendover, a quaint country town of the Aylesbury Vale district in Buckinghamshire. The scenery was picture postcard perfect and the good vibe gig feelings of the York gig continued as we finally reached The Division One Club, right out in the middle of nowhere on a country road. The Club itself was barn like, friendly and intimate and memorable also, for the appearance of fellow Scot Bill Drummond arriving backstage to hang out.

This guy was a good few years older than us and had already been the manager of Echo And The Bunnymen and The Teardrop Explodes (c/o of Zoo Records) so this guy had some sound experience of the wheelings and dealings in the big badass world of rock 'n' pop. At that time of summer 1986, he'd signed a one-off album deal for Creation Records and produced a true individual lp called 'The Man'. One track particularly stood out for me and that was 'Julian Cope Is Dead' in response to Julian Cope's 'Bill Drummond Said' track on the 'Fried' album. He sung the vocal in an Ivor Cutleresque kind of detached, droll way with cool backing from The Triffids on guitars and drums. It is an instant stone cold classic off an lp that no one bought – sod yer Proclaimers '500 Miles' pish, this was the real deal!

Before the night's gig took place, Tam had disappeared up Cobbler's Hill forra saucy, frothy romp in the fields with a local groupie maiden. When Tam eventually toddled down the hill (with a great big sheepish grin) we all gathered outside the venue to break into a slow round of sarcastic applause for his nefarious adventure up on the hill. Speaking to Tam recently, he said he nearly got his ass fried doing the deeds, as both of them unwittingly were lying right beside an electrically charged perimeter fence with sparks flying in all directions (in more ways than one). That's what happens sometimes when you bend down and touch the rainbow!

IT'S A HYPERDELIC WORLD

One Sunday night in October 1986, Primal Scream found themselves sharing a bill with music art provocateurs supreme, Psychic TV in the Town And Country Club, London once more. It wasn't exactly up there with Einsturzende Neubauton supporting Showaddywaddy in the Kilburn Ballroom for sheer downright audacity and strangeness but it came damn near close. Gazing once more at the fluorescent gig poster of the gig that I still possess (pink background with blue spiral in the middle) the 5 band bill sure makes a strange sight to behold. Psychic TV – Primal Scream – Shockheaded Peters – The Godfathers with The Shamen propping up the bottom of the bill.

Out of all the bands who played, The Shamen were the first out of the lot, to break free from the underground, to storm the Top 20 charts and even achieve a Number 1 years later with 'Ebeneezer Goode' (one fucking annoying record). Back in 1986 The Shamen were just another bunch of Charlie Cosh chancers riding the latest bandwagon, trying to hitch a lift on to Creation Records but no one there dug them enough to sign them up. Psychic TV had been kicking around since 1981 when Genesis P-Orridge and Peter (sleazy) Christopherson split from the so called 'wreckers of civilisation' Throbbing Gristle and hooked up with Alex Ferguson (no, not him) from Alternative TV to produce an avant garage bastard mix of experimental, provocative sounds and vision – a true pop gospel of mind alteration. By 1986 Psychic TV had already released a couple of albums that were more influenced by The Velvet Underground sound, such as 'Force The Hand Of Chance' and 'Dreams Less Sweet' on Stevo's 'Some Bizarre' record label that came with a more high end, hyperdelic pop production sheen than with his previous Throbbing Gristle releases. But could they really top "20 Jazz Funk Greats" as a warped, sicko album title, complete with band posing dangerously on the edge of Beachy Head, a well known suicide spot near Eastbourne? In 1985 Psychic TV released the superb hypnogroove 'Godstar' a rifftatastic Stonesy homage to Brian Jones whom Genesis P had a peculiar fascination for – a perfect blend of the demonic mixed with the angelic. Apparently at the time The Rolling Stones management demanded to hear an advance tape of the song before it was released. Psychic TV sent a hard copy to their hallowed offices, accompanied with a sticker bearing the message "BRIAN JONES DIED FOR YOUR SINS!" I would love to have seen 'The Glimmer Twins' reaction on first coming across this artefact! 'Godstar' (great title) itself was a total Stonesy blast with a Keef riff to die for with Genesis P in fine poppy vocal form.

'Thee Temple Ov Psychick Youth' was an esoteric offshoot of Psychic TV that had no particular object in their mystical manisfesto but to find your true identity – thee true will in life! There was to be no worship of false gods or idolatory here only a philosophy based on ancient pagan techniques blended within a base of modern technology taking in magick, video, music and poetry – hyperdelia! A true 'Exploding Plastic Inevitable' for the modern age! Without doubt Psychic TV were the first truly multi-media happening, that I'd ever experienced in a live situation. If only I was 10 years younger, I would've been able to catch The Velvet Underground at The Dom in 1966 blowing everyone's mind to pieces with their own original, unique take on the multi-media, mind bending experience of projections, light shows, dancers, poetry and avant garage musicians all synched in, as one entity.

After the soundcheck, hanging out backstage Genesis P dropped by and introduced himself to the band. Straight away he grabbed a seat and sat down beside me as we started to chat away, about music in particular, with his penchant for appreciating Scottish guitar players coming as a neat surprise. His present riffer Alex Ferguson was born in Scotland. Talking away to Genesis P, he came across as a real friendly approachable guy who was one of the most gen up guys I've ever met in the big, bad nasty world of rock 'n' roll. On a par with meeting Joe Strummer backstage at Dundee Caird Hall in January 1980 on the London Calling Tour (Oi! Stop that bleedin' name dropping!) With some people, you just happen to connect straight away in an instant, freestorming on a variety of subjects with the hours just drifting on by. Joyce X was a major Psychic TV fan at the time and turned me on to their 'Dreams Less Sweet' album which contained their acidic poppy tunes and was more accessible on the ear. I dug their concept and sound to a point of chaotic magick but I could never turn in to a card-carrying conscript. Only one band could affect me this way The Cramps – 'The Legion Of The Cramped'. Marc Almond – Rose McDowall and Duglas Bandit were all active members of 'Thee Temple Or Psychick Youth' at one point, whose doctrine also contained the influential thoughts and words of those avant garde visionaries: Burroughs – Crowley and Gysin – a counter culture holy trinity, of society's true outsiders!

Our gig itself went down well with the assembled Psychic TV heads but I remember skipping out seeing The Shamen and The Godfathers as they were our musical rivals at the time and god knows what Shockheaded Peters sounded like? By the time we'd all finished our sets, there was a real buzz of anticipation amongst the crowd hitting fever pitch as their satanic majesties requested the pleasure of Psychic TV onstage now! On first viewing it was a mesmerizing explosion of exotic dancers, multiple lysergic visuals and crazy day-glo costumes of lunatic abandon in amongst the songs. Girl about town Leigh Morrisson was living it up in London at the time and turned up at the gig in a buttoned up duffle coat, sweating profusely! Leigh described the gig as "satanik, like a bloody ritual, with candles blazing and hooded cloaked figures darting about". To me that sounds like a perfect description of a KLF video! I remember watching the show from the wings and thinking to myself, if this happened outside in the real world, everyone would've been locked up for charges of degeneracy ha! It was a freeform explosion of sexuality and magick, almost evangelical like and totally mad as a shit house queue! The whole experience possessed also a hippiefied flower punk vibe but was modernized and updated for the late 1980s generation. At the end of the gig we all trooped down to the Psychic TV dressing room to thank Genesis P and his merry gang of freaksters for an unforgettable concert. Those guys were so ahead of their time (at least 5 years) that a couple of years later they released an acid house album in 1988 under the alias of 'Jack The Tab'. More power to 'the wreckers of civilisation' – true visualizers in amongst the parasites!

JANGLEHEAD KNOW YOUR PLACE!

When Primal Scream finally signed their garage souls away to major record label, Warner Brothers in October 1986 little did I realise that tambourinists were at the bottom end of the pay scale, just next to the rhythm guitar players aka The Brat. By then, we'd already nearly signed to Chrysalis Records but they offered a pittance in return for the whole Primal Scream package so they got blown outta the picture. The Jesus And Mary Chain were already on Warner Brothers care of their subsidiary label Blanco Y Negro label and now it was our turn, along with The Weather Prophets and Edwyn Collins (Don't Shilly Shally anyone?) Felt were the other band who were meant to sign their souls away on the newly christened Elevation Records subsidiary but Lawrence spectacularly sabotaged the big deal by dropping a tab of acid at a showcase gig for Warner Brothers representatives, hitting freakout city and blowing their big chance of a major cheque book record deal. Looking back, maybe Lawrence had paid a visit to his local Brummie fortune teller and then decided against signing his fragile, battered soul to a corporate music machine, of never ending targets, deadlines and squeaky swivel chairs for the damned future! I now wish I had paid a visit to my local Glaswegian fortune teller too. Right now, I would love a good rake in the Warner Brothers archive to pluck out our signed contract from back then just to see what we actually signed up for, on that written piece of photocopied paper. It was all a bit of a blur to be honest, now you see it, now you don't and a total anti-climax – a real one way ticket to palookaville! There was to be no setting up tables outside of Buckingham Palace ala Sex Pistols style or even getting the chance to visit the Necropolis to sign our life away on a slab of gravestone ala Cramps style on Bela Lugosi's grave! Here's your bleedin contract suckers, read it over with your phantom lawyer and then sign on the dotted line – thank you very much please! Bang went your diy ethos in one hurried scrawled signature. Back then we were all so bloody innocent and naive when it came to the serious business of major record companies and how they operate. Raw working class musicians from the tenement streets of Glasgow with zero guidance from no one, we were all just winging it on a prayer. The Warner Brothers deal comprised of £55,000 – for one year only. This payment included the production of one album, two singles, publicity material, mega video costs, touring budget, new instruments, van hire and oh! our wages! I wonder who costed this project? Mr McGoo! Talk about cogs in a wheel? This was control and manipulation on a major scale operating on a low budget! The Weather Prophets managed to wangle a £75,000 deal as part of their one year package. I know Alan McGee thought The Prophets had more hit potential than Primal Scream at the time so maybe that was the reasoning in their larger payment deal? I thought it was a strange decision at the time, considering that Primal Scream were the band on Creation that had started to attract an ever-growing band of youthful, fanatical followers with a burgeoning setlist of potential pop hits for the future, at their disposal.

Our new label mates on Warner Borthers in October 86, producing million selling platters to the masses were Paul Simon with 'Graceland', Madonna with 'True Blue' alongside hoary old rockers Van Halen – ZZ Top and Dire Straits – Supertrampinwhitesnakinbollocks! the lot of them. The only rockin' fuckers missing from that hit list were U2! No pressure then on Primal Scream, to produce a stone cold classic album alongside the above, all for the princely sum of £55,000 – Kookie! Kookie! Lend Me Your Comb…..

Did someone just mention wages there? As we departed from our scarlet pimpernel combo of cockroach lawyer and leech accountant (never to be seen or heard of again) we decided to visit the local pub to celebrate and get down to the real nitty gritty, ie our wages for the coming year. It was during this sobering conversation that I learned that there was to be no such thing as the equal pay act going down, in this merry band of musical musketeers. The deal was also non-negotiable people! The songwriters Jim Beattie and Bobby Gillespie were on £100 a week, Tam McGurk and Dungo to be on £75 a week and myself and Stewart May (aka The Brat) were to get a measly £50 – just about enough to keep both of us hooked and from claiming on, in the local job centre as an unemployed decoy duck painter! There were a couple of right on radical socialists in Primal Scream at the time but when it came down to the serious matter of money and who gets what – those precious Karl Marx principles went right out that red door – slammed shut! It was a simple case of 'Mr Tambourine Man' look good, keep it zipped, don't make waves and know your place! Beforehand I never really got involved in the music and money side of things concerning Primal Scream (I preferred to spin records instead of making records) but all of a sudden I just felt like a £50 a week tambourinist! I knew I wasn't in Primal Scream myself for my musicianship but I did make up for it in other ways. I fitted in with the public image of being a Primal Screamer ie the look and attitude. Live onstage I was the upfront tambourine dude, injecting some energy into the live situation and I was also being used for press photos as part of the whole Primals package caboodle. It was all about complete control, wear the right gear and play the right records – all for £50 a week! It was for me a musical straightjacket that I wasn't particularly keen on. At times in The Action House, I felt that I was being spied on by the secret music police aka Herr Harte, who was still operating as Bob G's all-seeing-eye, who reported back to him, all the comings and goings of everything that was happening in Silverfoilcity in regards to how I lived financially and being with Joyce X. Let the madness begin…..

JULIAN COPE MEETS PRIMAL SCREAM IN DOWNTOWN ENGLAND

In late October, Primal Scream had managed to blag our way onto a small scale Julian Cope tour as support act. The 5 dates were Leeds Polytechnic – Birmingham Irish Suite – Bristol Bierkeller – Canterbury Kent Uni and finally touching down on the Saturday night at London Astoria. Ah! The might and power of a major record company backing behind you! Since we hadn't played a gig forra couple of weeks and were feeling a tad road rusty, we hired out The Red Star Communist Club in the Gorbals and got down to the serious business of rehearsing a polished set to satisfy The Copehead army of new recruits. There was gonna be 1,000 peepers, every night checking out your every move and since it wasn't our audience, we had to try twice as hard to get the sound and vision across. By October, 86 the old turtle shell of 'Fried' had been discarded on a slagheap outside of Tamworth and in came a new superslick, pounding rocky sound complete with a new fresh faced backing group going under the alias of 'The Two Car Garage Band' ha! The Copehead's recent single 'World Shut Your Mouth' had just recently shot into the Top 20, crashlanding at Number 19 and producing another memorable TOTPs performance with The Namdam perched on a green bolted microphone stand for optimum popstar effect. All of a sudden all the old Teardrops teenyboppers appeared out of the musical woodwork along with a newly acquired batch of Smash Hits teenies. Just where was this invisible, dormant crowd only a couple of years ago? (1984 to be precise) when he released the superior 'World Shut Your Mouth' and 'Fried' lp's, which it seemed only hardcore Copeheads at the time snaffled up, ie me and The Cumbernauld Garage Crew. Julian Cope was now signed to Island Records, a much bigger name and company (than his previous one, Mercury Records) and you could almost feel the mighty push of

Island Records now behind him, willing him on, to sell more music to the masses. He sure did like to fly in the face of fashion and his new album release came under the sacramental name of 'St Julian' complete with faux crucifixion pose on the front album sleeve. Another couple of singles were released also from the 'St Julian' lp but bombed bigstyle chartwise: 'Eve's Volcano' and 'Trampolene'. The greatest things about these 2 singles were the b-sides which produced a couple of blistering high energy cover versions of Pere Ubu's 'Non Alignment Pact' and The 13th Floor Elevators '(I Got) Levitation'. But the best b-side recording of the lot was one of his own compositions – 'Mock Turtle' which for me is classic Cope and would've fitted perfectly on the 'Fried' album previously.

From the wings of the stage, it was interesting to watch The Namdam work the crowd, in his new pop guise persona. With a newly shorn barnet and black leather jacket (Jamie Lee Curtis anyone?) he cut a dashing figure onstage, clutching onto his bolted mikestand for life, as he ripped through the deranged 'Reynard The Fox' and 'World Shut Youth Mouth' single which proceeded to raise the biggest cheer of the night, surprise surprise!

Backstage Julian Cope was surprisingly aloof and reserved for the first couple of gigs in Leeds and Birmingham. We tended to hang out mostly with his new hotshot guitarslinger in town, one Donald Ross Skinner, as he was more chatty and approachable and dug hanging out with The Primals. Me and Bob G amazed him one time raving about an obscure Namdam track and then singing it to him, word for word that left him gobsmacked in our fanatical knowledge of The Copehead's varied back catalogue including his Teardrop years.

The Bristol Bierkeller gig was memorable for two facts. The return of 'The Rich Bitch' and the meeting of 2 young anal, anorak Primals fans. This young couple got talking to us outside the venue and seemed to be scarily in awe of us but not in a good way. They actually followed us to the local Indian restaurant and get this – just to watch us eat! Bob G went over to them and had a friendly word in their ear that there was nothing exciting about watching a gang of guys stuffing their hungry faces, gorging on a lamb dopiaza curry!

We weren't superhuman, superhero superstars! Just 6 dudes on a musical kick looking for the good times. You don't mind chatting to fans, receiving gifts or even writing fan letters, it's a good buzz to feel appreciated but when it gets to these strange little episodes, it's time to set the 45 record straight. There's good weird and bad weird and that incident definitely slots into the latter.

After the soundcheck, 'The Rich Bitch' suddenly made one of her rare appearances and boy did she leave an impression! She was kitted out in full showjumping horse riding gear: tight jodhpurs, riding jacket, black boots and one riding crop to complete the whole kinkoid fantasy – Holy Bondage! 'The Rich Bitch' also produced a full hamper of goodies, full of tasty beverages and sandwiches. She also presented me with an original 1960s pink and black jumper top, which fitted in perfectly with my mode of style back then – the lady sure had good taste! I sometimes pondered whatever happened to 'The Rich Bitch'? Does she still live in the Plymouth area? Did she follow any other bands? Is she still living the Anita Pallenberg lifestyle? Answers on a rare postcard please.

Our next destination was Canterbury, deep in the heart of the Kent countryside. On the way there, we broke down in the middle of nowsheresville and ended up supping beers in some random country pub with all our gear, until the recovery guys came along and gave us a replacement van to get to the gig on time! Arriving there, we had missed our chance of a soundcheck and by this time the crowd were already swelling in numbers so we had no choice but to humph our gear onstage, plug in and spontaneously wing our way through our short set of velvet pop tunes to a bemused audience of fresh faced pop kids who had probably never experienced this kind of gig happening before. When Julian Cope finished his set for the night, he seemed in a more relaxed frame of mind by this time even christening me as 'The Nonsensical One' due to my penchant for talking Glasgwegian garage gobbledegook which he plainly never understood one word of ha! I quizzed him about the upcoming Suicide gig in London Camden Palace, the next night as we both had a night off to kick back and tear it up in Londinium. He was a massive Suicide freak but he had to fly somewhere in Europe to take part in some kids tv show on the same night – drat! The Namdam then proceeded to spend the rest of the night hanging out with us, smoking and drinking jamming it up into the late hours. London calling boppers once again.

This was to be the first time that I had seen Suicide live again, since the infamous Glasgow Apollo gig in July 1978 supporting The Clash and it was strange to see how an audience reaction had changed since those years – all 8 of them. On this particular night the crowd were lapping up everything the electronic punk pioneers could throw at them. I actually preferred it when Suicide were in full on antagonistic, baiting the audience mode as it produced a more thrilling, excitable spectacle. If you've lost your lust for life, the only solution is SUICIDE. You've paid your dues and I suppose they deserve the adulation after everything they've been through over the years. No more chairs, bottles or even hatchets this time round. The rest of the Primals posse had never set eyes on Suicide in a live gig setting before (apart from an unappreciative Bob G at The Clash gig in 78) and gauging from their wide-eyed reaction, had never experienced anything like Suicide before with their sinister, throbbing beat that pummelled your senses into oblivion. Suicide left the stage to a psychotic loop of screams that seemed to reverberate throughout the whole venue and seemed to last forever as everyone stood rooted to the spot thinking they would come back out for an encore but Suicide don't do encores! These guys are true original innovators and a one-off bunch of provocative ghost riders of the night that once seen were never forgotten.

At one point before the gig started, I took a wander up to the balcony and my gaze fell on Lloyd Cole who I shot down with a withering contemptuous sneer for subjecting the music world with his self indulgent take on pop music which I detested. The next day perambulating down Camden High Street, I bought a bootleg cassette of the Suicide gig and it sounded excellent, real raw electric power but through the years I must've thrown it away during the great cassette clear out, a major pity as old cassette tapes have made a bit of a comeback again. If you don't dig SUICIDE – you're dead anyway!

Our final destination on The Namdam tour was London Astoria, right in the heartland of the city centre. A couple of Julian Cope fanatics came along to the soundcheck and gave him a couple of remote control Dinky cars to indulge The Namdam in his other favourite pastime, ie collecting vintage toy cars. He had just entered toy car heaven and in his childlike element as we watched him control race the buggies about in the vast cavernous hall. It was fun to watch as us eager Copeheads had already read of his passion for all things Dinky related and here he was – living out his toytown fantasy to appreciative Julian Cope heads. By the time we arrived at The Astoria we were suffering from end of tour blues as the gig passed by without any memorable incident apart from the fact that the whole front row of the stage was composed of diehard Japanese fans with one girl in particular, leaning on the stage, swooning, not once taking her gaze off me, through the whole gig, according to the gospel of Bob G. And I never even noticed! I must've been blinded by the lights! It turned to fun later on as we were packing our gear away, a couple of girly Japanese fans appeared and started to scream at me and Bob G as we're busy lugging our kit into the back of the tour van. It was hilarious and ridiculous at the same time and I just couldn't take the whole fanship scenario serious – psychedelicamania on a small scale once again. I mean I was a £50-a-week tambourine player living in Glasgow but down here in London, girls were screaming at you as if you were a major league rock star! Strange game this pop star malarkey business! A couple of weeks later a similar scenario took place, only this time it was in a record shop (with Joyce X in tow) doing a serious bit of vinyl crate digging. Flicking through some lp's, I could spy a couple of young Japanese girls nudging each other and giggling amongst themselves "Ah! Martin St John – Primal Scream!!!" I looked over at Joyce X who was getting the hump so we made a sharp exit and split. My lasting memory of The Astoria gig was Chrissie Hynde appearing backstage hanging out with The Copehead and offering him the support slot on the upcoming Pretenders tour in America – just like that! One instant American tour – we were definitely still at the small end of the scale when it came to gigging and releasing records and getting hits!

Years later, I ended up in The Astoria once more but this time as a punter, to see The Cramps perform their very last gig in the UK in 2008 before Lux Interior died a couple of years later. The Astoria is now being pulled down, part of some regeneration project going on at the top end of Tottenham Court Road – another concert venue bites the dust all in the name of shitting progress. Hark! Did I hear someone at the back shout "There's an album to be made" – in Wales of all the places! I am the passenger……

ABORTED SONIC FLOWER GROOVE ALBUM IN ROCKFIELD

Right after the Julian Cope tour, we were shunted off to Rockfield Studios, somewhere deep in the Welsh Rye Valley near the English border. As we threaded our way through the bucolic Welsh countryside I found out through Bob G that I wouldn't be laying down any tambourine beats on the 'Sonic Flower Groove' album and this revelation sent me in to a silent downer for the rest of the journey. There were a hundred and one thoughts suddenly going through my confused headspace "Am I not good enough to cut it in a recording studio?" "Are they trying to edge me out subtly?" "Will I get the heave ho?" It wasn't a pleasant feeling and deep in my stomach pit I could sense the start of something ominous taking seed. Maybe they just wanted me to hang around, there for the Dr Feelgood factor, keep the good vibes flowing, a second opinion in the studio and don't ask questions about the money situation. It was a strange, unsettling feeling which suddenly cast some major doubts about where I stood in Primal Scream – no explanations!

Rockfield Studios was situated just outside the country market town of Monmouth and was only around 36 miles from Cardiff, the largest city in Wales. The studios were set up by a couple of brothers, Kingsley and Charles Ward in 1964, who had the foresight back then to purchase a collection of disused farm buildings which by 1965, had been converted into the first residential recording studios in the world. In 1969 Dave Edmunds caught local rockabilly rebels Shakin Stevens And The Sunsets at a live gig and one song in particular stood out in their repertoire, an upbeat version of 'I Hear You Knocking' by Smiley Lewis. Dave Edmunds was so inspired by this rockin remake, he took to Rockfield Studios to record his own distinctive take. The result was a major hit and the first one to emerge from Rockfield Studios.

The studios themselves had 2 recording areas: 'The Quadrangle' and 'The Coach House' (where The Primals shacked up). The place provided a calming atmosphere in which to create and kick back and came complete with their own individual bedroom quarters, games room en-suite bathrooms, communal living room, canteen and not forgetting the hi-tech, all mod cons studio itself, with no expense spare.

Just get a load of some of the inspiring classic albums that have been created down the years at Rockfield Studios: Dr Feelgood – 'Down In the Jetty' Flamin Groovies – 'Shake Some Action' and The Barracudas' excellent debut lp 'Drop Out With the Barracudas'. If these superb albums don't inspire the creative musical juices, you might as well close this book now and sling it in to your nearest, available charity shop! Motorhead also recorded here in the mid 1970s along with Queen who partly created 'Bohemian Rhapsody' here as well, we'll skip that fandango! The studios themselves produced a natural acoustic sound and the amount of bands who have actually laid down tracks here is simply astounding. A hefty Scottish contingent have recorded some might fine slabs of vinyl also: The Teenage Fanclub – The Skids – Altered Images and the excellent 'Empires and Dances' album by Simple Minds. How could Primal Scream not be inspired by that roll call of innovative recordings? In the mid 90s Oasis recorded 'What's The Story (Morning Glory)' lp also at Rockfield along with fellow Number 1 albums in the charts at that time of Black Grape and The Charlatans. It seemed to possess the Midas touch emanating from the recording boards and all we needed to do was tap into some of that inspirational creative energy and start laying down some tracks of our own – fast! After recording various radio sessions, completing a couple of singles and constant gigs along with multiple rehearsals, you'd think as a band that Primal Scream would be ready to kill it in the studio, as we had a ready-made album in the offing but sometimes things just don't turn out the way that they're supposed to and that's Buckaroo my friends.....

Our producer for the 3-week studio session was one Stephen Street – bad choice as it turned out. Initially we had tried to rope in either Stephen 'Tin Tin' Duffy or Dave Stewart (The Eurythmics) but we failed at both attempts. Pity, coz I reckon that David Stewart would've been the appropriate dude to sprinkle some of that magic fairy dust on 'Sonic Flower Groove' and bring it up to the poptastic standard that we had envisaged the album in our head to be. Looking at Stephen Street's credentials up to that point in 1986 as the top producer of The Smiths, you'd reckon him and Primal Scream would make a perfect hand in glove arrangement but right from the kick off, there were tasty, fiery disagreements about how we visualized the album. The problems were never resolved and as each day and week went by the resentment and antagonism on both sides grew worse.

The days then just turned into never-ending sessions of ping pong with occasional trips into Monmouth to relieve the recording process tedium. It was there that we came across a local pub called The Griffin (home from home) and instantly this turned into our rock 'n' roll headquarters as most of the other music heads from around Monmouth also seemed to hang out there on a regular basis, with some right old dodgy muso dinosaurs propping up that bar! At one point, we were all convinced that Keef Richards had a hideaway house here, as this dude (who was his doppelganger) used to pass us by, beeping his horn in his flashy Rolls Royce buggy. The game was up when we spied this cat visiting his local laundromat. We thought hold on! Keef Richards wouldn't be seen dead doing his dirty washing in public, right in the middle of a busy country market town! When we eventually got chatting to this cat, we found out that he was the current guitar player in Robert Plant's backing band. How fucking disappointed were we? (There were no major Led Zep fans in The Primals at that point in time). This cat was always trying to get us to jam with him but us garage cats were too young and snotty to get in to that ol hoary groove with him. At one point, he even wanted to start up his own band with Tam as his resident drummer ha! The other old rocker who we got acquainted with in The Griffin was that shady guy outta Showaddywaddy (short hair and shades) who occasionally shared vocal duties with that rubber lipped 70s style Ted upfront. Tam got friendly with this dude and at one point, he invited Tam out to his country mansion, so that he could pick up a small consignment of porno videos to keep us sex starved, horny young droogs satisfied forra couple of weeks. Tam was totally gobsmacked when he chapped his door and this beautiful, stunning blonde answered it. It took Tam a couple of seconds to realise this was the Showaddywaddy dude's wife! Tam thought, surely he must've picked her up at the height of the 70s, Ted revival bandwagon as there was no way this Les Battersby clone could've pulled a delectable honey like that in the real world.

One night hanging out in The Griffin, Tam and The Brat got chatting to these 2 American chicks and managed to sweet talk them into coming back to our country pad. Tam's lumber for the night came complete with a bag of kinky sex toys and moustache. The rest of us (me, Bob G, Dungo and Beattie) were in a half pished, silly mischievous mode (as we hadn't scored) so we managed to set up some kind surveillance setting, acquiring some cameras and sound recording equipment into the bargain. The sounds coming outta Tam's bedroom were pretty scary, a lot of moans, dragging chains and whiplash sounds reverberating around his lair. When Tam finally ground to a steamy halt, we chapped his door and he finally appeared, James Bond style with spunky towel wrapped around himself with a great big dirty grin on his face and he then started to chat to us about the kinky goings on trying desperately to stifle his laughter as the rest of us were bursting into stitches of uncontrolled jollity all around at the ridiculous situation. Meanwhile at The Brat's lair, there wasn't a lot of action going down if truth be told. The silly things you get up to, to kill time and to wipe away the boredom of being stuck out in the middle of nowheresville trying to desperately convince ourselves that we were here to make a fucking classic lp. As Dungo was laying down some bass grooves and the rest of the gang were trying to find their musical mojo, the ping pong sessions got more competitive and heated and ended up being more important than the actual music being recorded. One night lying in my bed, I could hear Bob G and Dungo (out in the living room) having a whispered conversation which struck me as a bit strange, as I thought that Bob G and Beattie were the close buddies and that Dungo was real chummy with Tam? I couldn't really make out the meat of the confab but it felt real conspiratory, Guy Fawkes like, as if they were discussing some apocalyptic scenario that was gonna happen real soon..... A couple of other groups were also recording at Rockfield as we were there. The Voice Of The Beehive one week and the next week were those outer space bandits The Hawklords. We never bumped into the latter band, they must've been hiding out in their silver machine somewhere, out in the kosmos?!?! Meeting up with The Voice Of The Beehive, they appeared friendly and chatty, in a laidback Californian style. Their drummer at the time was Woody (ex Madness then) but I never got to meet him, pity as I could've had a right good natter about his Nutty Boys' days well into the night. It was funny to see The Voice Of The Beehive finally crack the charts in 1988 with their Bangles influenced 'Don't Call Me Baby' on TOTPs. Sometimes you've gotta ride that pop bandwagon when it's hot as next to no time, you're yesterday's papers, in a faded copy of an old NME, lying in the gutter!

After 2 weeks of not a lot of music being created or recorded, we were beginning to wonder if we'd been struck down by the curse of The Teardrop Explodes! They had arrived at Rockfield in the early 80s to record their third album (after 'Kilimanjaro' and 'Wilder') but never quite got round to finishing it off. David Balfe initially titled it 'Be Prepared To Become A Whirlpool' which is a really funny and druggy album title but it must've been an explosive batch of acid that they were all getting mangled on as The Teardrop Explodes aborted their third lp and a couple of months later, finally imploded in a fug of crazed, schizoid drug taking and internal in-band fighting. Maybe sending The Primals a batch of mind melting acid might actually improve our attempts at producing a pure pop masterpiece! I eventually left the ping pong, cabin fever madness behind after the second week with some money in my pocket (£200 tamby wages) and decided to hook up with Joyce X and visit an obscure town in deepest Derbyshire called Matlock. The reason for ending up there was solely for the fact that it had a cable car system running overhead, throughout the town, which gave the place a peculiar, exotic feeling, of living in a snow capped mountain resort, only without the actual snow. It was a welcome relief to get away from the claustro, country antics of the Primals entourage. At one point, just before I departed, Alan McGee turned up with a bottle of champers to celebrate I don't know what?!?! Also in tow were James (Meat Whiplash shop) and 'The Rich Bitch'. Apparently she finally got her hooks into a Primal Screamer, Dungo, being the only spare single guy about the place and by the sounds of things, couldn't quite believe his luck that he'd copped off with an older cougar style groupie, getting to live out his Mrs Robinson's fantasies. Meanwhile in Matlock.....We managed to find a central bed and breakfast joint with possibly the most intense, uptight sonafabitch landlady this side of bleedin England. Before we turned in for the night, she demanded that breakfast was at 8am sharpish and notta second later. Well true to form we slept in and crawled downstairs half an hour later to be confronted with a very irate, bolshy landlady who point blankly refused us our breakfast, since we never made it up in time to catch her fucking, precious continental brekky. Joyce X and the landlady then proceeded to have a screaming match which resulted in us being ejected from her premises. Talk about an unfriendly, obnoxious person! This person would give ol Basil Fawlty a good run for his money in the downright rude stakes. After packing our bags, we hit the streets of Matlock to search for another more hospitable lodgings for the night. We found one within minutes, that we didn't have to set our bleedin alarm clock for 8am – Lord love a duck! Matlock itself felt like a real small town village and once you'd taken a cable car ride and explored some Roman ruins that was it really. Since it was Saturday night, we decided to hit the only bar come disco in town for some small town musical action. To make it that lil bit more interesting, we popped a tab (out of that never ending supply) grabbed a few drinks and plopped ourselves down for a spot of people watching. It looked like some sorta soul shindig roadshow happening as the dj proceeded to pump out a selection of chart hits and soul tunes to the pissed up townies of Matlock. It was one of those Saturday night joints where everyone hung out, the token goth couple, a pair of mods, some hipcats and a table full of really hyped up annoying soul boy knobbers in colourful matching t-shirts, with one guy in particular super annoying with his unfunny, loudmouth tomfoolery antics. If ever a guy deserved a Glasgow kiss, it was this hyper dick knobhound! Thank fuck that was our last night there!

By the time I arrived back in Glasgow, all hell had broken out in Rockfield Studios – Tam and The Brat had gotten the sack – for apparently not being able to cut it live in a recording studio. It seemed that Tam and Stewart were the fall guys who took the rap for all the shambolic shenanigans that had taken place in Rockfield over the last couple of weeks. After 3 weeks of ping pong, guitar masturbation, no vocals or drums laid down, Tam and The Brat found themselves the whipping boys for the whole sorry mess. A complete utter waste of £20,000 with a half completed album lying in the tape vaults. After the third week was over and everyone was back up the road, Tam was called to a showdown meeting with Alan McGee and Bobby Gillespie to be told that his services as a drummer were no longer required. According to Tam, he quoted that the real reason he got the silver bullet from Primal Scream "was an apparent clash of personalities with Bob G", the ultimate controller at the heart of the Primals universe. They used Tam's supposedly inadequate drum skills as an excuse to eject him from the world of Primal Scream as Tam was at times forthright in his views, saw right through the fakery and told it straight to your face – no bullshit. Tam had picked up some bad vibrations at the rehearsals before everyone set off for Rockfield and this matter caused some unresolved friction between the two, until now. Tam's in yer face approach to life didn't sit too well with lead mouthpiece Bobby Gillespie. He pushed the buttons in the Primals cosmos and Tam just found himself to be another cog in the wheel and used as the main scapegoat for what was really happening in the studio. One of the main reasons for the aborted half finished album lay in the simple fact that Bob G couldn't produce a decent vocal to use and at one point during the sessions he accidentally spilt a whole cup of coffee right over the mixing desk soundboard, resulting in the recording session being abolished and our wages flushed down the toilet pan with it, due to requiring more money to start all over again. Bobby Gillespie's vocal range was also found out at the studio as he couldn't hit some of the high notes that were required for a couple of the tracks. His normal range was mid range to low. Surely if Tam and Stewart were really that bad at playing their instruments, you'd initially have just hired a jobbing gang of musicians ala 'wrecking crew' style to complete the album. It worked for The Byrds and their first album – 'Mr Tambourine Man'.

Tam McGurk's drumming throughout his short but action packed Primal Scream career was bang on the snare drum. If you listen to the 2 early singles (a-sides and b's) radio sessions and live bootleg recordings that he played on, he was more than capable of cutting it as a drummer, who was on the beat and in the drumming groove Topper! Have a listen once more to 'It Happens' (the b-side to 'All Fall Down') for proof of his snappy military style fills at its best, especially right at the end of the track. When Tam was told to depart from The Primals, all he was left with was a set of well battered drums, a bruised ego and a horrible feeling of emptiness and utter despair. Not long after, he split from his long-term girlfriend and decided to try his luck in London where he eventually found employment – from drummer to plumber, in just a matter of months!

Tam's suspicions were aroused earlier in the recording studios at Rockfield when Andrew Innes had suddenly appeared out of nowhere, strapped on his guitar and proceeded to lay down some guitar tracks. I would love to have gotten Stewart's side of him getting the bullet too as there's always two sides to every story punks! (I tried to contact him through social media but no joy).

Word finally got out the scrappy leftover tapes were to be scrapped and that the whole album was to be re-recorded once again with that hurricane fighter pilot Mayo Thomson at the controls in the producer chair. This meant that the rest of our scanty wages were then to be plunged into this new attempt at 'Sonic Flower Groove'. For 3 months only I got to be a fully paid up tambourinist and it just had to be too good to last. I even think that Bob G's and Beattie's music publishing royalties were also raided for the new album. It was a complete disaster from day one, inexperience in a major recording studio, wrong producer in the hot seat, bad management and ineptitude and an unforgettable bad experience all round.

The start of 1986 had started on such a high with the excellent London ICA gig and by the end of 1986 it had ended on such a downer. Surely things could only get better as a new year beckoned with 1987 on the horizon….. May the sun shine bright on you!

TOP 20 TURNTABLE SOUNDS – 1986

1. The I.D. – Boil That Kettle Mother
2. The Jesus And Mary Chain – Some Candy Talking
3. Ronettes – Here I Sit
4. Sonic Youth – Starpower
5. The Gun Club – Jack On Fire
6. 23 Skidoo – Fuck You G.I.
7. Johnny Thunders – Hurtin'
8. The Cramps – What's Inside A Girl?
9. Felt – Ballad Of The Band
10. Wire – Mannequin
11. Richard Hell – Don't Die
12. The Byrds – My Back Pages
13. Wimple Winch – Save My Soul
14. Ramones – Howling At The Moon
15. The Seeds – The Wind Blows Her Hair
16. June Brides – In The Rain
17. The Jacobites – Shame For The Angels
18. The Byrds – Ladyfriend
19. Nobody's Children – Good Times
20. The Weather Prophets – I Almost Prayed

GREETINGS FROM GLASGOW

Who'd have thought that after all the palaver in Wales, I would end up on the tv screen on some obscure Channel 4 arty crafty programme called 'Down The Line' in early 1987? God knows how McGee pulled that one off? In early January we found ourselves in a disused cavernous studio in Parkhead, shooting a couple of videos for the show. Since we had no drummer now, Paul Harte filled the vacant drumstool slot ala Chas And Dave shuffling style complete with homburg hat. (Now no drum rolls to blow your cover!) In between the songs, the production team set up a couple of short interviews, with McGee in one of them and Bob G and Beattie in the other. Not many people I know have actually seen this clip or can barely remember our baptism of tv eye fire. I've still got the 10 minute clip on an old vhs video tape and I keep swearing that one day I'll get round to uploading it on YouTube forra laugh. Dave Belcher (from Glasgow Herald) was the interviewee and he'd already written about The Primals in The Herald concerning the Bobby Gillespie clones suddenly appearing everywhere you went and he had also written up a live gig review of the London ICA gig from 1986. Looking at the interview again is a total cringe factor. Bob G answered the questions in an unnatural static manner with a silent Beattie beside him looking like a 1960s henchman from the film 'Alphaville'.

The McGee interview was notable for the memorable quote that he spat out in regards about bands on the current music scene of 1987. He cracked "that they all should be given acid baths specially Bros!" This line had me in stitches when I first viewed it on the box as it just looked out of context on this dullsville, sedate art programme that no one hardly saw. Looking at the video recently one other particular moment sticks out. When the cameraman was slow tracking a shot to the video of 'Gentle Tuesday' I let off a real howler of a creeping fart, which the others in the band caught a real whiff off and this sent everyone laughing into themselves at the sheer bare-faced cheek of my stinky stunt! I couldn't see the anonymous cameraman's reaction as he was hidden behind this giant film camera but you the viewer can watch the clip in all its odourama glory once more, if you ever get the chance to viddy Primal Scream's first ever tv performance. The line up for that tv performance was Martin St John – Tambourine, Bobby Gillespie – Vocals, Jim Beattie – Rhythm/Lead Guitar, Robert Young – Bass and Paul Harte – Drums.

Straight after that, the rest of Primal Scream (no Harte) departed to London to restart 'Sonic Flower Groove' part 2 and since there was to be no gig action over the next couple of weeks, I decided to start up a club night myself (along with Joyce X) called 'The Superstar Club' (in homage to the Andy Warhol Factory years). I was also pretty rooked again due to my band wages being docked so it was real lucky around that time that Joyce X found employment as a chambermaid in ultra posho West End hotel, One Devonshire Gardens. Starting up a psychedelic garage club on a Wednesday night, situated on a quiet street down a basement gay club (called Stepps) in hindsight now, looks a surefire loser! It ran for 2 nights only – no promoter of the year award for us. Since it was a crappy midweek slot, it was a free hire. You took the door, they took the bar. Obviously influenced by the success of Splash 1, I continued with the cassette compilation format and no dj. It was hassle free and you weren't stuck with a pair of headphones flipping records over every couple of minutes. When Joyce X was on the door dealing with people coming in, a lot of the regulars were still turning up and not paying as they all supposedly knew the manager, who always let them in free. Most of them turned up in the hope of hearing some Bronski Beat and Erasure megamixes and were surprised to say the least when they came across people out on the floor frugging away to the 13th Floor Elevators and The Chocolate Watchband. We'd plastered posters all over the city centre and spread the garage gospel but it was just too underground and off the beaten nightclub centre track to attract people on a midweek slot. It was doomed to disaster and after just 2 nights of 'The Superstar Club' – it ground to a halt.

Back in The Action House in Byres Road, there was a drastic change in the group dynamics in early March as Big Paul suddenly decided to depart and Jim Lambie suddenly decided to move in, to keep the rent money flowing. Harte then moved out of his small room to move into Big Paul's larger room and Jim moved into Harte's old room and at once, proceeded to turn it into a Joe Orton inspired shrine with one wall bedecked in a cut up collage of religious imagery. Down with the swastika and up with the crucifix! As time went on, Big Paul had been spending less time in Byres Road and eventually he just got sick of all the hangers on that used to turn up out of nowhere, talking shit, that you just couldn't get rid of when the bleary eyed morning came round. Some people just weren't very good at taking hints. I was also spending less time in Silverfoilcity as my relationship with Joyce X deepened and I tended to spend more time in her Hillhead Street basement pad. I still had creeping doubts in my mind, especially since Tam and Stewart were given the big push and I expressed these concerns to Bob G who assured me that everything was cool with me, I wasn't going anywhere. I told him that I was unhappy that Tam and Stewart had to leave but it didn't seem to bother him – nothing personal just business matters.

Dropping in to Grant and Billy's next door one night around that time to catch TOTPs, it came as a pleasant surprise to see Iggy Pop shoot into the Top 20 with a cover version of 'Real Wild Child'. What was really exciting was seeing 'The Igster' jumping up on the piano and shaking his action man torso to a crowd of boppin disbelievers in the audience. That's how to make a dramatic impact popkids! And come to think of it I don't remember ever seeing Iggy on TOTPs ever again after that inspiring appearance…..

APRIL SKIES AND GOODBYE SILVERFOILCITY

The Jesus And Mary Chain finally shot into the Top 10 in April with funnily enough a song called 'April Skies' which to me was their most exciting single release to date so far. By then April 1987 they had already ditched their trademark dirty ass feedback fuzz sound. In December 1985 riding on the success of 'Psychocandy's' plaudits in the press, they released 'Just Like Honey', a new radical departure in sound which made a pleasant change from their previous singles of noise drenched sounds. I'm sure Karen Parker (Bob G's chick) wrapped her vocal cords around the harmony of the original 'Just Like Honey' track and who'd have thought that nearly 30 years later sultry Hollywood actress Scarlett Johansson would have a bash singing it live onstage with The Mary Chain recently, at a show. In July 86 The Mary Chain released another killer single in 'Some Candy Talking'. It also entered the charts but never achieved any Top 20 action which is a bit of a surprise as it's extremely catchy in its slow narcotic build up and orgasmic rush of guitars crescendo middle bit. That unholy trilogy of singles proved to be their Everest moment, chart wise and songwriting wise. A couple of years later, they did release a street sass song called 'Sidewalking' that was a superb slice of swaggering pop also but it never even kissed the Top 40.

Hanging out in Silverfoilcity infrequently myself then I would bump into Jim, who was always enjoyable company to have around. He was a switched on guy, confident with it and he certainly knew where he was going! He was intensely passionate about his art at which he was creating, on a more serious and regular basis back then. But sometimes the good times have got to end at some point and me living in Silverfoilcity had finally run its course. Maybe there was some kinda weird silver karma thing happening what with the recent death of Andy Warhol and me now departing Silverfoilcity once and for all. As me and Joyce X were packing up to leave, Harte and Louise appeared in the kitchen and within minutes a screaming match kicked off with Harte and Joyce X getting heated up about the kitchen kettle and who it belonged to? It had all boiled down to this…..Boil that kettle mother and make mine a breakaway. Joyce X was in a particular feisty mood and didn't like to be beaten ever! (She wasn't a dedicated former Scottish gymnast champ for nothing). One kettle later, we were brewing up in Hillhead Street, my new permanent home and such a relief in a way, especially after that dramatic exit of psychodrama city back in Silverfoilcity. Literally as I was coming in the front door with my belongings, Joyce X's flatmate Diane was being shunted out the back door, no questions asked. When Joyce X made her mind up about something, ain't nothing was ever gonna change it! Since Harte and Bob G were still close buddies, word would've automatically got back to his ears about the Silverfoilcity showdown stushie with Joyce X. All of a sudden she would be scarred as public enemy Number 1 – a Bébe bitch from hell, hellbent on splitting up the band, Yoko Ono style! I could now see why Big Paul had split the month before from The Action House, that phase of your life was now over. I never even gotta proper chance to say my goodbyes to Grant and Billy next door as it had been such a sudden departure all round.

Looking back, reminiscing, it was an excellent time to be young, free and single for the first 2 years of living in Silverfoilcity and I wouldn't have swapped those experiences for anything (apart from a lottery win). Living with Joyce X in Hillhead Street was definitely a more relaxed time in my life and with Joyce X working during the day and not much band action going on I took to creating mixed media pieces of art, using a concoction of collage, paint and old picture boards which were heavily influenced by The American batch of pop artists such as Jackson Pollock – Andy Warhol and Robert Indianna. Myself and Joyce X also bought a couple of bikes, so we took to the West End backstreets, freewheeling in a carefree manner in the beautiful spring weather with not a care in the world. But come mid May it was soon to be London calling once more as our first major single release on Warner Brothers 'Gentle Tuesday' required some press attention!

GENTLE TUESDAY AIMS FOR THE TOP FORTY

Hitting London once more, this was to be our first experience at creating a video for the soon to be released single 'Gentle Tuesday' our first record release on Elevation and our third release in total since May 85 of 'All Fall Down'. The rest of Primal Scream in the meanwhile had finally completed the second version of 'Sonic Flower Groove' plus recorded and completed the 2 b-sides for the 12-inch single release: 'Black Star Carnival' and 'I'm Gonna Make You Mine'. By this time Andrew Innes had joined The Primals on rhythm guitar and the drum stool was taken up by several session drummers. So it was all systems go on the propaganda front to create the all important video and to whipsmart some press fever in the music weeklies. For some unexplained reason, Primal Scream had spent a small fortune on an ultra large backdrop that we used in the background for the video and also for the back sleeve of 'Gentle Tuesday'. It was that large and an awkward size, that we couldn't get it into the back of the tour van so that we could use it, as a visual stage accompaniment. A major faux pas there and another glorious waste of Primal Scream dosh that seemed to be dwindling by the day. I was that boracic I had barely 2 pennies to rub together and to get to London, I had to borrow the train fare off Joyce X's mum. For interior shots, the production company hired a large studio, that had us miming along to the video. That tedious process practically took up a whole day's filming where by the 14th take, you'd actually lost the will to live anymore. Talk about sucking the soul out of a song? Then some bright spark looking at the playback images suggested that we hadn't shot enough interesting footage to complete the video so they then suggested that we continue the shoot in wait for it – deepest Gloucestershire, for some pastoral, summer-kissed exterior shots. Heading out into the sweet summer breeze the next day, we managed to lose a car that was following us that had the soundman, drummer and Dungo in it. So it was left to the cameraman/driver to complete the promo video along with me, Beattie and Bob G striking various scowling, pouting poses for the camera. We eventually came to a bucolic lush laden green field and set to work to finish it off. The scenery and surroundings reminded me of The Pink Floyd video for 'Scarecrow' which they also shot in a luscious green field in the country, only ours was without the whacked out, surrealist touches. At one point I climbed up a tree (caked in make-up and guyliner) trying to look all innocent and wistful, wishing I was stalking the streets of Los Angeles, Sunset Strip 66 instead. Near the end of the shoot, the cameraman lay down on the ground as I proceeded to circle him with my tambourine trying desperately to look my koolest in the red hot blazing sunshine. Bob G and Beattie were also sweating like bitches in their leathers and shades. The camera dude managed to get a couple of supercool shots of Beattie's Rickenbacker guitar in all its ringing, gleaming glory, which looked pretty ace in the completed video – and that's a wrap! Since no one in the late 80s possessed a mobile phone back then (only drug dealers and office twats) we all decided to head back to the town of Gloucester and lo and behold the first pub we came to, we found the rest of the gang, supping away, with not a care in the world ha!

Hanging out in McGee's lair in Tottenham later that night we were pleasantly surprised to see Lenny Kaye taking up some couch space. I don't think he could quite believe that there were that many guys attached to Primal Scream. "My God! There's a helluva lot of you's guys!" He probably felt mildly intimidated by the sheer presence of 6 speed-talking Glaswegians firing questions at him from all angles of McGee's living room. To us young garage cats he was like a god like figure – the guitar hero in The Patti Smith Band and more importantly he was the first dude to compile a selection of great lost psychedelic punk tracks and call it 'Nuggets' in the early 1970s. Lenny Kaye possessed that kool laid back New York drawl that had us garage cats lapping up his every word, a real genuine sound guy. The reason he was on McGee's couch in the first place and in London was that he'd just been picked as record producer for the forthcoming Weather Prophets album – 'Mayflower'. Looking back in hindsight, I wish to fuck that Lenny could've sprinkled some of that magic fairy dust on 'Sonic Flower Groove' too, as he would've been a perfect skin for us – G.L.O.R.I.A.

With the imminent release of 'Gentle Tuesday' in June we suddenly got caught up in a never ending, whirlwind tour of music paper interviews mostly in London. In May the NME ran a 1-page feature on Primal Scream that sounded as though it was written 2 years ago, complete with an innocent, yearnful looking Bob G pic to drool over popkids. It looked as though it was just in that week's edition to fill up a space. Flicking through that copy again, in the singles review, was a taste of the competition that 'Gentle Tuesday' was soon gonna be up against. The Beastie Boys – 'No Sleep Till Brooklyn', ABC – 'When Smokey Sings' and U2's bombtastic 'I Still Haven't Found What I'm Looking For' – just how could the guitar velvet pop of 'Gentle Tuesday' really compete with these monolithic beasts on 45? Meanwhile on the gig page diary, at Fury Murrays, The Voice Of The Beehive were getting ready to strut that stage.....

By early June the battle was on for the prestigious front cover of the latest NME edition with Primal Scream neck and neck with Trouble Funk – it was all go-go-go! Guess who won? Yip! Feckin Trouble Funk.

According to an insider on the NME at the time, the editor came to the conclusion that Trouble Funk were more current and relevant to the music scene of that time – Primal Scream wait your turn! I suppose it made a surprise change from having LL Cool J on the front cover, as he seemed to be on every fucking music mag cover in town around those hip-hoppin times – I'm gonna knock you out! Inside the Trouble Funk issue The Primals still managed to pull off an informative 2-page spread that also contained a neat colour length picture of myself, Dungo, Bob G and Beattie posing it up inna greenhouse setting in kinky Hampstead Heath Park. I was up the back of the photograph, staring into the distance, trying to perfect my innocent little lost boy look as the rest of The Primals gang got to display a myriad of various poses. It was in this article that I got to be described as 'a tambourine flaying skeleton in leather gloves' which is a pretty neat description all round and one that I'm immensely proud of – skeletor to a tambourine beat! The writer also makes out 'that we're a downright strange bunch to be in a band' – he got that spot on too ha! Also in that week's NME edition, the fagend of the C86 explosion reared its ugly head with the likes of Talulah Gosh and Baby Lemonade clogging up the review pages also. Back on the gig diary 999 were getting ready to punk it up at Daddy Warbucks stage in Glasgow.

Out of the blue Bobby Bluebell (The Bluebells) called on the phone to find out if we'd be up forra interview for a new local Glasgow magazine called CUT. For once I got to speak my musical mind in a Primal Scream interview – hooray the tambourine man speaks! It made a change for once to speak up and express a point of view. Bob G at one point praises me for being a fanatical music lover and not a musician which is factually spot on but if I was being pedantic I could also say that Bob was a good songwriter but no singer! The article takes on a tone of how we perceive ourselves in a modern way without being totally branded a 60s influenced pop group. Near the end of the interview Bobby Bluebell asks me if we'd like to have lived in a different decade and in a blinding flash I go into a freeform spiel about how I'd love to have been hanging out in New York in 66 to catch The Velvets and then hop in my time machine to Detroit 69 to see The MC5 and The Stooges and then zoom forward back to New York once more in 1972 to catch The New York Dolls and then hop in to my tardis for a final dash, landing in Londinium 76 just in time to catch The Sex Pistols tearing it up! I think this hurricane journey of music left Bob G speechless as he barely gotta word in edgeways ha! My other stand out quote in the interview was 'I'm just there for the image – strictly a live guy!' There endeth my one and only attempt at a Primal Scream interview. On the front cover of CUT was the obligatory Hipsway staring back at us – opium for the masses man! Inside was a full blown advert showcasing a Genesis gig at Hampden Park. Glad I never lived near Mount Florida at that particular time in 1987 and having to suffer that ol prog rocking nonsense – pass the razor blades Phil! Having a gander at the singles reviews section, there's a couple of interesting releases being unleashed that month: James King – 'The Right To Be Wrong' (neat title), The Pastels – 'Crawl Babies', My Bloody Valentine –'Sunny Sundae Smile' and Danny Wilson's – 'Mary's Prayer' – I think you can already guess which one of them entered the top 20? I wondered whatever happened to that magazine CUT? It must've got shredded somewhere along the line…..

THE BEAUTIFUL END (AKA I WASN'T BORN TO FOLLOW)

With the Primal Scream juggernaut in full flow for the forthcoming single release 'Gentle Tuesday' on June 14, I found myself back on that London train once more – for the last time! During the journey, I felt I was under the spotlight from the rest of the band in regards to recent heated events such as the Silverfoilcity incident and the premature ejaculation of Tam and Stewart which still grated my conscience. As the light bulb kept swinging back to and fro, I got the horrible feeling that I was drifting away from Bob G, Beattie and Dungo on the band front. Their egos were beginning to take off for different planets, even though my own ego was sometimes adrift in the twilight zone but I always made sure my Chelsea boots were firmly grounded on the floor, I think?!?! Sometimes you've gotta talk up and say you're piece even if it pisses people off! If you can't be yourself, why be somebody else? I could sense that they were a touch taken aback by my honest forthright views on everything that had happened recently as up until then I had kept my big mouth zipped and played the game.....

The latest press junket was a one-page interview in The Record Mirror and a healthy double-page spread in The Melody Maker. It was back to the 'say nothing, look cool' scenario once more and keep it zipped tamby man! For the Record Mirror feature I'm up the back of the photo once more, this time gazing forlornly up at an old ripped 'n' torn Sex Pistols 'Bollocks' poster (fading fast) down a lane of Oxford Street somewhere. The interviewer described Primal Scream as "crushed velvet guitar pop" ready to gatecrash the Baroque Top 40 Chart party at any moment now. If only! Once again we were up against the mighty dollar push of LL Cool J gazing out on the front cover with other single reviews including The

Beatmasters with 'Rok Da House' and The Pet Shop Boys with 'It's A Sin' – you're telling me daddio! There's a humerous bit in the article where the interviewer asks Bob G if he's sexy enough to compete with George Michael, Nick Kamen and Boy George in the pop charts. Bob G then goes on to say that if he was a current pop chick devotee, he wouldn't want to shag any of them but then mentions Rowland S Howard as the dude that they should all want to fuck ha! Must admit, gotta agree on that one! Also on the singles page Boy George is on reviewing duties and proclaims The Weather Prophets 'She Comes From The Rain' 45 as perfect for his "indie moods" which also reminds him of Lou Reed. I suppose any publicity is good publicity even from the former king of chameleon pop! Over on the albums review page a certain Peter Paisley is slaughtering the recent Biff Bang Pow lp – 'Oblivion' "as a badly stoned Lloyd Cole album" – now that's just downright evil! This Record Mirror edition came out in July just after I'd left Primal Scream and the Melody Maker feature came out even later, in late August 1987. Reading them after departing, was a definite unreal peculiar moment, as if I was still in the band – very strange! The photograph in The Melody Maker was a full length distorted pic that wasn't particularly flattering. The interviewer described me "as a tousled and quizzical Rod Hull lookalike to Bob G's Emu". Gotta give the guy full marks for that surreal, incisive snapshot description. Looking at the photo, I can actually see the bizarre connotation of the comment, staring me right in the face. If there were any strings being pulled, it certainly wasn't Rod Hull who was pulling them! In this group band dynamic, Emu was definitely the supreme string puller of all decisions. The writer must've received an advance tape copy of 'Sonic Flower Groove' as he's particularly scathing in his appraisal describing the album as "too much like the early Byrds recordings and not enough of 'Younger Than Yesterday's more experimental moments". At the end of the article he lumps us in line with Husker Du, The Smiths and The Jesus And Mary Chain as a full stop in the line of development, in regards to classic underground pop with attitude. Bob G is once more in the hot seat having to defend Primal Scream's credentials of their vision and stance explaining that as well as The Primals 1960s Byrds and Love fixation, they are also influenced by Scott Walker, Tim Hardin and Gene Vincent! It was a bizarre article and photo to end my Primal Scream tambourine career with, that's for sure boppers!

Also getting slated in the lp reviews section was The Mary Chain's second album release 'Darklands'. Just how could they have topped their first classic lp 'Psychocandy'? At least Primal Scream were in hot company in the features pages, as that delectable 'angel with big tits' Marianne Faithfull was spilling out her sister morphine confessional guts all over her article.

The Friday following 'Gentle Tuesdays' release on the Monday, the disc found itself being selected forra review blasting on Radio 1's 'Round Table' evening programme. Guest reviewer for that week's show was none other than one of my old punk rock heroes from yesteryear – Joe Strummer of The Clash. Well old Joe boy did not dig the jingle jangle pop of 'Gentle Tuesday' one little bit and proceeded to slate it bigstyle! At least he never smashed it over his kneecap, like what happened to The Mary Chain's 'Upside Down' when it first got reviewed by some 'Bat outta hell' satin bomber wearing Radio 1 twatto dj with shit taste in sounds! The very next day 'Gentle Tuesday' got aired on Saturday morning's The Chart Show as that week's new release, to watch out for, eager-eyed popkids. It was around then that we were holed up in some recording studio near Waterloo Station and they never had a tv, so we had to hit the nearest café pronto to catch it. We ended up grabbing a cuppa in this greasy spoon caff and asked the proprietor really nice if we could switch channels to catch The Chart Show? Oh! the glamour of it all. This is the real down to earth world of the budding popstar (well tambourinists anyway) sitting in a greasy café, with barely a shekel to your name, watching yourself disbelievingly masquerading as a pop star, up a tree, caked in make-up, bashing a tambourine for all I'm worth – nothing!

Having a good swatch on YouTube recently, 'Gentle Tuesday's now copped a kool 52,000 hits and back then if that was transferred into actual sales, you'd be zoomerating up that Top 40 chart in no time. 'Gentle Tuesday' later on also found itself being comped on 'The Children of Nuggets' selection, an updated take on the original 1970s 'Nuggets' compilation. On the 12-inch release of 'Gentle Tuesday' was a nifty little tune called 'Black Star Carnival' along with a stomping cover of 'I'm Gonna Make You Mine' by The Shadows of Knight. 'Black Star Carnival' is a superlative, melodic mid pace tune that for me personally outshone the a-side, once again. It has so far achieved 6,000 hits on YouTube and deserves wider attention. Bob G's vocal in mid range suits the song perfectly and is an unknown gem in The Primals back catalogue. Also propping up the b-side was our rocking, driving cover of 'I'm Gonna Make You Mine' which has racked up an impressive 16,000 blasts so far but the original Shadows Of Knight version blows us away with 24,000 viewings. I don't' remember laying a tambourine track on any of the above records which is a major pity as they still hold up to this days as 2 of my favourite early Primal Scream recordings. It probably had something to do with being on a major record label and getting some hired muso in to do the business as I was just a tad too offbeat in my own idiosyncratic way…..

On the Monday of June 22nd, Primal Scream set out on another short headlining tour that took in Brighton, Birmingham, Nottingham, London, Manchester, Bristol and Leeds only I never quite got to Manchester….. Whenever we got together as a band, a simmering nervous tension built up, producing a definite power cut in the atmosphere. Bob G, Dungo and Beattie proceeded to lord it up on their songwriter's publishing, enjoying the rock 'n' roll lifestyle and bragging it up to yer face, belittling you without any hint of shame. I was now receiving zero wages, no gig money and getting handouts from Joyce off her meagre wage, just to get by on a daily basis. That whole Three Musketeers manifesto had been well and truly shredded, it was the old pals act closing ranks on the outsider. In a dead end job you detest, at least you know your enemy, with these guys it was worse. It was every sucker for themselves. Originally I thought (naively) that we were all on the same kick but since the Warner's deal went through, their true colours shone bright. Money! Fame! Ego – The whole Orson Welles Complex! As an added touch of spice and drama, the main support act for the tour was The Electric Cowboy aka Paul Harte ex Primal Screamer and ex Byres Road flatmate of yore! The other support act forra couple of dates were Loop who had just recently signed to Jeff Barrett's new record label Head Records and were eager to hit motorway city with their zinging, throbbing Suicide influenced grooves. Our first gig on the tour was in the grand, ornate setting of Brighton Pavilion. From Glasgow's grotty Venue Club (scene of first gig) to this princely palace was a large step up in gigging venues over the last couple of years. Before we got to the venue McGee had spotted Joyce X wandering around the streets of Brighton so the tour van pulled up, Joyce X got in and then – complete silence! The Brighton gig itself wasn't as frenetic and wild as previous ones, maybe it had something to do with the large sterile grandness of the venue itself which produced a subdued atmosphere. I still possess the original tour itinerary brochure from the tour and written down as the members of Primal Scream were: Bobby, Jim, Robert, Andrew, Gavin and Dukes. They couldn't even get my nickname correct – it was Joogs you dunderheids! A familiar name popped up on the roadie schedule – The Crusher! I wonder if this crazed, loonball ever recovered from his first acid trip in Glasgow? Our next stop was Birmingham Burberries with Joyce X still barred from the Primals tour entourage (that old no chicks in the van while on tour routine). Karma certainly entered the picture that day, as Joyce X caught the train instead and our van then managed to break down on our way to the gig. He moves in mysterious ways?!?! The gig itself was a complete blast with crowd and band psyching in as one with Bob G rolling about the stage, living out his Jim Morrison fantasies while I was bashing and rattling my tambourine in to a jingle jangle frenzy. Joyce X had managed to acquire a room in the same hotel as the band were staying in, so I decided to shack up in her room forra couple of nights since we had a free day off to hang out in Birmingham the next day. Well this innocent act on my part didn't go down too well with Bob G, Dungo and Beattie and it proceeded to bring out all their nasty, spiteful, childish behaviour in them, when they came back pished on the second night. Late at night 'the gang of 3' appeared at our room door inna threatening, drunken intimidating manner shouting and banging on our door acting pretty much like a buncha pissed up, laddish arseholes out on a bender – an act of pure aggression that pissed me off bigstyle. They were extremely jealous of Joyce X being around and seemed to be directing all their pent up hatred towards her, all because she was young, took no prisoners and stuck up for herself. She certainly wasn't bowing down to these egotistical braggarts of the night! The green-eyed monster had reared its ugly head and they just couldn't handle the fact that someone's girlfriend had appeared on the road, paying her own way without any support from Primal Scream. The 'code of the road' had been well and truly broken! It was all about power and control now. By the time I got to Nottingham the next day the atmosphere was even more frosty. By this time I was full of total disgust for these guys, that they could sink so low in their petty pranks and behaviour. Jeff Barrett was tour manager for the tour and was oblivious to what was going on behind the scenes. But someone must've told him about the previous night's shenanigans as I remember everyone hanging out at the soundcheck and Jeff telling the rest of The Primals that Joyce X wasn't a bad girl but I don't think they took this piece of information onboard. Only Jeff, Andrew Innes and Douglas (Mary Chain) were really talking to us at this point.

By the time we arrived in London the next day, to play at The ULU venue in Bloomsbury, I'd decided that this was to be my last ever gig as a member of Primal Scream. I'd been stabbed by the night of the long knives once too many and it was now time to depart, exit stage right, in style and on my own personal terms. The way that they treated Joyce X as the black-hearted she-devil, was the last straw in their drinks, as by this time in life, I'd really grown to resent them. I was a dead man walking and my one-way ticket had been well and truly punched and was now expired. It was Victor Mature or bust! Time to make a crucial executive decision to retain my sanity. It was truly the end of a jingle, jangle era for myself. When the new hired drummer Gavin and Andrew Innes (the new rhythm guitarist) were receiving payment for their services, and I was getting sweet Fanny Blankers Koen zilch, you knew the game was up. I had been a trusting, faithful member of Primal Scream for a solid 3 years from 1984 – 87 – a time of all sharing the same mattress, huddled up in the back of frozen tour vans, bonding at Record Fairs, buying up Seeds albums, getting high on lsd, raucous live gigs and a near death van crash had all boiled down to this – the living screaming end, sweet fucking Gene Vincent! A guy could only take so much jealousy, spite, pranks, backstabbing, snideyness and obnoxious behaviour before you hit the cracking up, broken stage. It should never have really come to this sorry end. If only someone had gotten us all together and thrashed out the problems and tried to resolve the situation (instead of excluding me from all the major group situations) maybe things might have sorted themselves out in the long run. Sometimes guys just aint very good at facing up to serious matters and resolving them!

Back at the gig I managed to rip a poster off the wall as a memento of my last appearance onstage. The support acts were now: Phil Wilson, The Electric Cowboy and Loop with Primal Scream due onstage at 10pm – student time at The ULU. It's now called The Venue and since the ULU days over the years, it has also managed to launch the careers of Arcade Fire and Goldfrapp amongst others. At the soundcheck a strange chill shot through my rockin bones, knowing in myself that after performing over 65 live gigs, giving it 110% to the Primal Scream cause, that this very gig was to be my final garage pop swansong! I could feel the festering resentment simmering, a different kind of tension just bubbling away under the surface. There were no more easy smiles or onstage chit chat going down and I just didn't feel part of the last gang in town anymore. I felt and looked aloof and morose, a stranger in a strange land with an ominous feeling of dread hanging in the air. If I'm gonna go, I might as well go out in style in tip top fashion, dressed to kill, belted, buckled and booted! Leather strides, suede waistcoat and Cheslea boots complete with luxurious bouffant barnet. Just before Primal Scream were ready to hit the stage, I actually felt nauseatingly sick at the thought of rattling that tambourine for one last time, to a packed crowd of Friday night, pissed up jangle heads! I gotta bad dose of feverish palpitations so I ran to the side of the stage (to get rid of the pent up nervous tension and crap that was building up inside) and proceeded to vomit and retch up all the rage and fury of the last couple of days. I was totally drug fee but I felt as though I was on another planet and another world in my head. Recently someone posted the whole gig on YouTube in all its fuzzy 38 glorified minutes. I couldn't believe that after nearly 28 years later, someone had just discovered it in their video archive. It's not of the best of quality but it still captures the sound in all its raw, crude moment in time. The gig starts real slow and sluggish and it takes to about half way through the set for The Primals to find their garage mojo. By the time we tear into 'Imperial' near the end, the guitars are blazing away in a burst of pure sunshine pop ecstasy with myself cutting loose, flailing away like a jumping jack punkoid skeleton, with my wristy's taking a severe pounding bashing my big white metal tambourine furiously. We then keep the mood on an upbeat groove and kick in to a storming version of 'I'm Gonna Make You Mine' by The Shadows Of Knight that has by this time, got the near thousand capacity crowd, screaming and yelling for some more action and sounds, as we all trundle off stage silently. The set is ending just as we are enjoying the gig but Bob G has been struggling with his voice throughout the gig as the thumping drums, throbbing bass, ringing guitars and my tambourine bashing are obliterating his vocals in to a screeching primal scream! Within minutes, we are hollered back on by the hyper excited crowd. Looking at the video in hindsight throughout the whole gig, I've not uttered one word and I am desperately trying to avoid eye to eye contact with Bob G, in case he can see right through my aftershow le grande exit! Normally it's all grinning smiles and knowing winks but now it's just scowls a go go along with a horrible feeling of encircling doom ahead.

After the gig, I grab my tambourine case and split quickstyle, with no goodbye and hole up at a secret address in London with Joyce X. The flat belonged to Jim Lambie's girlfriend at the time. Jim was at The Primals gig and I confided in him how I was feeling and he gratefully decided to put me up for the night. Awakening the next day, it was time to depart from the rockin' rollercoaster, it had run its course and this ghost rider on the highway had come to its final journey. I never asked for money throughout the whole tour, even though The Primals were now earning good gig money and packing the venues out. Everyone else in the band were getting their sweaty palms well greased but all I was left with, was one battered tambourine case, and one confused, bewildered mind with notta penny to my name. Time for Johnny On The Spot to resign and depart this cackle factory once and for all.

The next night's gig was once again at The International in Manchester and was promoted by the legendary club promoter, one Roger Eagle. Now sit down and listen to this Roger – I won't be turning up at your venue, all aboard the runaway train to Glasgow now! Apparently at that night's gig there were a couple of shouts from the crowd "Hey! Where's the tambourine guy?" At least I was noticed by some of the Primals fans and I was actually acknowledged as being part of them, especially in a live gig situation. Jumping onboard that train to Glasgow and leaving all the twisted, headfuck mindgames behind was a feeling of complete utter relief, that I had my own life back again – I felt liberated and cleansed. I just wasn't prepared to be dangled on a guitar string any more like a rock 'n' roll puppet in a band called Primal Scream.

The next day someone phoned at Joyce X's pad to enquire where I was? I just spilled out my guts that I despised them all and didn't want anything more to do with them. In a blinding, spiteful rage I decided to take my bittersweet revenge on them for the crap that they had put me through over the last couple of months. I'd been in the Warner Brothers office the month before and received a pre-release tape of 'Sonic Flower Groove'. I put an advert in the NME stating that I had the complete finished recording of 'Sonic Flower Groove' for sale (I hadn't, only a few tracks) to the highest bidder. It was designed to put a rocket up their arse and make them think that I would sell it before it got its proper release in October. Obviously no one was that bothered as I received no takers! Within a few days Dungo and Gringo (sound a right pair of cowboys) appeared at our abode in Hillhead boozed up, inna demanding, threatening manner asking that I hand the tape back. I refused and it then turned into a heated slanging match with eventually Joyce X and Dungo facing off to each other. A neighbour had called the fuzz, who arrived sharpish to send the goon squad on their merry way into the dark night. I was spittin furiously at Bob G that he had sent his brother and Dungo round to do his dirty work so I phoned him and gave him a shower of abuse in regards to his cowardly act. That was the last I ever saw or heard from Bob G and Dungo. Over the next few months it was a constant ping pong battle of lawyer's letters getting batted to and fro. At the time of my departure from Primal Scream, it felt like a really slow, drawn out horrible divorce that grinded on for the next couple of years with nothing getting resolved.

I was suddenly back to being Johnny Nobody again – a walking exile on main street, pounding the hilly west end pavements once more – Everybody's been burned!

The setlist for my last ever Primal Scream gig on June 26th 1987 comprised of: Treasure Trip – Sonic Sister Love – Gentle Tuesday – Silent Spring – May The Sun Shine Bright On You – I Love You – Tomorrow Ends Today – Imperial – I'm Gonna Make You Mine and Imperial once more for an encore.

Diary entry for July 1st 1987 – NOTHING HAPPENS ANYMORE!!! Also in my diary from around then was a curio entry: 'Bobby Gillespie got gobbed on in The Griffin' and shortly after that incident, Bob G and Dungo moved to Brighton.....Welcome to the big bad world of rock 'n' pop beat boppers!

TOP 20 TURNTABLE SOUNDS – 1987

1. The Velvet Underground – I Can't Stand It
2. Husker Du – Eight Miles High
3. Primal Scream – Black Star Carnival
4. The Dukes of Stratosphere – Vanishing Girl
5. Third Bardo – 5 Years Ahead Of My Time
6. Captain Beefheart – Diddy Wah Diddy
7. The Sonics – The Witch
8. Teddy And His Patches – Suzy Creamcheese
9. Electric Prunes – Ain't It Hard
10. The Jesus And Mary Chain – April Skies
11. Tim Buckley – Dolphins
12. Balloon Farm – A Question Of Temperature
13. Julian Cope – Mock Turtle
14. ? And The Mysterians – Girl (You Captivate Me)
15. Lulu – To Sir With Love
16. Chesterfield Kings – Outside Chance
17. The Poets – That's The Way It's Got To Be
18. Left Banke – Pretty Ballerina
19. Felt – Final Resting Of The Ark
20. The Pleasure Seekers – What A Way To Die

TOP 5 PRIMAL SCREAM COVERS

1. The Sex Pistols – Belsen Was A Gas
2. Subway Sect – Nobody's Scared
3. Them – Gloria
4. Suicide – I Remember
5. Shadows Of The Knight – I'm Gonna Make You Mine

AFTERMATH

In August, a couple of months after I'd left, Primal Scream released 'Imperial' (a personal live fave) which again like 'Gentle Tuesday', never made a dent in the Top 40, so the Boy George's and George Michael's of this world could breathe a sigh of relief once more. It was also around then that they popped up on an instantly forgettable Beeb programme called FSD, playing 'Imperial' in a live studio setting. Watching the clip at the time, I couldn't help thinking that there now appeared one almighty gaping hole on stage where I used to be. Bob G was now also taking up tambourine duties – stick to the songwriting!

In October 'Sonic Flower Groove' finally got released – to a whimper! I couldn't bring myself to buy a copy so Grant gave me his freebie copy as it wasn't really his kinda record. On first listen, I thought the songs were just too mr clean and well produced. I wanted a bit of dirt in the eye – perfection at times breeds boredom! Most of the songs on 'Sonic Flower Groove' had been gigged furiously over the last couple of years and I must admit (apart from a couple) I preferred them raw in a live setting or on a spontaneous radio session, stripped of over-produced trickery. I've listened to the songs quite a lot over the years and for some fun baby fun, I've compiled my own personal selection of songs (that would make up a more enthralling, thrilling album) which are comprised of a mixture of original lp tracks, b-sides and radio sessions.

SONIC FLOWER GROOVE
(21st Century Remodel Version)

A SIDE
1. Gentle Tuesday
2. Subterranean
3. Silent Spring
4. Black Star Carnival
5. Bewitched And Bewildered

B SIDE
1. Spirea X
2. Imperial
3. It Happens
4. Velocity Girl
5. I Love You

That's my own take on a much improved 'Sonic Flower Groove' that now possesses more bite, energy, buzz and variety to the selection. If any Primal Scream fan out there wants a true flavour of what The Primals could produce from that exciting, embryonic line up from 1984 – 87, this is the playlist that should capture your heart and put a smile on your face – the toppermost of the poppermost! Right now with modern technology, there's an electronic company online that can transfer your bona fide perfect playlist on to vinyl, for your own personal collection to savour.

In 1988 the year after 'Sonic Flower Groove' bombed and The Primals were extinguished on Elevation Records, Jim Beattie left the band. I was shocked and taken aback by this decision as he had started the group originally and came up with the name as well. It must've been a real bad situation back then, when you actually leave your own band! (I tried to contact Beattie to get his side of the story but to no avail). Maybe it had something to do with Primal Scream's new departure in sound, out with the Byrdsian 12 string sound and in with a contrived MC5 style that just didn't cut the mustard one little bit to my critical ears. I hoped and prayed that the 45 single release of their second lp 'Primal Scream' 'Ivy, Ivy, Ivy' wasn't about Poison Ivy of The Cramps cos if it was, it was sacrilege of Ben Hur proportions. If you require a genuine tribute to Poison Ivy, check out The Gun Club's – 'For The Love of Ivy' – a swamp punk classic.

One track of their second lp proved to be their saviour. The last track was called 'I'm Losing More Than I'll Ever Have' which seemed to prick up the ears of electronic producer-come-dj Andy Weatherall, who took the track, constructed a dancey backbeat, plucked out a couple of inspired samples, hardly any Bob G vocals and voila! One instant Top 20 hit at last in 1990. 'Loaded' (the new remade track) got so huge that you couldn't escape hearing it every time you went out in the town blasting outta car stereos, in the pub and clubs. All of a sudden I couldn't escape the bastards ha! The crazy thing is when I was in Primal Scream, I always had a gut feeling that they would break on through to the chart side of life at some point but only with me in them! Little did I know who could've predicted that 3 years later after I'd departed, that they would have their Mount Everest moment. Only 2 original members were still left from the original 5-piece combo and it was a strange surprise to find out that Dungo had now switched from bass to lead guitar and instantly transformed overnight into a rockstar lovegod called 'The Throb' complete with straggly Musketeer hairdo intact.

The third album release, in 1991 was 'Screamadelica' which contained an even greater selection of singles in 'Come Together', 'Don't Fight It, Feel It', 'Higher Than The Sun' and 'The Dixie Narco EP' which also comprised of 'Movin On Up' and the kool instrumental groove of 'Screamadelica' – a non album track. All of a sudden I wanted to be back in Primal Scream again, they were that good! I thought 'Movin On Up' was a total joyous rip off of Stephen Still's 'Love The One You're With' but with added gospel soul backing singers for effect. I wasn't surprised when 'Screamadelica' lifted the annual Mercury Music prize award the next year in 1992 as it had practically taken over the charts, airwaves and nightclubs as one of the most dynamically exciting lp's of the year. I bought the 7-

inch single of 'Come Together' as a fan and for me Bob G's vocal is bang on the bongo beat, no high notes or screeching on this gem of a 45 single. My actual favourite track on the album was the electronically charged dance rhythm of 'Don't Fight It, Feel It' which is a superb singalong tune to shake yer ass to, out on that dancefloor. In December 1992 I found myself at Sheffield Arena to catch Primal Scream and The Orb play a gig for the miners benefit benevolent fund (good to see The Primals were still keeping it real). This was to be the first time that I had seen Primal Scream live again since I'd left them 5 years previous and it was one mighty, acid-soaked surreal experience to behold. I went there (with no accommodation booked) along with a couple of friends at the time, Louis and Adrienne and as soon as we arrived at the Arena, we popped a couple of tabs and then proceeded to hit the nearest bar forra pint and bite to eat. As we were drinking, eating and coming up on the acid, all offa sudden we were sitting transfixed at the big screen which was now showing 'Who Framed Roger Rabbit?' Cartoons always make more sense on hallucinogenics and when Jessica Rabbit wiggled her way onscreen – wowsa! (Steady!)

By then it was time to enter the Arena and catch The Orb, who were just about ready to dub out our minefields and send us all into a never ending huge pulsating orbit in space. In October I went to see The Orb at The Barrowlands and it was a total mindsnapper offa gig and right now in Sheffield they were sending my eyeballs pivoting a go go once more, in to another head fuck dimension. Their dubbed out version of 'Singing In The Rain' was the reverberating climax to an excellent, psychedelic set of chilled out dubtronica that took us all nearly higher than the sun. Watching Primal Scream, taking to the stage (with a huge entourage of musicians) in this new danced up phase, was one strange feeling. Through the acid, I could just about visualise myself onstage shaking my maracas, rattling my tambourine and even playing some bongo drum action in amongst the throng of assembled hired musicians. Looking at Primal Scream from an objective point of view, this appeared to be a natural progression from 'Sonic Flower Groove' to 'Screamadelica'. Without a doubt the electronic wizardry of Andy Weatherall made

'Screamadelica' come alive with his knowledgeable production skills that turned Primal Scream, once more, into instant press darlings. The Sheffield set mostly consisted of tracks from the recent album (nothing from the 1st two lp's) and they sounded even more amazing live as they kicked off with a butt shaking 'Movin On Up' followed by 'Don't Fight It, Feel It'. Also at one point, they played the 10 minute instrumental 'Screamadelica' track that was a personal fave of mine. The whole Arena was grooved out (including ourselves) we just never stopped dancing – the beat, groove and rhythm was that goddamn infectious. There was a real surprise for the encore, when Hooky out of New Order joined The Primals on stage for a superb bass heavy version of Joy Division's 'Atmospheres'. There endeth the night after one superb piece of rockin, electronic dance extravaganza – just hope the miners got their dosh! From an innocent bunch of garage pop hopefuls to full blown stadium dance rockers, it was an unbelievable journey that absolutely no one could've predicted in the month of Sundays. During a lull in one of their songs, I let out a trademark awheh! scream just to let them know that Martin St John was in the building and watching them! I think it took quite a few people around us by surprise at my howl from my acid drenched soul directed at the stage! They had made it! I hadn't! Game over....

When 'Loaded' first appeared in 1990 I thought it would be a flukey one off hit single as a couple of their main contemporaries from around 1985 had already stolen a march on them by releasing some ace dance based tunes – The Stone Roses and The Happy Mondays. I was a major fan especially of the uber stoned beats and lyrics of The Mondays in particular who released some killer club 45s in 'Wrote For Luck, 'Kinky Afro', 'Loose Fit' and not forgetting the 2 treasured covers of 'Step On' and 'Tokoloshe Man' by John Congos. Boy! Were these guys cooking up the warp factor to the max? '24 Hour Party People' right enough!

And talking of The Happy Mondays and that freaky dancer Bez himself, the one question people always hit you with, when you tell them that you once played in Primal Scream was "And what instrument did you play?" When you tell them a touch of maraca shakin', a bit of tambourine bashing and some dance steps you literally see the blood drain from their face and then their eyes suddenly light up "like Bez outta The Happy Mondays sorta thing?" Sorry to disappoint people but I was doing my thing on stage long before Bez popped an ecstasy and performed his spazzed out dance routine. Good luck to Bez for riding that spaced out, maraca bandwagon for all it's worth and even getting a celeb career out of it but I think entering the world of politics might just be stretching it too far but then again 'The Monster Raving It Up Ecstasy Party' would definitely get my vote....

Trying to explain to some non-music blockhead that you once played in Primal Scream before 'Screamadelica' exploded also produces a quizzical expression as if they had just appeared outta planet Jupiter with 'Screamadelica'. I knew when I was taken on that I was that live guy who was there to spark some dynamics into the live situation and since I got into music myself around 1970, I've tended to dig people who weren't particularly musically minded but added another dimension to the outlook of a band. Some of my fave raves over the years have been Mickey Finn out of T Rex, Chas Smash of Madness, plus The Clappers out of Gene Vincent – always watchable and a true part of the whole group experience.

Looking back on Primal Scream's recordings after 'Screamadelica' they seemed to have reverted back to hit and miss mode once again. In 1994 they released the more rock influenced album 'Give Out But Don't Give Up'. Watching that cringeworthy programme of the 1990s, The Word and all those bussed in fruggin, fashionistas shakin' their tushes to 'Rocks' was one truly embarrassing sight to behold! It was totally derivative and real clichéd into the bargain with the cringe factor turned up 100% to the max. About the only song I dug on the whole album was a track called 'Jailbird' which I bought as a cd single as it contained The Toxic Shock Mob remix version which was a serious mind shredder with one potent brew of studio trickery going down in the cd package. The one other album that grabbed my attention was

'Vanishing Point' which was released in 1997 and produced the ace bass heavy rumblings of 'Kosalski' the last of the 7-inch records that I snaffled up of theirs. I actually prefer the dub version of the album called 'Vanishing Dub'. It's a stone cold menacing classic of a cd, notta million miles away from Massive Attack's 'Mezzanine' lp. In the year 2000 Primal Scream released a record called 'Exterminator' that was that rotten I actually took it back and demanded a refund, it sucked a big one, a real false record with not one goddamn tune on it to shake yer rockin' bones to. In 2002 'Evil Heat' was released, more of the same kinda stuff and unlistenable, apart from one beautiful tune in 'Autobahn 66' which has a real neat melody cutting through the song and was obviously influenced by Suicide. From the outside, looking in, I can safely say that Primal Scream as a rock 'n' pop band don't really rock my world. I certainly wouldn't classify them in the first division category of rock 'n' roll greats such as The Rolling Stones – The Clash – Iggy Pop – The Cramps – Suicide – The Ramones and Nick Cave – that's for sure popkids!

Since I left Primal Scream over 28 years ago, my moptop mugshot still pops up occasionally in old Primals articles from that 1984 – 87 period. (God's strewth I even get a royalty cheque of around 20 spondoolas every year for my musical services rendered.) In one article I came across in my 1992 diary, I am brandishing my gigantor white tambourine on stage with a pic of Bob G in the middle of it. The accompanying caption goes something like this – 'Things you must never say: "Hey Bobby! Whatever happened to that geezer who used to play tambourine?" He must've been well sick of that line over the year…..Primal Scream have certainly left a hefty Chelsea boot imprint on my mind. The Bad Daddy (Airdrie face about town) once famously quoted "That I certainly gotta good innings over the years, blagging my way onto multiple guest lists due to my association with Primal Scream" ha! I can't really argue with that one! I only ever got a chance to see them live again over the ensuring years a couple of more times since the Sheffield Arena gig in 1992. One was at T In The Park '94, outside on the Sunday headlining, where they performed a high energy set that had everyone boppin' about in the rain, like crazy loons! The third and last time was in one of the large tents in Glastonbury '97 where by the looks of things they had finally crashed burned and seemed to have lost their musical mojo, in amongst the muddy, mired fields of Glasto.

Last year I was extremely saddened to hear of the sad death of Dungo aka Robert 'The Throb' Young, who was the original bass player during my time in Primal Scream. My last memory of Dungo in the real world was of him turning up at my abode in a threatening manner and not a pleasant one but that was 28 years ago and time is a great healer that I believe in which should bring everyone together, but seldom does, even funeral get-togethers can't even achieve this impossible task at times! Reading Dungo's obituary in the Glasgow Herald I can't quite believe he never even reached the age of 50 before he departed from this earth. When I e-mailed Tam (the drummer) about Dungo's death, he felt totally gutted that his once former compadre in The Primals had died so young. We proceeded to have a good ol' chinwag together about the good times in the early days, hanging out on the road, getting up to all sorts of mischievous hi-jinks out on motorway city. As I'm flicking through the back pages of my memory box, I sometimes feel lucky to be still alive myself as I ponder there but for the grace of god what I would've turned out like myself, if I'd stayed in Primal Scream and rode the full 'Screamadelica' bandwagon of money, fame, adulation, groupies and drugs? Would I have had the mental capacity to handle the fallout and end up as just another rock 'n' roll casualty statistic like Dungo?

Dungo was one of the youngest members of the band and when I first met him at the time of '84 summer, he was a total Joy Division freak, who years later got 'Heart And Soul' tattooed in tribute to his musical heroes. He possessed what I would describe as a melancholic, destructive side to his personality whereby he was willing to try anything once, just for the sheer hedonistic thrill of the experience. I'd heard through the garage grapevine that Dungo had acquired a nasty addictive heroin habit during the post fame of 'Screamadelica' and this led to him finally leaving Primal Scream in

2006 and never to return. His nickname of The Throb only seemed to have appeared once he took up guitar duties, once Beattie had left in 1988. I must admit during my tenure in The Primals I didn't spot any of 'The Plastic Casters' (all the way from Chicago) chapping his door forra sample or come to think of it, any of our doors ha! Being young, naïve and up for every twisted stunt going, living the 24 hour party lifestyle non-stop for nearly 20 years, certainly must've taken its toll on Dungo's health and lifestyle choices at some point in his life. In retrospect, now, I have no regrets in jumping that train back in '87 and skipping out the 'Screamadelica' rollercoaster rubber room antics of the early 1990s. R.I.P. Dungo aka Robert 'The Throb' Young – 49 years old.

Ten years after I'd left Primal Scream in 1987, I suddenly found myself joining another band in 1997 called The Mount Vernon Arts Lab aka M.V.A.L. for short. It was really the brainwave of one guy, Drew Mulholland, with me helping him out on live happenings and bedroom recordings for added effect. I'd first met Drew in the back of a transit van going to a Primals gig in Sheffield in 1986. He was there with an old school pal of mine from the past, Denny Little, who just happened to know the driver and came along forra ride – all 150 miles of it to Sheffield. Speaking to Drew recently, his first impressions of Primal Scream were that they gave off a frosty, unfriendly vibe and he said "that I was the only friendly, talkative one amongst the gang". In M.V.A.L. Drew played an assortment of instruments such as drum machines, guitar treatments, Vox tape recorder, bass guitar and the VCS3 analogue synthesizer, which produced an unearthly sound which I was only just beginning to discover myself. I helped out on toy whirly, maracas, theremin and my old white tambourine, which was dusted off once again. As you can imagine with this selection of instruments, at times it produced one helluva deranged, dubbed out, amped up aural experience. The main influences at the time seeping into our thoughtwaves were Krautrock, Joe Meek, The BBC Radiophonic Workshop and the ethereal soundscapes of Delia Derbyshire, which were a major inspiration especially. It was a total change in musical direction for me and once again I felt my creative batteries were recharged. Also kicking around on this arcane underworld scene were Add N To X – Sonic Boom – Disinformation – Scanner – Broadcast – Stereolab and Electroscope. All these entrancing musicians were captivated by the vintage electronic sounds from the 50s, 60s and 70s and soaking up these exhilarating influences they managed to produce a weird out creative sound akin to some supernatural beast that had just escaped from the film set of 'Quatermass And The Pit!'

Over the 3-year period that I was an active member of M.V.A.L., I thoroughly enjoyed the experience once more of being that live guy on stage, at times donning a full skeletor outfit as I'm freaking out on the theremin to a bemused crowd of onlookers, who had no clue that I was once the former tambourine man in Primal Scream of yore, and I liked it like that, in disguise and creating merry mayhem on stage.

Since I left Primal Scream in 1987, I've managed to see quite a lot of my old heroes live on stage: Sky Saxon – Alex Chilton – Roky Erikson – The Sonics but one gig for me sticks out for being particularly memorable and that was the LOVE gig in King Tuts in the early 2000s. Arthur Lee was finally released from prison in 2001 after several years behind bars forra firearms offence – truly vindicated at last! Once released, feeling musically invigorated, he contacted Johnny Echols (original LOVE guitarist) and assorted members from Baby Lemonade and toured Europe under the banner of Love with Arthur Lee. Myself and fellow Love freak Derek Lee were the only 2 lucky fellows to have managed to acquire a couple of rare gig tickets for the prestigious gig at King Tuts Glasgow forra truly eventful, momentous gig, which straight away shot into my all time Top 5 gigs. As Arthur Lee appeared on stage, he still looked the koolest, charismatic freak to ever come outta The Sunset Strip with his bandana and black hat combo intact on his napper. I was slightly disappointed that Johnny Echolls never had his original double necked guitar in tow but I suppose you can't have everything punk! The last time that Arthur Lee had stepped on stage in Glasgow was in the early 1970s with another incarnation of Love in what is now The Garage nightclub in Sauchiehall Street (Electric Gardens maybe?). I've still yet to meet anyone on the gig scene who was at this particular gig just to compare notes on the Love setlist from that night. Back to the King Tuts gig and when Love blasted straight into 'My Little Red Book' with Arthur Lee on tambourine, it was one of the greatest moments in rock 'n' roll for me personally. I was sober as a judge and when music is this exciting and stimulating, who needs drugs to reach a higher state of nirvana. The gig was total heaven from the word go, with Arthurly's vocals in great condition and top form psychedelic shape. The screams and adulation of the gathered Love freaks nearly blew the roof right of King Tutty Wah Wah's as the crowd and band synched in as one in perfect subversive harmony. Johnny Echolls and Baby Lemonade were also cooking it up as they served one almighty, righteous garage punk inspired set. Every tune was kicked into shape with a mean, snarling beat with bags of attitude a plenty. There was to be no fishnet horn section a la 'Forever Changes' tonight daddio! The gig was that momentous, no one wanted it to end, we were all blessed that night to have witnessed one of the greatest gigs of our lives and for an encore Love produced a superb, heart warming singalong of 'Everybody's Gotta Live' which possessed a real John Lennon vibe to it. When the gig did finally end quite late, Derek had to fly inna taxi pronto to Cumbernauld to get him up the road but I hung around, shooting the shot with a fellow Love freak basking in the afterglow of a buzzing gig. Just as I was about to split, someone mentioned that Arthur Lee was upstairs talking to fans and autographing memorabilia. I shot upstairs straight away and joined a short queue to have a quick chat with Arthurly. Waiting there, I felt as though I was about to meet my maker in the old confessional box, preparing to spill out my rock 'n' roll sins over the years! When it finally came to my turn to meet him, he shook my hand and personally thanked me for coming to the gig and supporting him. Arthurly spoke in a hushed, gentle tone of voice and for once in my goddamn life I was rendered speechless and the only thing I could nervously splutter out was "Please stay out of jail Arthur, we need you!" He smiled back and said "I'll try" and then signed my prized gig ticket as I then departed up the road, floating on cloud 9 all the way to my bed in Govanhill. LOVE had been such a big influence back in 1984 when Primal Scream were discovering all these amazing, undiscovered gems of records from the 1960s and to catch them live many years later was an unforgettable experience which still resonates in my memory to this day.

Coming to the end now, (honest) whenever I'm walking down the bottom end of Byres Road, I sometimes stop at No 97 and wonder who actually lives there now and what the flat looks like? I bet there is certainly no trace of Silverfoilcity left there now! I've always visualized one of those blue plaques hanging outside the close with the inscribed message: 'At one point in the 1980s both Primal Scream and Sheena Easton once lived here – but not at the same time!' If only Sheena had hung around long enough we could've perfected a right good mash up of '9 To 5' mixed with 'Velocity Girl' – now there's a thought!!!

My philosophy in life – keep your feet on the ground and your head in the twilight zone!
AND THE TAMBOURINE BEAT GOES ON…..

'The Psychedelic Kid' ponders his next move – pop artist maybe?

Printed in Great Britain
by Amazon